Frustrated Empire
US Foreign Policy, 9/11 to Iraq

Frustrated Empire
US Foreign Policy, 9/11 to Iraq

DAVID RYAN

Pluto Press

LONDON • ANN ARBOR, MI

First published 2007 by Pluto Press
345 Archway Road, London N6 5AA
and 839 Greene Street, Ann Arbor, MI 48106

www.plutobooks.com

British Library Cataloguing in Publication Data
A catalogue record for this book is available from the British Library

Hardback
ISBN-13   978 0 7453 2389 3
ISBN-10   0 7453 2389 8

Paperback
ISBN-13   978 0 7453 2388 6
ISBN-10   0 7453 2388 X

Library of Congress Cataloging in Publication Data applied for

10   9   8   7   6   5   4   3   2   1

Designed and produced for Pluto Press by
Chase Publishing Services Ltd, Fortescue, Sidmouth, EX10 9QG, England
Typeset from disk by Stanford DTP Services, Northampton, England
Printed and bound in the European Union by
CPI Antony Rowe Ltd, Chippenham and Eastbourne, England

For Heidi, Daniel, Hannah and Luca

Contents

Acknowledgements

I would like to acknowledge the support and encouragement of Ziauddin Sardar for the original suggestion to undertake this project and for ongoing discussions. I am also grateful to Scott Lucas and Liam Kennedy for opportunities to present this material and for ongoing support. Lloyd Gardner and Marilyn Young continue to provide encouragement. My sincere thanks to Anne Beech, Judy Nash and Elaine Ross at Pluto Press for their engaged and very helpful assistance on all aspects of the book from its inception to the concluding stages. Their editorial work and suggestions have been invaluable. The *European Journal of American Culture* originally published a version of Chapter 2. I am grateful for their permission to reproduce it here. I would also like to acknowledge the support of the Department of History, University College Cork, and the College of Arts, Celtic Studies and Social Sciences, University College Cork.

1
Broad Contexts

Shortly after 9/11 President George Bush explained to his audience in the National Cathedral, Washington DC, that the conflict began 'on the timing and terms of others'. He seemed certain that: 'It will end in a way, and at an hour, of our choosing.'[1] He was wrong. He would not control the timing or the geographical scope of the new 'war on terrorism'. In a very short time the action and reaction would arouse forces and sentiments beyond US control and US strategies. The sense of limits to US engagement, deemed so crucial by US strategists after Vietnam, were elusive because US objectives were vague, broad and encompassed issues unrelated to 9/11 and because opponents, and the plural is important, had very different agendas. The defined limits in the US reaction were shunned because the Bush administration pursued a wider agenda. They sought nothing less than a thorough re-engagement of US power and the demonstration of its application in war. The strategies that embraced limits haunted and aggravated several people in his administration since the mid 1970s. US military power had been rebuilt after Vietnam. Beginning in the later years of the Carter administration, and accelerating under President Reagan, US military power and its disparity between that of its conventional rivals shaped US policy in distinct ways. With this re-militarisation power gravitated back to the executive branch, despite the lessons and adjustments after Vietnam. Buttressed by 9/11 such concentrations of power facilitated certain myopic and unwise opportunities.

The humiliating defeat in Vietnam placed a range of inhibitions on US foreign policy. Some constraints were lifted with the end of the Cold War, others after 9/11. For some of Bush's key principals war was a policy of choice; it could contain the pervasive Vietnam syndrome.[2] For Donald Rumsfeld, the Secretary of Defense, the reaction had to be broad. Bush began to conflate US problems and opponents. The rhetorical strategy was echoed in cultural discourse. Lumping disparate opposition was a familiar Cold War strategy. Al Qaeda was conflated with the Taliban, terrorism and Islamism, and the infamous phrase of the 'terrorists and the tyrants'[3] led the United

States into a myriad of conflict that will probably take decades to subdue. In the process all sorts of new forms of resistance were created. By August 2004, George Bush admitted that 'I don't think you can win it.' The Democrats were quick to make political hay during an election year, and the White House hurried in to limit the potential damage and signs of defeatism. But Bush was probably right. The breadth of US objectives lay beyond its capabilities. Just as the Cold War eroded the traditional sense of victory, the ends to these conflicts would be elusive. There was no clear line to cross or border to restore. When President Bush Sr decided to end the 1991 Gulf War on conventional terms, stopping short of the march to Baghdad, the Vietnam syndrome was compounded by that decision. Paul Wolfowitz, Rumsfeld's deputy, felt that frustration acutely. In 2004 Bush was quick to restore the narrative of victory: 'I think you can create conditions so that the – those who use terror as a tool are less acceptable in parts of the world.'[4] Yet the US actions provoked and enhanced the violent responses that the US troops struggled to quell in Iraq since 2003 and again in Afghanistan in 2006. The application of such force was bound to provoke reaction and resistance. US troops were not welcomed as expected; internal resistance, external antipathy and anti-Americanism spread rapidly; political opposition and diplomatic resistance featured throughout the world and at the UN to anticipated US actions.[5]

The narrative Bush advanced implied US innocence. They had been attacked out of the blue (a phrase that takes on new meaning after 9/11). That narrative obfuscated and deterred broader and deeper understandings of why 9/11 took place. Though the atrocities cannot be justified, understanding is important.

Narratives are important. They create the framework and the stories that help us understand how our world works. 'Our world' is often defined or understood to the extent that people share and assimilate the dominant cultural narratives. Narratives are important because they relate a story; they provide the audience with a framework, a beginning and an end. Narratives keep people together and they set them apart. They justify what we do and undermine and cast doubt on what others say and do. Ultimately, narratives or the cumulative stories we tell ourselves, our culture and our nations, sustain an international order that is often cruel and unjust. The stories of 'others' seem strange and incredible because they do not comport with our understanding and 'our' world.

LONG-RANGE US POLICY TOWARDS THE NEAR EAST (1958)!

Decades ago in 1959 William Appleman Williams wrote that a part of the tragedy of American diplomacy was that: 'If the United States cannot accept the existence of such limits without giving up democracy and cannot proceed to enhance and extend democracy within such limits, then the traditional effort to sustain democracy by expansion will lead to the destruction of democracy.'[6] If one of the philosophical gambits of US diplomacy rested on James Madison's injunction to extend the sphere to ensure the survival of democracy in his tenth Federalist paper, Williams' reflections anticipated danger. Americans had to learn to live within limits. Their failure to do so would produce 'empire as a way of life'. US officials struggled with the proposition, with their identity, and more importantly for current purposes, with the perception of their identity. As they supplanted European powers in the Middle East, especially in the late 1950s, after Suez, the National Security Council identified a range of interests, issues and concerns. Metaphorical parallels are never as straight as geometric requirements, but there are remarkable parallels nonetheless. Even as Washington assumed the position of the pre-eminent Western power in the region it worried about its identification with its 'colonial' allies: 'Since the British-French-Israeli invasion of Egypt in November 1956, the United States has been the undisputed leader of Free World interests in the area', a National Securtiy Council strategic paper opined. There was tacit recognition of this by European powers. Still, Washington could not separate itself from these Europeans and an identification with 'the powers which formerly had, and still have, "colonial" interests in the area'. Thus, the 'Western alliance makes the United States a target for some of the animus which this situation generates'. It worried about a range of issues, the US stance and the local perceptions of it. The tragedy in many ways is that those issues, albeit without the Soviets, remain largely on the table, and little has been achieved to ameliorate the tensions across the Middle East, especially after the 1967 war. Given the history and consequences the further tragedy of the Bush administration's response to 9/11 is the myopic tendency to fall back into old ways and not to explore readjustments in policy. Old stories were forgotten.

In January 1958, just over a year after the Suez crisis, the National Security Council drew up an extensive document on 'Long-Range U.S. Policy toward the Near East'. Obviously, it identified that 'the

Near East is of great strategic, political, and economic importance to the Free World. The area contains the greatest petroleum resources in the world and essential facilities for the transit of military forces and Free World commerce.' If the area fell under Soviet influence, US security would be jeopardised. Moreover, the 'strategic resources are of such importance to the Free World, particularly Western Europe, that it is in the security interests of the United States to make every effort to insure that these resources will be available and will be used for strengthening the Free World. The geographical position of the Near East makes the area a stepping-stone toward the strategic resources of Africa.'[7]

The National Security Council was aware that their interests did not accord with much aspiration throughout the Middle East. It observed that the 'current conditions and political trends in the Near East are inimical to Western interests. In the eyes of the majority of Arabs the United States appears to be opposed to the realization of the goals of Arab nationalism.' The Arab–Israeli dispute was important and US opposition to 'Arab aspirations for self-determination and unity' while there was 'widespread belief that the United States desires to keep the Arab world disunited and is committed to work with "reactionary" elements to that end'.[8] It is little wonder that after Arab nationalism was largely contained and options for free secular expression were so curtailed that eventually, and especially after 1979, 'the mosque and Islamic charitable organisations became the only sections of civil society that had not been bought or broken by dictatorial regimes'. Toby Dodge concludes, 'It is hardly surprising ... that rising resentment took a religious form,' which obviously benefited al Qaeda.[9] The US support for the repressive regimes was clearly recognised in internal memoranda in the 1950s: 'Communist police-state methods seem no worse than similar methods employed by Near East regimes, including some of those supported by the United States.'[10] The public and private narratives were at odds. The National Security Council was aware of its assets in the region. They made reference to the tradition of philanthropic and educational efforts, 'the respect which is engendered by our military power; our own revolutionary tradition and our identification with the principle of self-determination; the abundance of our wealth; the advancement of our science and technology', which all contributed to the positive views of the United States. Still, and perhaps more pertinent they recognised that:

The tendency in the area is to ascribe the blame for the gap between the present living standard and popular desires with respect to economic progress and development to external factors such as 'colonialism', unfair arrangements with the oil-producing companies, and a desire on the part of the West to keep the Arab world relatively undeveloped so that it may ultimately become a source of raw materials and the primary market for Israeli industry.

These words remain extraordinarily pertinent nearly fifty years later. Anticipating trends of our times its suggested policy guidance included: 'provide Free World leadership and assume, on behalf of the Free World, the major responsibility toward the area; acting with or in consultation with other Free World countries, particularly the United Kingdom, to the greatest extent practicable, but reserving the right to act alone'.[11]

IRONIES OF 'OUR' TIME

Despite these acute observations we have lived with stories for decades now about the growth and dispersion of liberty, democracy, self-determination and the benefits of a particular socio-economic system based around capitalism. One US commentator, a former employee of the US Department of State, went so far as to proclaim the 'End of History'. There was, according to this account, no further possible ideological development. Liberal democratic capitalism represented the highest form of political maturity.[12] Such notions were incorporated into the US National Security Strategy of September 2002, in which the United States was considered to be the sole surviving model of progress. This sense of superiority and orientalist outlook on others from afar and above resonates widely in Western culture and in the more ethnocentric North American political culture. The twentieth century was, to many commentators, following Henry Luce of *Life* magazine, the 'American Century'. It was characterised and sustained by the ideologies advanced in the meta-narrative of US history and foreign policy; creating a nation and a world in pursuit of life, liberty and happiness.

There are huge ironies in three broad themes that characterised the second half of the twentieth century, a period that coincided with the apogee of American power. After 1945 European empires collapsed. The rise of the Third World not only shaped the Cold War but also was devastatingly shaped by it.[13] Often aspirations directly clashed. India's first Prime Minister and founding member of the Non-Aligned

Movement, Jawaharlal Nehru, signalled, 'we propose to stand on our own legs. We do not intend to be the playthings of others.' Certain areas of the Third World were crucial for US strategic pre-eminence, especially Europe, the Far and Middle East; others were crucial in so far as they either contributed to or undermined US credibility. Guatemala in the early 1950s was an important symbolic case in point. The feigned hysteria concerning the communist threat in Guatemala in 1954 provides a distant echo in 2002. It was clear to many inside the belt of influence in Washington DC that the various orientations of the Third World countries 'might well determine the outcome of the Cold War'.[14] Yet the US had a very ambivalent relationship towards the processes of decolonisation and Third World nationalism.

Second, since 1945 world population has exploded. The earth sustained over 2 billion people in 1945, and had grown to over 6 billion at the end of the century. Yet despite this phenomenal growth, and widespread use of narratives on democracy or of the use of the word 'democracy' or 'democratic' in country titles, most people have had a very poor experience of this phenomenon. While 'democratic transitions' are widely noted and rightly celebrated, Washington has too frequently sided with forces that have suppressed democratic aspirations. A central grievance throughout the Middle East stems from Washington's support for authoritarian and sometimes brutal regimes that have frustrated democratic aspirations since 1945.

Finally, since 1945 the world economy has developed rapidly. The magnitude of global wealth and the wealth of nations has grown exponentially. Yet the figures and the daily realities of global poverty are stark. Inequalities within and between nations have become more obvious and wider. The exercise of democratic rights and practices is inextricably linked to certitude on security and standard of wealth. The connections with and between various forms of freedom are important. Political freedoms can promote economic freedoms, which in turn can contribute to social freedoms; 'freedoms of different kinds can strengthen one another', Amartya Sen argues. His 'freedom-centred' understanding of economics and development is very much focused on individual agency. 'With adequate social opportunities, individuals can effectively shape their own destiny and help each other. They need not be seen primarily as passive recipients of the benefits of cunning development programs', he contends.[15] Yet too often individuals are treated as subjects for development rather than as autonomous active agents. One often hears of the need to 'pacify' their collective desires and objectives. How bitter it must be to hear the words, 'freedom', 'democracy', 'self-determination', repeated – mantra like – in US rhetoric when direct encounters with US force, military or economic, or with that of the so-called 'national security states' and authoritarian regimes it supported and supports, would suggest other conclusions. How does one restore the narratives of liberty, democracy and self-determination or reconcile them with the growth and spread of US power? How does one restore agency to these meta-narratives of US diplomacy that would move the masses to the ideological and teleological terminus associated with the 'End of History'?

When the US occupation of Iraq in 2003 and its extension of military bases throughout the region and into Central Asia after 2001 was characterised as a new form of colonialism or at least imperialism, many Americans blanched. How could the United States be considered in such terms? Were they not the first in the modern period to break their colonial ties with Britain, declare their independence, and form a new system of government 'deriving their just powers from the consent of the governed'?[16] Were they not the nascent power to enunciate the Monroe Doctrine in 1823, precluding European colonialism from the Western hemisphere? Were they not the nation created by Abraham Lincoln, constituting a government of, for and by the people? Were they not the nation that had advanced the prospects for self-determination through the policies and rhetoric of President Wilson's Fourteen Points? Or down through to Franklin Roosevelt's promotion of the Four Freedoms, as the 'arsenal of democracy' and the champion of decolonisation during the Second World War and through the benign agenda of the Atlantic Charter? Had the United States not led the way through its decolonisation of the Philippines in 1946 and then secured the West through Soviet containment? Warren Kimball writes:

Historical memory is part of what nations are all about, and a visceral dislike of colonialism is part of the American self-image. The conventional wisdom in the United States has long been that colonialism, with its suppression of political freedom, has generated discontent, conflict and eventually revolution.[17]

US historical memory of course privileged a particular narrative over other stories of the past. The same period could be recast as the time when US power was consolidated at home, when they moved from 13 states on the Atlantic seaboard to the creation of a vast empire spanning a continent, in the process displacing European colonial powers, the Mexicans and Native Americans. Another benign narrative formed around the concept of 'manifest destiny' from the 1840s onward, but this was a parochial and ethnocentric proposition. Though colonialism might appear anathema to the US tradition and its formal ideologies, it was thoroughly a part of their historical experience during the nineteenth century. Though in the United States it might be characterised differently in school texts, Osterhammel identifies 'border colonization' as the '*extensive* opening up of land for human use, pushing a "frontier" into the "wilderness" for agricultural purposes or to attain natural resources'.[18] What could be more American? When Thomas Jefferson and James Monroe considered the form of government for the new territories, Monroe asked directly whether their government should be 'upon colonial principles' with a governor or should they be left alone to exercise their 'inalienable rights'?[19] The colonial option was more attractive. By the end of the century US colonialism and imperialism spread overseas, through the acquisition of Spanish territories in the Caribbean, the Philippines and hegemony over Cuba and Central America. Though formal colonialism was eschewed after the Second World War, Washington set about creating conditions in the post-war world in which a US 'preponderance of power' would prevail.[20]

Despite US ideologies and much collective memory it was never clear that the United States stood for anti-colonialism or for self-determination, the consent of the governed or democracy. The exceptions are far too numerous to make that exceptional claim. While Western narratives privileged certain experiences, nationalists around the world drew other conclusions.

Washington usually had to balance its aspirations to pursue strategic preponderance with freedom and self-determination. Franklin Roosevelt compromised on his promotion of decolonisation to keep the wartime alliance and the major European colonial powers intact.[21] President Truman faced derivative dilemmas on the issue as he decided not to push hard for decolonisation during the emerging context of the Cold War. Such instability might provide too many opportunities for communists or the Soviets; moreover, nationalists were widely regarded as no better than communists during that period. The metropolitan colonial powers were far too important to US strategic objectives relating to containment. Moreover, through increasingly integrated economies, colonialism represented a means to continued stability for a while.[22]

But Washington realised the prospect was temporary and that ultimately its association with colonialism would be costly. On the eve of African decolonisation, in 1957, Eisenhower's National Security Council (NSC) opined that care should be taken to 'avoid U.S. identification with those policies of the metropolitan powers, which are stagnant or repressive, and, to the extent practicable, seek effective means of influencing the metropolitan powers to abandon or modify such policies'. And 'emphasize through all appropriate media the colonial policies of the Soviet Union and particularly the fact that the Soviet colonial empire has continued to expand throughout the period when Western colonialism has been contracting'.[23]

Neither the colonial powers nor the independence movements trusted Washington. US traditions suggested that to maintain stability in the Third World, to win allies there, it had to support decolonisation; and yet potentially such independence could provoke instability in an increasingly hostile environment. Moreover, if independence movements leaned towards Moscow then Washington considered that decolonisation and self-determination were incompatible.[24]

While the process of decolonisation rapidly increased the number of nation states in the world, advancing at least the symbols of self-determination, the rapid growth in world population since 1945 outpaced the spread and entrenchment of democracy or the possibility of providing consent to the form of government under which people lived. The poorer states were soon 'disillusioned with this formal notion of equality ... Decolonization, and access to international institutions, did not result in a more substantive equality.'[25] Self-determination, whether related to political rights and freedoms or to the economic structures, and having the necessary means to effectively participate in society, are crucial. When anti-American attitudes were expressed, it was not because people *fundamentally* opposed values and concepts advanced by the United States, but that the United States had betrayed these values in its Middle East policies and history. The Pew Global Attitudes Project found that 'despite soaring anti-Americanism and substantial support for Osama bin Laden, there is considerable appetite in the Muslim world for democratic freedoms'. People wanted more freedom of expression, press freedoms, multi-party electoral systems, equal treatment under the law and so forth.[26] These freedoms were denied by regimes supported by the United States since the 1940s.

In the economic sphere, in the aftermath of September 2001, surveys found that there was considerable resentment against the United States because 'majorities in most countries also see U.S. policies as contributing to the growing gap between rich and poor nations and believe the United States does not do the right amount to solve global problems'.[27] Washington was conscious of the problem. After 9/11 there was a limited focus on the issue of world poverty as a causal factor. For instance, David Clark, a former advisor to the then British Foreign Secretary, argued that in the longer term the United States would have to reflect on 'the lessons to be learned from this sickening episode'. The attacks 'took place within a political context that we ourselves have helped to shape. Something rotten has happened to relations between the West and the rest. In many parts of the developing world a deep sense of alienation has begun to manifest itself in a hatred of the industrialised countries and the US in particular.' And 'the world's poor experience the daily immiseration of their lives, often the result of policies imposed on them by the West, while images of our good life mock them via the global media'. And finally:

If there is one positive outcome from this week's events, it must be the beginning of a new dialogue with the developing countries to address that crisis and give them a real stake in a common future. If we ignore these lessons and treat the upsurge of extremism as a security threat requiring a stiff military response, we will end up creating greater division and more bloodshed. That, and not the murder of thousands of innocent civilians, would be the terrorists' real victory.[28]

The argument went further than the direct act of killing. Ted Honderich proposed a wider view on the process. He argued that obviously the acts of terrorism involved the shortening of lives, and ran into some controversy when he also pointed out that the global economic order, largely designed in the West, involved taking economic decisions that resulted in the significant shortening of lives, especially in Africa, but elsewhere too. Behind each of the millions of impoverished lives and those with life spans that averaged thirty years, is a person: 'each of them had a name, and hopes'. Honderich writes:

The disparity in living-time between these two well-defined sets of human beings is not something we see clearly. We are not faced with it. We do not see it as we saw the awful killing at the Twin Towers. By way of our screens, we were there, and we brought our own experience and knowledge with us. It was people like us on the planes. Seeing an emaciated child on television is not the same.[29]

Redistribution of global wealth was and is crucial. Though of course the means of doing so remain highly contentious and are at the centre of the debate on development and the creation of wealth and poverty. The Bush administration recognised the importance of development, but questioned the efficacy of aid: 'Decades of massive development assistance have failed to spur economic growth in the poorest countries', its National Security Strategy explained. Such aid even served to perpetuate misery by supporting failed policies and reducing the pressure to reform. Still, it recognised, 'A world where some live in comfort and plenty, while half of the human race lives on less than $2 a day, is neither just nor stable. Including all of the world's poor in an expanding circle of development – and opportunity – is a moral imperative and one of the top priorities of U.S. international policy.' Still, the central gist of the strategy was that: 'Free markets and free trade are key priorities of our national security strategy.'[30] It did not mention the failures of that system. No doubt the extraordinary growth in global wealth since 1945 has occurred in areas that practised a sort of freedom of commercial exchange, but that same system also contributed to the relative poverty, impoverisation and inequality both between nations and within them. Wealth and poverty are central to the stability and the legitimacy of both domestic and international orders. US policy planners recognised early that the American way of life was privileged. Director of the State Department's Policy Planning Staff, George Kennan, observed in 1948 that 'we have about 50% of the world's wealth but only 6.3% of its population. ... In this situation, we cannot fail to be the object of envy and resentment. Our real task in the coming period is to devise a pattern of relationships which will permit us to maintain this position of disparity without positive detriment to our national security.'[31]

This disparity was compounded still further by the vast population growth in the Third World from some 2 billion in 1945 to over 6 billion now. Oil revenue has relieved some Middle Eastern countries from the extremes experienced elsewhere, but the situation promises to be even more acute with expectations of significant population increases over the next few decades in the region. The United Nations Development Programme (UNDP) argued that 'globally, the disparities between rich and poor nations can be even greater. But since the kinds of institutions and mechanisms that can redistribute income *in* countries are generally absent, it is hardly surprising that the gap in global opportunities has widened in the past three decades' (emphasis in original). The disparities are reflected in stark figures. The North, with about a quarter of the global population, 'consumes 70% of the world's energy, 75% of its metals, 85% of its wood and 60% of its food'. The process was exacerbated during the 1980s, when global growth rates were higher than the previous decade and the growth of relative poverty was even greater.[32] Development requires that these barriers are removed. Amartya Sen observes that 'despite unprecedented increases in overall opulence, the contemporary world denies elementary freedoms to vast numbers – perhaps even the majority – of people'.[33] Things only got worse in the 1990s. It is ironic that, in the decade most associated with globalisation and economic boom in the West, by the end of the decade the poor had become even poorer: 50 countries suffered a fall in living standards. The decade created even further divisions between rich and poor. The richest 1 per cent of the world's population collected the same income as the poorest 57 per cent; and the richest 25 million Americans received the same income as roughly a third of the world's population, 2 billion people. The report indicated that while 9/11 had created a 'genuine consensus' that poverty was the world's problem, reflected in Bush's 2002 National Security Strategy, the UNDP urged the West to abandon the notion that the free market solution is appropriate for all countries.[34] Despite the so-called 'third wave' of democracy, which spread through southern Europe in the 1970s, Latin America and the Caribbean in the 1980s, Eastern Europe, the former Soviet republics, South and South East Asia and Central America during the 1990s,[35] it is a further irony, given this demographic explosion that in our age of democracy, most people on earth have little effective control over their economic and political destinies. Moreover, such trends have yet to reach the Middle East.

REGIME CHANGE AND THE PERILS OF NATIONALISM

In 1954 the Eisenhower administration overthrew the nationalist government of Jacobo Arbenz. Though narratives associated with Soviet and indigenous communism were rife at the time, the decisions also related to the regime's appropriation of United Fruit Company land, to the Guatemalan nationalism and to the challenge to US credibility outside the dominant Cold War context.[36]

Although one would not like to draw too many parallels between Guatemala in the 1950s and Iraq under Saddam Hussein there are a couple worth thinking about. The first is that in very different ways they both challenged the United States within their spheres of influence. While they pursued a different course to some extent, they were both characterised by that infamous term of the 1990s as 'rogue' states. The second comparison arises from the first. The US reaction was quite exaggerated. There has been a tendency, especially during the Cold War and after, to vilify the opponent and create enemies where resolution might have been found through negotiation. While there were significant differences and an array of concerns, in both cases US diplomatic rhetoric and public diplomacy came across as at times quite absurd and out of touch with reality. Such extremes of characterisation and language may in part be related to the Manichaean tendency in US foreign policy. This in turn could be related to the evangelical tendency to portray the United States as exceptional and at odds with various evil-doers. In part it might be related to the manner in which foreign policy initiatives are funded. Though the president takes decisions, Congress holds the powers of the purse: how can it resist a president's request if pitched in terms of good and evil? The sense of perspective is lost in the process. The reversion to Manichaean constructs dates back to the early days of the republic; it was recalled on numerous occasions: when Monroe announced his doctrine (1823), in US discourse on the Axis powers, when Truman announced his doctrine (1947), when Reagan deployed the rhetoric of the 'evil empire', when Bush Sr reconstructed Hussein as another Hitler (1990), or in the 'clash of civilisations' thesis (1993), and when the associations of totalitarianism and communism were melted into the phrase: 'axis of evil'. In 1947, when Truman sought funding for his doctrine in Greece and Turkey, there was some scepticism on why the United States would want to fund a fairly brutal European monarchy. The pitch had to be advanced in terms of the Soviet threat and a universal struggle, not localised, not particular, but one that concerned everyone. Truman too gave people a defining choice in world history between two ways of life. Senator Arthur Vandenberg confided to Truman officials that if they expected Congress to fund their projects on the edge of the Middle East, they would have to 'scare hell' out of the American people.[37] The resulting mixture of 'illusion and reality' pushed the United States down paths in which it had to confront a problem at once constructed as universal, with very limited means.[38] Over fifty years later Washington would again embark on an adventure in the Middle East, heady with the illusion of using Iraq as a demonstration for the promulgation of democracy in the Middle East, and soon confront the reality of the limits of its influence: military, moral and material.

Too often throughout the Cold War, US intervention in the Third World was interpreted as intervention to assist the forces of democracy and self-determination against the threat of communism and the Soviet Union. Communists or various forms of socialist or nationalist movements were involved in many of these revolutionary threats; some had links to the Soviet Union and others did not. Though the Cold War provided both US policy makers and the West in general with the necessary and legitimating meta-narrative, intervention was frequently conducted to avert a challenge to the system. A pattern was set early in the 1950s. Washington took covert, yet decisive, action against two regimes continents apart. Mossadegh was deposed in Iran for nationalising the country's oil industry. A report of the NSC Planning Board on policy towards Iran outlined its apprehension on the 'loss of Iran'. Amongst its concerns was the security of the Middle East, India and Pakistan; Soviet access to its oil; the loss would 'damage United States prestige in nearby countries' and weaken their ability and will to resist communism; oil would potentially be used as a 'weapon of economic warfare to disrupt the free world pattern of petroleum production and marketing'; and finally, it would 'have serious psychological impact elsewhere in the free world'. Hence, 'the problem of Mossadegh must be solved'.[39]

If Iran at least had the virtue of bordering the Soviet Union, conditions and characterisations were even more absurd in the Western Hemisphere. There was a strong tendency at the time to regard most Third World nationalists as communist. So to a large extent, it really did not matter what Mossadegh or Guatemalan President Jacobo Arbenz's objectives and ambitions were: they disturbed the prevailing order of things by trying to wrest their nations out of the periphery. While the oil in Iran was significant and would no doubt have forced the United States to realign its political commitments in the region, just as they ultimately had to in 1979 when the Ayatollah Khomeini grasped power, when certain assets of the United Fruit Company were nationalised in Guatemala the impact was relatively minor.

The purpose of moving the narrative briefly to Guatemala in the early 1950s is not only to illustrate another example of regime change at a crucial point in the history of US foreign policy when it was imperative to maintain the validity and centrality of the US centred system, but also to suggest that the process of regime change is nothing new. The novel factor in our times relates to the process of naming. The Bush administration was quite blunt about its intentions, as indeed was the Clinton administration, when it became the policy of that government to remove Saddam Hussein from power. Even the Reagan administration, an inspiration for President Bush, shied away in public from asserting that it was the intention to remove the Sandinistas from power, though of course that was the specific aim of the US funded *contras*.

Despite the widespread public and private references to the communist conspiracy in Guatemala, US officials were worried that economic nationalism would undermine the inter-American economic system.[40] Even if Guatemala followed Soviet directions, State Department official, Louis Halle, argued that its power, either political or economic, was so negligible that the degree of the threat would be quite limited.[41] The 'real threat' according to Halle was that 'it would injure the prestige of the U.S. and the cause of freedom to have any state in the midst of the free world take up and flaunt the banner of Communism'. He then made comparisons to Soviet client states challenging or seeking greater autonomy within the Eastern bloc. Halle argued:

The situation would be for us somewhat like the situation of the Soviet Union when Yugoslavia broke with the Communist bloc, although on a smaller scale because of the inappreciable power-position of Guatemala and the prospect that she could not make her desertion to the Soviet cause permanently effective. Guatemala's independence and defiance of the U.S., however, would certainly arouse a sneaking admiration among most Latin Americans and, as it continued, would invite emulation.[42]

Though Saddam Hussein did not provide a model for other Middle Eastern countries, there was a certain admiration amongst some protagonists of his stance in defiance of the West and particularly the United States. The US Ambassador to Guatemala, Edward Sparks, told his superiors that 'world opinion believes that the United States was responsible for the overthrow of the Arbenz regime ... [and] that we have a special responsibility for the success of the new government'. If Guatemalans did not believe that the new regime was more beneficial to them, then the US objectives would have failed.[43] Similarly, what the United States leaves behind in Iraq and its implications for the Middle East in the early twenty-first century is crucial for the region and for US credibility.

Despite fairly blunt internal assessments on Guatemala and the need 'to arrest the drift in the area towards radical and nationalistic regimes' that were exploited by communists,[44] Washington was troubled by Guatemala's defiance and potential example. They faced a dilemma. The National Security Council recognised that 'non-action would be suicidal' because Moscow's allies would not change their objectives and they realised that 'Guatemala would be defenseless' against US action; this was a doable project. However, intervention 'would violate solemn United States commitments and under present circumstances would endanger the entire fund of good will' they had generated. The National Security Council opined that 'loss of this good will would be a disaster to the United States far outweighing the advantage of any success gained in Guatemala'. If direct intervention was not possible, National Security Council officials were also aware of the 'hazards' of CIA operations. It was difficult to keep covert operations secret, and 'were it to become evident that the United States has tried a Czechoslovakia in reverse in Guatemala, the effects on our relations in this hemisphere, and probably in the world at large, could be as disastrous as those produced by open intervention'.[45] Still, Guatemalan autonomy caused offence to US policy makers. Director of Central Intelligence, Allen Dulles stated, 'in effect they have flaunted us and consistently got away with it. It is time they were brought to realize that this could not continue.'[46] It was imperative to impose the Cold War narrative to legitimate US actions. Guatemalan communism was central to the dominant message in US senior level speeches. For some it may have been a sincere belief, but the cynical manipulation of the issue was also apparent. US Ambassador John Peurifoy reported after a dinner with Arbenz that: 'I came away definitely convinced that if President is not a Communist he will certainly do until one comes along… .'[47]

Halle was concerned that too many decisions were taken 'in an atmosphere of urgency'. The parallels are striking. Staff were making decisions without enough 'basis of information and thought', and 'the concentration on what appears to be a local emergency' might cause problems on larger issues: 'the atmosphere of emergency breeds a disposition to exaggerate dangers, and this disposition is strengthened by the necessity of "making a case" in order to get effective action'. For Halle the inter-American context was imperative. Focusing on the economic relationship, he argued that the 'revolution in Guatemala is nationalist and anti-Yanqui in its own right. It is, in its own right, a movement for "social justice" and reform.'[48]

In an attempt to temper the official mindset, Halle argued that 'the evidence indicates no present military danger to us at all'. Though there were frequent references to the fact that Guatemala was only within three hours flying time to Texas and less than that to Panama, 'we may console ourselves that Guatemala's capability for bombing either is nil'. However, the 'Communist infection' might be contagious in the region. But, the 'infection'

could also spread through the example of independence of the U.S. that Guatemala might offer to nationalists throughout Latin America. It might spread through the example of nationalism and social reform. Finally and above all, it might spread through the disposition the Latin Americans would have to identify themselves with little Guatemala if the issue should be drawn for them ... not as that of their own security but as a contest between David Guatemala and Uncle Sam Goliath.[49]

Once the overthrow had started, Halle reported on the widespread belief that the United States was involved, which resulted in 'warm expressions of sympathy for Guatemala' and 'indignation against the U.S'. He warned 'that the widespread impression abroad is: (a) that the U.S. has become hysterical about the communist menace so that it is losing its head in dealing with it; and (b) that this is leading the U.S. to commit acts of international lawlessness'.[50] The parallels should be obvious.

But they are not solely linked either to Guatemala in the 1950s or to Iraq in 2003. One could tell a very similar story on the Reagan reaction to the Sandinistas, or Clinton's official reactions to such regimes. In another process of conflating enemies, in a precursor to the controversial phrase of 2002, 'the axis of evil', Anthony Lake, President Clinton's National Security Advisor, identified a few 'backlash' states, such as Cuba, North Korea, Iran, Iraq and Libya that assaulted the 'basic values' of the 'family' [of states]:

For now they lack the resources of a superpower, which would enable them to seriously threaten the democratic order being created around them. Nevertheless, their behaviour is often aggressive and defiant. The ties between them are growing as they seek to thwart or quarantine themselves from a global trend to which they seem incapable of adapting.[51]

CONCLUSION

Underneath this process of globalisation and its cousin, Americanisation, this century there has always been resistance. The forms it has taken have varied throughout the last century and no doubt will do so throughout this one. The narrative through which one understands the overarching explanation of the century and US foreign policy in it is crucial to how one responds. Because even though the US collective memory of their diplomatic history posits a benign power assisting with the process of decolonisation, self-determination, pluralism, liberty, democracy and so forth, other narratives take the same experience and advance explanations of neo-colonialism, overbearing influence, hegemony, the pursuit of economic access, dependency, US support for authoritarian regimes and intervention to curb democratic aspirations.

2
Framing September 11: Rhetorical Device and Photographic Opinion[1]

Signs that assume the function of interpretants have a special role in the exercise of power, because the capacity to assign cultural significance to signs constitutes an important aspect of domination. Power can determine ('regulate') the interpretants that will be admissible, emphasised, or expunged. It not only certifies that a sign and its denotatum are cognitively appropriate; it stipulates that this sign is to be used and who may so use it. It can also regulate which signs and interpretations are to be accorded priority and significance and which are to be played down and muted.[2]

HIGHWAY 8

Rowan Williams, now Archbishop of Canterbury, tells the story of how shortly after 9/11 he answered the phone, which presented him with a familiar dilemma. The voice on the line spoke in Welsh. Though Williams was conversant in it, he knew that if he responded in Welsh the conversation would continue in that language. He had some anxieties about coping with it given the gravity of the issue. 'It seemed a telling metaphor at that particular moment. Violence is a communication, after all, of hatred, fear, or contempt, and I have a choice about the language I am going to use to respond. If I decide to answer in the same terms, that is how the conversation will continue.'[3]

Many parallels sprung to mind in the days after 9/11 (the year is no longer necessary, because it has become a common cultural signifier that this date refers to an American tragedy, rather than to a Chilean one). I was sitting in the Ford Library, Ann Arbor, at the time, examining the documents on the US response to a set of crises immediately following the Vietnam War (the Mayaguez incident in 1975 and the Korean Tree incident in 1976), and the overriding message emerging from the Ford administration was that the United States needed to demonstrate resolve. Indeed, the then

National Security Advisor, Henry Kissinger, was informed '... I fear that we will only now begin to realize how much we need to shore up our positions elsewhere once our position in Vietnam is lost. We may be compelled to support other situations much more strongly in order to repair the damage and to take tougher stands in order to make others believe in us again.'[4] Seemingly, US credibility depended on the demonstration of resolve, that it could still project power. These sentiments found echoes on the eve of US interventions in Central America, Iraq, Bosnia, Kosovo, Afghanistan and Iraq again. Some of the same personnel were involved on several occasions. Following 9/11 the US framework emerged almost instantly. President Bush described the events as 'acts of war', which 'will require our country to unite in steadfast determination and resolve. Freedom and democracy are under attack.'[5]

In the days that followed 9/11, Washington and US culture more generally created the framework within which the United States would respond to these monumental crimes committed in New York, Virginia and Pennsylvania. Various symbols, devices, rhetorical strategies and images were employed that soon obscured the broader meanings of 9/11 and framed the US response within the benign narratives, the constructs of nationhood, and the images that would link 9/11 to the road to war; supposedly a war on terrorism, but one also with a more ambitious agenda. Rather than treating the acts as criminal, Washington chose to respond through violence. Rather than making the choice that might have ensured that the conversation would not continue in the same language, war was the preferred option from Afghanistan to Iraq, as though 'to persuade ourselves that we're not powerless'.[6]

A framework was constructed from which difficult issues and questions were excluded. The attacks were deemed to be against American freedom and Western civilisation, against tolerance and democracy. There was little consideration of the roots of such hatred and violence. There was initially sparse analysis of the US presence in Saudi Arabia, its stance on the Palestinian issue or its maintenance of Iraqi sanctions, to take just the immediate issues identified by bin Laden. Nor was there a pause for the thought that though such grievances cannot justify the violence of that clear blue September day, these sentiments were widely held in the Middle East and elsewhere, and that, in the words of Douglas Little, 'the attack on the World Trade Center was also a product of the unintended consequences of five decades of U.S. policy in the Middle East'.[7] The adopted framework neither explained the atrocities nor enhanced US interests or those of anyone else; it was both myopic and counterproductive.

It was by no means an accident that the four planes that took off on the morning of 9/11 had as their destination a set of symbolic termini. The World Trade Center and the Pentagon were clearly chosen because they also represented the imperialism of US capitalism and military might in the Middle East. There was an immediate struggle over these symbols.[8] It was imperative that they be resituated into the more benign framework of nationhood and the good things that the United States stood for. Thus the semiotic struggle of mid September 2001 saw Bush's rhetoric and the use of the flag and photography privilege a certain interpretation over others.

To this end a series of conflations took place that facilitated the military response. There was the pre-verbal deployment of the flag, which obscured divisions in US society and challenged anyone to question US unity. Enemies were conflated; Al Qaeda, with the Taliban, and terrorism with Iraq, to ultimately produce the comfortable phrase of Bush's 2002 National Security Strategy, 'terrorists and tyrants'.[9] There was the conflation of the attacks with US ideologies and benign narratives in Bush's rhetoric. And finally, the 9/11 photography enhanced the notion that these pictures depicted the beginnings of a dialectic of violence, rather than a product of US intervention and influence.

Foucault's analysis of the archaeology of knowledge throws significant light on the processes that occurred shortly after 9/11. From him we understand that,

what properly belongs to a discursive formation and what makes it possible to delimit the group of concepts, disparate as they may be, that are specific to it, is the way in which these different elements are related to one another: the way in which, for example, the ordering of descriptions or accounts is linked to the techniques of rewriting; the way in which the field of memory is linked to the forms of hierarchy and subordination that govern the statements of a text; the way in which the modes of approximation and development of the statements are linked to the modes of criticism, commentary and interpretation of previously formulated statements, etc. It is this group of relations that constitute a system of conceptual formation.[10]

THE FLAG AND FRAMEWORK: FABRIC AND FABRICATION[11]

The flag, 'Old Glory', was an almost omnipresent and powerful symbol in the early days after 9/11. *The Economist* observed, 'the whole country is aflutter with flags. They fly at half-mast from federal buildings. They fly from every other house and car you pass as you walk down the street. Huge flags decorate sports stadiums, tiny ones dangle from baby carriages. Wal-Mart and K-Mart have sold more than half a million flags in the past week.'[12] Vendors gave away miniatures of Old Glory to those who bought a bandanna in New York; the flag was soon draped over a section of the Pentagon; bodies on stretchers were sometimes covered with it; it framed the ticker-tape news on major networks; and perhaps most famously, it took centre stage in the fire fighters' Iwo Jima-like photograph on Ground Zero, taken by the *Bergen Record*'s, Tom Franklin. That flag was later flying on the *USS Theodore Roosevelt* south of Afghanistan and later it flew above Kandahar airport. Though Franklin initially saw the flag as a symbol of 'the strength of the American people', it soon became an enduring icon for the US war on terrorism. The echoes between Franklin's picture and Joe Rosenthal's Iwo Jima were obvious and immediate. The transfer of the flag to Afghanistan and its centrality to the Franklin photograph facilitated 'a shift from the local to the international, from the work of recovery to the work of war'. It moves the nation's attention from Lower Manhattan back to the Second World War and on to Afghanistan.[13]

Manufacturers could hardly keep pace with demand for the flag. It provided a symbol for the 'imagined community' that now stretched far beyond Lower Manhattan across the country and most symbolically to the Jean-Marie Colombani headlines of *Le Monde* (Paris) on 12 September 2001, which exclaimed, 'We Are All Americans'.[14] The flag perhaps, unlike any other symbol, sent a powerful pre-verbal message of unity, community and resolve. Such an icon, as Benedict Anderson has demonstrated with the evolution of the map as symbol, was 'instantly recognizable, everywhere visible, the logo-map penetrated deep into the popular imagination…', which formed a powerful emblem of nationalism.[15] The sense of shared grief and anger soon turned to resolve, and partly as a result of the shared expectations of Americans (opinion polls indicated that it would be a liability if Bush did not take action), and largely as a result of the employment of a rhetoric of war, that Transatlantic sense of shared sympathy and objectives diminished. European governments and many others began to express reservations about the US response and President Bush's belligerent rhetoric.[16] The recourse to war was not universally regarded as an appropriate response, but it was one to which the United States had become culturally accustomed.[17]

The imagined community, momentarily universal, reverted to the particular and the parochial.

The flag worked at an iconic, symbolic level to represent a nation that could gather around such signs. The flags sent the message that Americans across the continent were with those in Manhattan. But what did the flag actually mean? In its most immediate context it stood as a symbol of courage, strength and resolve. But it soon reverted to its more militaristic functions. In the context of the Middle East the flag meant something quite different. For some it stood as an imperial symbol when it flew over US military missions; in the streets it was burned frequently at demonstrations – clearly the flag invited different responses. The struggle over its meaning was therefore all the more important.

At the height of the Cold War and the paranoia of the early 1950s, Jasper Johns painted a series of flags, oil and collage on plywood. These paintings of a ready-made image outraged some, and confused others, but Johns suggested that they were symbols that were 'things that are seen and not looked at' or examined. The recreation of the image of the flag in Johns' work perhaps, for some, forced a greater examination of the flag and the symbol. What did it stand for? And for whom did it stand? Such questions in the context of the 1950s were quite provocative; they were no less so in 2001. The point of this detour to the early Cold War period is to illuminate various questions of belonging. Just as the Truman Doctrine advanced a Manichaean view of the world, so too Bush's warning, that you are either with us or against us, obscured those who were dispossessed and disenfranchised by the system. The work of Johns said nothing and yet asked these fundamental questions of what it meant to belong.[18]

The desire to include would find its way into acts of commemoration. Franklin's photograph of Dan McWilliams, George Johnson and Bill Eisengrein will be erected as a statue that will be installed in the New York City Fire Department. However, one Hispanic and one Black figure will replace two of the fire fighters to reflect the multi-ethnic character of New York City. Yet Willis observes, 'the desire to inculcate the statue with the spirit of multiculturalism also serves to assimilate America's non-white population under the universal blanket flag euphoria, in contradiction to the fact that the demonstrative display of flags has been a predominantly white response'. Many Arab-Americans put out the flag perhaps as a prudent act of self-defence, but according to Willis, 'most black and Hispanic neighborhoods have been relatively flag free'.[19] Old Glory was draped over the divisions within the United States and its 'imagined community' just as soon as it would be draped over the imagined transatlantic community.

The symbol for community was therapeutic to some extent, but also soon came to provide the symbol for war. The rush to the patriotic response limited the latitude of questions asked. The images of the flag were omnipresent – as a symbol of community, a community of grief and condolence, it is understood. But, as a rallying point for response and counterattack, it was more worrisome. The tendencies towards this instant, nationalistic response limited the examination of US foreign and domestic policies, past, present and future.

'THE THEM' AND OTHERNESS

Despite John Quincy Adams' injunction to go not in search of monsters to destroy, monsters have usually animated and provided US foreign policy with purpose. The existence of an alter ego, the 'other' has been vital to US social cohesion and mobilisation. It is nothing new or surprising in and of itself. Edward Said writes, 'throughout the exchange between Europeans and their "others" that began systematically half a millennium ago, the one idea that has scarcely varied is that there is an "us" and a "them", each quite settled, clear, unassailably self-evident'.[20] Dichotomies have been used throughout US diplomacy from the Monroe Doctrine, creating conceptual dualities in the old and the new world, in the Truman Doctrine, positing the existence of two ways of life and the need to make a choice at that juncture in world history. Head of President Truman's Policy Planning Staff, George Kennan, understood the effects of such supposed challenges on US society when, in his now famous essay, he wrote that they should welcome the challenge, because it would make the United States more cohesive.[21] The Cold War sustained that conceptual divide and enhanced the propensity to engage issues in terms of dualities, even though actualities are always far more complex. Still, despite the period of détente during the 1970s, US foreign policy seemed somewhat bewildered at the end of the Cold War. But it was not long before the pundits started to provide overarching explanations. Fukuyama's 'End of History' thesis provided grist for the mill and elicited a huge reaction: the United States had led the way to the terminus of ideological development. But as a source for motivation, it lacked the essential ingredient of the 'other'. More satisfying was Samuel Huntington's thesis on the 'clash of civilisations', which in part even talked about the 'west versus the rest'.[22] Though widely criticised in many regards, it was also widely referred to after 9/11 as Americans searched for an overarching understanding of what the atrocities meant. The dualistic approach to world affairs was enhanced through presidential rhetoric, when Bush explained, 'either you are with us, or you are with the terrorists',[23] which not only obscured conditions and understanding, but also found multiple echoes throughout US culture. As Said suggests, 'the basic paradigm of West versus the rest (the cold war opposition reformulated) remained untouched, and this is what has persisted, often insidiously and implicitly, in discussion since the terrible events of 9/11'.[24]

The United States and the world were given few clues about the direction of Bush's foreign policy prior to 9/11. There were instances of and more emphasis on unilateralism; the US pursued isolated and unpopular positions on the Kyoto Agreement, the International Criminal Court, the ABM treaty and so forth, but nothing positive was presented for some time. The administration missed the deadlines for the mandatory publication of National Security Strategy papers. Moreover, little was said on foreign policy in his inauguration. Bush warned 'the enemies of liberty' that Washington would 'meet aggression and bad faith with resolve and strength'. After Vietnam, such language had become familiar. Identification of these enemies remained vague. During the campaign Bush admitted not knowing who the enemy was. But he explained: 'when I was coming up, with what was a dangerous world, we knew exactly who they were. It was us versus them, and it was clear who the them were. Today we're not so sure who the they are, but we know they're there.'[25] Of course after 9/11 'the them' became abundantly clear, though the whereabouts of 'the them' and especially 'the him', bin Laden, was immediately problematical.

Within days a series of rhetorical strategies took place that merged disparate opponents. First, Bush made it clear that the United States would make no distinction between the terrorists and those who harboured them. From afar, within US political culture, it seemed as though al Qaeda and the Taliban were one and the same enemy. Certainly Washington now had problems with both groups, but it is increasingly clear that some form of action would have taken place against the Taliban had 9/11 taken place or not. More importantly, though, was the ability to transform a potentially open-ended, widespread campaign into something that had territorial definition. The ghosts of Vietnam may have had some influence. Just as they had tired of fighting the elusive Vietcong, the battle was moved to North Vietnam. Afghanistan provided 'a concrete territorial enemy, a target'.[26] Without the 'hype' of the fall of Kandahar and Kabul, the war on terrorism and the pursuit of bin Laden would appear inconclusive, frustrating, without closure. It was as if 'Old Glory' had to be hoisted at some location; it marked the end of a stage in the battle against the other. The use of the Manichaean rhetoric perpetuated the illusion that this highly complex struggle against terrorism could be reduced to territorial conflicts.[27]

More worryingly, on 9/11 the White House principals began discussions on Iraq. Secretary of Defense, Donald Rumsfeld, and his Deputy, Paul Wolfowitz, led the argument. Rumsfeld was given to quoting President Eisenhower to the effect that, 'If a problem cannot be solved, enlarge it.'[28] Secretary of State, Colin Powell, initially persuaded Bush to remain focused on Afghanistan for fear that the coalition partners would drop off.[29] Iraq was put aside for some time during the autumn of 2001 and during the war on Afghanistan. Reference to it was especially scarce during the period in October 2001 when progress in Afghanistan was slower than expected, casualties incurred and pictures of civilian casualties appeared in the US and European media.[30]

The conflation moved the so-called war on terrorism towards a greater focus on Iraq. Again, just as the Bush administration had problems with the Taliban prior to 9/11, some in the administration regarded Iraq as a long outstanding issue. The 2002 State of the Union speech joined the problems with the now infamous rhetoric that identified an 'axis of evil', comprised of Iraq, Iran and North Korea.[31] Though US foreign policy was now thoroughly engaged, it was not until September 2002 that the administration published its National Security Strategy paper, which presented an imperial agenda, filled with US exceptionalism and unilateralism. Clearly 9/11 helped the Bush administration to frame the purpose and the direction of its foreign policy.

WORDS AND NATIONS

President Bush's rhetorical response to 9/11 further limited the range of discourse deemed appropriate in mainstream US culture. Within days the 'power to persuade' had been used effectively to define the events, and in so doing to limit the scope of critical discussion, alternative explanations and understanding. The targets of the attacks were defined not only in terms of US geographical territory, but also on its ideological territory. American freedoms and, ultimately, the American 'way of life' were attacked. It was a short step to the rhetoric of war.

Bush effectively connected two referential discourses that encompassed influential elements of American nationalism. In the mid 1950s, Louis Hartz identified two sets of American nationalism that often clashed with each other, but nevertheless, at the symbolic level were and are mutually reinforcing. Nationalism is identified with and feeds off reference to the territory, the country, the flag, the state, the map as icon[32] and the numerous other symbols that evoke the nation. In addition, another set of ideas, ideologies, foundational myths and constructs have also evolved, more associated with the sense of civil nationalism, which are built around traditions of benign rhetoric, national celebration and various forms of storytelling.[33] After 9/11, the two nationalisms converged in the seamless conceptual associations employed in Bush's rhetoric. Some of the most potent symbols of American-style progress, civilisation, economy and power, the World Trade Center and the Pentagon, had been attacked. The attacks were considered an attack on America and its freedoms.

For the first time since 1812, mainland America had been struck. The rhetoric of war, rather than criminality, was privileged. The state was at war. And so, according to Bush, the terrorists were at war with American ideas. On 14 September, Bush informed the National Cathedral, the nation and indeed the world: '... our responsibility to history is already clear: to answer these attacks and to rid the world of evil. War has been waged against us by stealth and deceit and murder. This nation is peaceful, but fierce when stirred to anger. This conflict was begun on the timing and terms of others. It will end in a way, and at an hour, of our choosing.' And 'In every generation, the world has produced enemies of human freedom. They have attacked America, because we are freedom's home and defender. And the commitment of our fathers is now the calling of our time.'[34] There was little scope in the aftermath and its attendant atmosphere to suggest that these attacks had roots in US policy in the Middle East and US attitudes towards Arabs and Muslims.

A week later, to the Joint Session of Congress, on 20 September he stated:

My fellow citizens, for the last nine days, the entire world has seen for itself the state of our Union – and it is strong. ... Tonight we are a country awakened to danger and called to defend freedom. Our grief has turned to anger, and anger to resolution. Whether we bring our enemies to justice, or bring justice to our enemies, justice will be done. ... On September 11th, enemies of freedom committed an act of war against our country. ... Americans are asking, why do they hate us? They hate what we see right here in this chamber – a democratically elected government. Their leaders are self-appointed. They hate our freedoms – our freedom of religion, our freedom of speech, our freedom to vote and assemble and disagree with each other. .... Every nation, in every region, now has a decision to make. Either you are with us, or you are with the terrorists.[35]

It was much more than that, but some uncomfortable fundamental lessons could not be admitted. The Manichaean formula masked US support for the authoritarian regimes that it sustained in pursuit of regional stability, balance of power politics and access to Middle Eastern resources.

Building on the work of Lauren Berlant, Sandra Silberstein identifies the various rhetorical devices that facilitated the move from the attacks to the rhetoric of war. Berlant developed the concept of the 'national symbolic' that incorporates a tangle of concepts and symbols relating to language, political space, a shared legal and experiential condition and all the symbols that evoke America. Through the association of these factors with the language and the concepts employed the nation is continually being (re)created; the primary goal of the 'national symbolic is to produce a fantasy of national integration', expanding people's sense of identity from the personal and local to that of the national, the abstracted yet (somewhat) shared imagined community.[36] Somewhat, because the narratives of freedom, tolerance and democracy are obviously not shared by all Americans.

Yet Bush used the evocation of the 'other' to create greater unity at home. The US nation-building and nationalism works through a rhetorical 'convergence by divergence'. They are 'brought together through their contrast with a shared enemy'. So the rhetoric was filled with references to unity: 'Americans from every walk of life unite in our resolve...', or 'our military', 'our financial institutions...', and 'the resolve of our great nation is being tested'. Though the rhetoric of war was almost instantaneous, and certainly significant sections of US culture expected some form of military response, the explicit use of the phrase 'war on terrorism' was first made in the announcement of the gathering coalition.[37]

More problematical are the rhetorical conflations that followed. A war against a territorial objective could only be fought in Afghanistan through the merging of the Taliban and al Qaeda, because of the refusal to draw distinctions between the terrorists and those who harboured them. Iraq was soon added through further duplicity. The rhetorical strategies that sought to contain internal dissent and foster the sense of nationalism and unity are replete with selectivity. Bush's response to the question of why they hate us was limited to the issue of their hatred of US freedoms. The US presence and history in the Middle East since 1945, its support for Israel and its sanctions on Iraq were beyond the conventional boundaries of discussion. US history and interests were omitted from other references, especially, 'In Afghanistan, we see Al Qaeda's vision for the world.' Or later still the demonisation of Saddam Hussein ignored the US relationship with both Iraq just days before the 1990 invasion of Kuwait or the US relationship with the Taliban through the summer of 2001. Moreover, Silberstein points out, no justification is provided for why war should be the inevitable response to terrorism. Alternatives are not advanced or considered. At most there is the distinction between Bush's intended actions and those taken under the Clinton administration. Bush would not settle for a short and symbolic use of missiles as Clinton had done in 1998. Bush rhetorically prepared the country for a long war in which US casualties were likely; the war on terrorism would not be another Kosovo (fought largely with airpower, resulting in no US casualties).[38]

Finally, there was little in the rhetoric that considered the consequences of responding through war, beyond vague but resolute assurances that it would result in a US victory. September 11 was presented as the beginning of a sequence of events that was yet to unfold. The past had been obscured and the future was painted in broad brush strokes that avoided the issues of generating further anti-Americanism, and the possibilities of maintaining the cycle of violence as opposed to seeking another language through which to respond. The myopia of this kind of rhetoric did serve the sense of US nationalism, but echoing Rowan Williams' opening anecdote: 'If I decide to answer in the same terms, that is how the conversation will continue.'[39] Several voices around the world tried to temper US responses after 9/11. Allies grew restive with the belligerent rhetoric and the resort to a military response. Others questioned the contexts through which Washington presented the issues. Still others questioned the tactics. General Merrill McPeak, the Air Force

Chief of Staff during the Gulf war, argued that airpower was ill suited to this kind of threat, 'You have to ask, "What's the endgame?" You want to come out with a safer, more secure environment, and it's not clear that a massive air attack, unleashing the dogs of hell, will result in an aftermath that's more secure.'[40]

Despite the widespread misgivings amongst allies and high-profile military personnel, Bush's rhetoric had set a course from which it would be increasingly difficult to extract the United States. Language was used not just to communicate, but also as an 'instrument of power'. Following Eric Wolf and Pierre Bourdieu, the relationship between language, power and authority invested Bush's words with an aura of competence and legitimacy. His words implied 'the power to impose reception' of his exclusive framework.[41]

GROUND ZERO PHOTOGRAPHY

Many pictures of 9/11 conveyed the horror of the attacks. An impromptu exhibition, which took its name from E. B. White's *Here is New York*, started in a shop window in Soho and then moved indoors gathering pictures from famous and unknown photographers, which were hung, unframed, on lines. It later moved to the Corcoran Gallery, presenting a multiplicity of not only images, but perspective, interpretation and response.

Yet, there was a simultaneous move towards closure and an attempt to promote certain interpretations and impose a certain framework through the pictures of 9/11 that echoed the sentiment of resolve and national values that were being developed in official rhetoric and through the choice of depiction in the mainstream media. As Susan Sontag and others have long argued, photographs do not provide a static view of the world, a window into the past. While they do provide evidence, it is an evidence that is often selective and incomplete, 'in support of dominant ideologies and existing social arrangements. They fabricate and confirm these myths and arrangements.'[42] To photograph is to frame, and to exhibit is to select. The process is of necessity the result of a sequence of choices, made by the photographer, publisher, picture researcher, layout designer, artistic director and editor. The pictures that remain etched in our memories have been heavily influenced by the need to capture the 'decisive moment' championed by Henri Cartier-Bresson and in Robert Capa's adage, 'if your pictures aren't good enough, it's because you're not close enough'.[43] But proximity and moment were captured, choices were made to downplay the more harrowing images that were available, in strong contrast to images of foreign wars and atrocities. While the absence of the body was a result of the collapse of the towers, the depiction of even some of these images, especially by the *New York Daily News,* ran into a storm of controversy.[44]

Instead, the dominant images after the initial implosions generated feelings of unity, resolve and heroism. They made connections with the US past: one thinks not only of Franklin's picture of the fire fighters and the flag, but of the heroic images of the workers at Ground Zero amongst the immensity of destruction. The image of the standing piece of framework, still against the chaos, acquired a totemic quality. The presence of the flag features widely, and is especially evocative, in Joel Meyerovitz's 'The Flag, Midnight',[45] a picture in which a huge flag, torn and in flutter is draped from a damaged building. The meaning given to the picture depends to a large extent on the viewer providing the picture with context, to give it a past and a future, in a sense to frame it within webs of significance and a narrative of the past, and promises of the future; it is 'to reinsert the discontinuous instant into a durational continuum'.[46]

The effect of much of the 9/11 photography was to privilege a certain continuum over alternatives. That context was being created by the various protagonists involved in the selection and representa- tion of that day and thereafter, and the rhetorical framework advanced through Bush's response and echoes throughout the media. 'The problem is not that people remember through photographs but that they remember only the photographs' Sontag argues. The still image is generally seen as far more evocative in the mnemonic process than that of the moving image and other sources of information. But photographs do not necessarily enhance understanding: 'narratives can make us understand. Photographs do something else: they haunt us.'[47] Yet photographs do delimit certain interpretations and exclude certain considerations. Given that all memory, even collective memory in a broader space, is local, the cumulative effect of the photography enhanced the notion that 9/11 was the start of the process. The narrative in the United States begins as an attack on freedom, American values and way of life. The naming of the site, Ground Zero, enhanced the implication. Such framing ignores and excludes the nightmarish dialectic scenario that these attacks had something to do with US policy in the Middle East: Saudi Arabia, Israel and Iraq. As such it precludes the options of reconsidering the past, its policies and preferences.

Instead, the nation moves on. The narrative becomes one of resolve and determination. The cover page of the 24 September 2001 edition of *Time* magazine, its title now in red, white and blue, captured the prevailing atmosphere. Bush stands upon the rubble, a flag hoisted, bulhorn in hand, next to fire fighters and other workers. The masthead read 'One Nation, Indivisible', backed up by the resolution of the subtitle, 'America digs out – and digs in.'[48] Such resolution, and the cultural echoes of another 'good war', were enhanced by Franklin's Iwo Jima-like image, replicated on magazine covers around the world and ultimately distributed in Kandahar inscribed with the words: 'freedom endures'.[49] Before they got there, weeks into the coalition bombing of Afghanistan, Bush fortified the nation with words of resolve and determination: 'I told the American people many times ... that this is a struggle that's going to take a while, that it's not one of those Kodak moments. There is no moment to this; this is a long struggle and a different kind of war.'[50]

The efforts to frame 9/11 within the preferred US context were advanced through a renewed attempt at cultural diplomacy. Many photographers were excluded from Ground Zero, their cameras and equipment confiscated because, as the police warned, it was a crime scene where photography was prohibited.[51] The work of Joel Meyerowitz, who did negotiate his way through, was subsequently used to create a travelling exhibition backed by the US Department of State. The exhibition, heavily influenced by personnel previously involved in the advertising and public relations industries, was according to Under Secretary of State for Public Diplomacy and Public Affairs, Charlotte Beers, an attempt to 'counter ... "the myths, the biases, the outright lies" being presented about the United States throughout "the Muslim world"'. Her intention was to specifically send a message around the world through the photographs as a 'visceral reminder' not only of 'devastation and death' but also of 'strength and resolve'.[52] As Liam Kennedy argues, 'resolution is the predominant structure of feeling in these photographs, there are few images of grief or pain. ... Meyerowitz's images crudely animate Beers' message as one of heroic redemption.'[53]

The exhibition reinforces the narrative that the terrorist attacks were on US freedom and values as opposed to the totemic symbols of its commercial power and military reach. As the exhibition opened in London, juxtaposed with an exhibition of the Blitz, the connections between the wars, their purpose and their meaning were enhanced. As Kennedy shows, Lynne Cheney made this explicit at the London exhibit with references to their 'shared difficulties', 'common values' and 'freedoms that were attacked', and the reminder from the Blitz that good would win in the end.[54]

As Sontag has argued, 'to photograph is to frame, and to frame is to exclude'.[55] Like the infamous *New Yorker* cartoon of its own city, there was little to know or understand beyond the Hudson River. The photography excluded the past, which facilitated the process of avoiding the difficult questions and potential lessons. This was not a narrative about the United States as protagonist, but that of victim, initially, but then of a resolute nation.

NATIONHOOD, NARRATIVES AND IDEOLOGY

The early and important construction of the narratives of 9/11 had and will continue to have a profound impact on the outcomes and actions taken throughout the world. The narratives that emerged, especially from the White House, found deep resonance in the US media, print and visual, and along with the flag and the definition of the enemy, they worked to galvanise domestic support.

In the context of these observations the narratives that emerged said a great deal about and to the individuals in the United States and helped them to locate themselves amongst the bewildering events that had just taken place. They also provided an explanation for conflicts that were about to unfold. Clearly visible in Bush's rhetoric was another important function of narratives: to 'reveal deep fears, perceived threats, and past grievances that drive a conflict'. By linking the terrorists' hatred for the United States with US freedom Bush was clear, if thoroughly misguided. Ross argues that 'narratives are important because they privilege certain actions over others'. Framing the actions of 9/11 within a narrative of war, as opposed to a criminal and terrorist act, facilitated the pursuit of certain actions and militaristic responses, and precluded a more imaginative and effective pursuit of the perpetrators, or at least those who worked with them. The narrative of war had deep resonance in US culture and was privileged as a response above all others.[56]

War provided the United States with a greater sense of national unity and purpose. But through Bush's rhetoric and the emergent narratives, the terrorism was juxtaposed against the benign framework of US history and diplomacy. Not only did the definition of the enemy enhance the Manichaean outlook, but the stories told by the president, newscasters, articles, op-ed pieces in the papers and magazines, further buttressed the basic dichotomy. This is not to suggest that other views were not present, but they were marginal to the thrust of the social preference. The explicit and insidious strategy conjured up the vocabulary of civilisational conflict; freedom, tolerance and democracy had been attacked according to such stories. The narratives provided both closure and explanation. They made connections with referents to the past in US foreign policy that most Americans were familiar with. They told stories about freedom, democracy and self-determination. They promised to bring justice to the world. They worked through multiple layers of reinforcement. The words employed were significant. Contexts and settings were important: whether Bush delivered his speeches in the National Cathedral or in the House of Congress, the locations sent messages. So too on the occasion when Bush climbed above the crowd in New York standing besides a fire fighter, bull horn raised, the crowd chanting 'USA, USA', when Bush let them know, '... the people who knocked these buildings down will hear all of us soon'.[57] The situation is largely regarded as a moment when Bush found his voice among the people. The mood was one of defiance. In the video sequence on the White House website one can hear the injunction, 'go get 'em'. The early and official narratives served as 'gatekeepers ruling in or out options for groups, decision makers, and politicians'. They reflected how the protagonists understood the impending wars and their own motivations. The stories provided 'in-group support and solidarity that promote negative images of the enemy, escalatory actions, and offer little room for accommodation'.[58]

At issue was the centrality of the US identity. It was imperative to place the events in the framework of the benign narratives rather than talk about the US support for authoritarian regimes across the Middle East for five decades, or to ponder the US support for Israel, or its interventions, or its sanctions regime in Iraq. All such connections had to be denied. Just to reiterate: such connections can in no way justify the acts of 9/11, but it is impossible to understand the events without this context. Coverage in the European press provides far more critical distance, with suggestions that Washington not only needed to examine its Middle East policy, but also to examine issues of development and the global structures of inequality. It was somewhat surprising to hear these criticisms so soon after the events, but beyond their obvious relevance, there was a sense that these authors and politicians were attempting to convey messages to slow the rush to war.[59]

The traditional narratives of the United States and US foreign policy are built around a series of myths. They relate to stories about liberty, democracy, self-determination, individualism and opportunity. It is not that all of these attributes are missing, but the public rhetoric is particularly exclusive of other interpretations and facets of US history. The collective consciousness and collective memories reinforce these myths through symbols, metaphors, national celebrations, memorials, political rhetoric, schools texts, films and so forth. There are substantial exclusions and exceptions to these suggestions. Obviously, not all Americans share the attachment to the benign narratives, but they are still delivered without trace of irony or self-reflection. So the US identity and that of the 'other', the conflation of bin Laden, the Taliban and Saddam Hussein, were subject to gross reductionism. As the work of Emile Durkheim, through Maurice Halbwachs, demonstrates, such constructs and myths are indispensable as 'integrative' and stabilising forces. They are vital to social organisation; they ensure solidarity and social cohesion.[60]

The United States and US foreign policy are mediated by the various ideological constructs, inspired and sustained by culture and society. The constructed collective memories ultimately secure the sense of historical place, in a bewildering present, and serve as a basis for moral action 'intended to shape a better future'. Such ideologies arise from a series of symbols, beliefs and values, which together provide US culture with certain structures of meaning.[61] These ideological constructs are as much a part of the thinking of policy makers as the general population. The narratives that emerge from their public rhetoric become one of the primary devices used to represent the past in US political culture. These narratives provide the essential context and framework to understand the US response.

'Nations themselves are narrations.' This was perhaps never more important in constructing the 'imagined community'. To that end it was important for Bush to reduce the character of the United States and that of its enemies to basic polarities, which make no contribution to analysis and understanding, but are essential to cohere and motivate society. As Renan put it: 'Getting its history wrong is part of being a nation.'[62]

3
Orientalism and the anti-American Sentiment

'As the Afghan bombs fall, the hate spills forth from the impoverished alleys of Quetta like blood from a festering, badly bandaged wound. In Palestine, the fury of a dispossessed people briefly flares, only to turn inward upon itself as if in self-disgust. From Jakarta to Cairo to Tehran, the symbols of the west's and, specifically, America's perceived economic and cultural domination are assailed. The world is no longer safe, it seems, for McDonald's.' ... The alleyways of Quetta are impoverished, as in so many developing countries, because there is no economic justice in a world run from Wall St. The Palestinians burn American flags not because they support Bin Laden but because, despairing of redress, they fall into his trap. The rage expressed in Egypt and other Arab countries is directed outwards because corrupt, oligarchic regimes deny their people the freedom to rage at them, as well they might.[1]

Is it an irony of monumental proportions that 9/11 came about because of an intense anti-Americanism and, in the aftermath of the international outpouring of sympathy, global anti-American sentiment intensified still further? The Bush administration squandered its opportunity to build on world-wide sympathy, and instead responded in the 'same language'. It constructed that wondrous 'imagined community' and set it against an 'evil' and imagined 'other'. As Washington promoted a policy of retribution in the name of all the virtues associated with its traditional and ideological nationalism, it encouraged its antithesis: anti-nationalism and widespread anti-Americanism. Both discourses, Orientalism and Occidentalism, were and are far too essentialist and reductionist; they fostered further the supposed differences with facile explanations of current events and rather than providing opportunities for greater pluralism, dialogue and engagement, they undermined the common ground between moderates in both 'West' and 'East'.

Colombani's headline, 'We Are All Americans Now', rang true in many ways, briefly. Rajeev Bhargava eloquently submitted:

For one moment, the pain and suffering of others became our own. In a flash, everyone recognised what is plain but easily forgotten: that inscribed in our personal selves is not just our separateness from others but also sameness with them; that despite all socially constructed differences of language, culture, religion, nationality, perhaps even race, caste and gender, and over and above every culturally specific collective identity, we share something in common. Amidst terror, acute vulnerability, and unbearable sorrow, it was not America alone that rediscovered its lost solidarity but, across the globe, almost everyone who heard, saw, or read about these cataclysmic events seemed to reclaim a common humanity.[2]

It was a bitter irony in March 2003 when the *Guardian* carried a headline to an article by the Egyptian editor, Hani Shukrallah, 'We are all Iraqis now'.[3]

There are many and varied forms of anti-Americanism and they must be understood in the contexts within which they arise. So too, the US views of Arabs, peoples from the Middle East, and even Islam must also be understood within the context in which they arise. The views of 'self' and 'other' are often counterposed, creating essences that rarely accord with a more complicated and integrated reality. Lewis Lapham, editor of *Harpers,* captured it well, 'No sum of historical justification can excuse the attack on the World Trade Center and the Pentagon, but neither can we excuse our own arrogance behind the scenes of shock and disbelief. Enthralled by an old script, we didn't see the planes coming because we didn't think we had to look.'[4] Such was the US imagination of itself, some very basic questions needed revisiting.

WHY DO THEY HATE US?

Bush attempted one of the first responses. He provided words of comfort, but he also constructed a framework that obscured more than it revealed. He misled his audience by suggesting that, 'they hate what we see right here in this chamber – a democratically elected government. Their leaders are self-appointed. They hate our freedoms – our freedom of religion, our freedom of speech, our freedom to vote and assemble and disagree with each other.' He did not point out that many in the Middle East saw another America, one that supported authoritarian regimes, which suppressed democracy and freedoms. Bush continued, 'these terrorists kill not merely to end lives, but to disrupt and end a way of life. With every atrocity, they hope that America grows fearful, retreating from the world and forsaking our friends. They stand against us, because we stand in their way.' Certainly they sought to disrupt a way of life through the attacks, but also through the symbolic resonance of the targets: icons of US commercial and military might. The subsequent rhetorical juxtaposition is worth examining. Certainly there was the desire to see the United States retreat somewhat; specifically from their military bases in Saudi Arabia, but more generally from their presence in the Middle East. But the use of the phrase, 'we stand in their way' echoes the containment thesis that captivated US culture and the minds of US policy makers for a couple of decades between the Second World War and the Vietnam War, rather than illuminating the advanced presence of the United States throughout the region. And finally, there was that ludicrous and facile conflation of their identity: the terrorists were lined up with the big enemies of the twentieth century, as if the world were so simple that everything the United States fought derived its inspiration from the same sources. Bush asserted: 'We are not deceived by their pretences to piety. We have seen their kind before. They are the heirs of all the murderous ideologies of the 20th century. By sacrificing human life to serve their radical visions – by abandoning every value except the will to power – they follow in the path of fascism, and Nazism, and totalitarianism. And they will follow that path all the way, to where it ends: in history's unmarked grave of discarded lies.'[5]

The United States would fight these 'enemies of human freedom',[6] Bush told his audience at the National Cathedral. And back at Congress: 'this is not, however, just America's fight. And what is at stake is not just America's freedom. This is the world's fight. This is civilization's fight. This is the fight of all who believe in progress and pluralism, tolerance and freedom.'[7] These words must be placed in the rhetorical framework that reinforced the benign meta-narrative of US history, culture and foreign policy. That narrative may have provided consolation, but it did little to advance understanding. If the intention was to reassure and uplift, fine within the context, but it also had the effect of blocking enquiry and a real debate on the nature of US interests in the Middle East, the use of its power, and the domestic control of its foreign policy.

The rhetorical framework exacerbated two immediate problems. First, an exceptional and exclusive US identity was constructed. The axiomatic association of the United States with such concepts of freedom, justice, tolerance, democracy and so forth, not only obscures an understanding of the United States held by many in the Middle East and elsewhere, but also denies many of the histories developed within the United States, whether these are the revisionist interpretations of US diplomatic history, or others advanced by African-Americans, women and other so-called hyphenated-Americans. The concepts of freedom, tolerance and democracy are unrepresentative of their experiences.

Second, a Manichaean world-view was advanced. Despite the widespread denials to the contrary, the rhetoric used conjured up and enhanced the notion of a 'clash of civilisations', associated with Bernard Lewis', 'The Roots of Muslim Rage,'[8] and Samuel Huntington's controversial *The Clash of Civilizations.*[9] The implications of the sentence: 'Either you are with us, or you are with the terrorists' constrained the latitude of options available to those who were appalled by the acts of 9/11, but similarly were resolutely opposed to the US response and resort to war in Afghanistan in 2001 and then Iraq in 2003. While such binary sentiments were somewhat shared by authors like Huntington, who argued that the 'clash of civilisations' would also be a real test for the concepts of nationalism, of what it meant to be an American, and the West,[10] the problem with such a constructed discourse is that it is not only reductive, simplistic and enhances the supposedly essential qualities of both the United States and the 'other', but, like most orientalist discourses, it tends to approach 'a heterogeneous, dynamic, and complex human reality from an uncritically essentialist standpoint; this suggests both an enduring Oriental reality and an opposing but no less enduring Western essence, which observes the Orient from afar and, so to speak, from above'.[11] This hides historical change. Moreover, this essentialist discourse not only feeds, but also mirrors that of the anti-American rhetoric used in the Middle East.

Realities, of course, are much more complicated. Those trying to promote a sense of an enduring American national identity have had to deal with the difficult issues of the Civil Rights movement, black liberation, feminism and increases in non-white immigration in the post-war period and so forth. A post-orientalist approach 'suggests that the category of nation is not in itself adequate for understanding the histories we have often presumed to be "American"'.[12] Broader than this, the concept of the West as a unitary entity or that of the 'Islamic threat' are similarly infused with so many internal differences and contradictions that the complicated histories of their development and encounters with each other are simply elided to advance the Manichaean discourse of opposition.[13]

ORIENTALISM AND THE CLASH OF CIVILISATION

If various forms of Occidentalism have been of primary consideration since 9/11, it is no less important to examine US Orientalism. In many regards the Occidentalism that feeds so much of the anti-Americanism at the periphery is mirrored in the condescending Orientalism exhibited in US culture and policy-making circles. It is important to note that even though US attitudes towards Middle Eastern peoples and Muslims more generally have taken on particular forms, they are not exclusive to the region or the religion. US policy makers have exhibited similar attitudes towards Native Americans, Latin Americans and East and South East Asians at various points of encounter.[14] While these attitudes do not necessarily drive US policy, they certainly influence the manner and demeanour of its conduct.

The outlook must be put in historical context to understand the prevailing US attitudes towards the Middle East and Islam, which are too often taken together. Little argues that in order to understand the past half-century of the US encounters with the Middle East, one must first understand US cultural baggage. Looking at popular culture in the eighteenth and nineteenth centuries, he points out that 'Muslims, Jews, and most other peoples of the Middle East were "orientalized" and depicted as backward, decadent, and untrustworthy. By 1900 anti-Semitic and anti-Islamic sentiments were as American as apple pie.' After the Second World War, anti-Semitism 'abated somewhat, and Jews were "westernized" while Arabs and Muslims were "demonized" as anti-Western terrorists'.[15]

'Arabs, Africans, and Asians who grace the pages of *National Geographic* are backward, exotic, and occasionally dangerous folk who have needed and will continue to need U.S. help and guidance if they are successfully to undergo political and cultural modernization.'[16] Some examples illustrate this point. The White House counsel, Clark Clifford, opined that Washington would appear 'in the ridiculous role of trembling before threats of a few nomadic desert tribes' if it cowed in the face of Arab hostility to US recognition of Israel. In 1949 a CIA psychological profile indicated that the Arabs were 'non-inventive and slow to put theories into practice' and 'skilful mainly at avoiding hard work'. Eisenhower argued, 'Nasser embodies the emotional demands of the people of the area for independence and for "slapping the White Man down".[17] As late as 1971 a CIA handbook reported that 'the Arab fighting man "lacks the necessary physical and cultural qualities for performing effective military services." The Arabs were thought to be so clearly inferior that another attack would be irrational and, thus, out of the question.' Just days before the Arab attack in 1973, despite warning to the contrary, the CIA reported a 'ho-hum' day in the Middle East.[18] Said's work in *Orientalism* (1995), *Culture and Imperialism* (1993), and *Covering Islam* (1997) has built up a study of the relationship between power and discourse on this issue and demonstrates that the stereotypes of Arabs and Islam serve to justify Western cultural and economic imperialism. Yet simultaneously, 'lurking behind all of these images is the menace of *jihad*' with the fear that Islam will take over the world. Such views contrasted the democratic Israel against the homogeneously undemocratic Arab world, whose inhabitants were implicitly associated with the Palestinians and were all, therefore, terrorists.[19]

Said not only examined the body of writing in the United States, France and Britain to comment on its Orientalism, he also linked these writings to power and explored their symbiotic relationship. The 'communities of interpretation' are central to the ability of the policy-making community, understood in the broad sense, including politicians, journalists and commentators, marketing strategists and corporations, to categorise, identify and to use these entities for cultural mobilisation or to frame a certain outlook. Rarely was the concept of 'Islam' deployed in US culture or media prior to the oil crisis of the early 1970s. After that it became a frequently abused term invoking negative associations.[20]

Such discourses facilitated the conceptual separation of the 'West' from 'Islam' in cultural debate, even though another more material interpretation and the pursuit of oil insisted on constant US engagement and integration. The dilemmas of both integration and conceptual separation are not new in US history and diplomacy, facilitating the beliefs in a US exceptionalism. The discussions of US exceptionalism have been closely related to the notion of an exclusive nation and nationalism. Islamism represents the constructed 'other' at this juncture in history. Similar discussions and concepts were deployed during encounters with Native Americans and later Latin Americans. The Monroe Doctrine of 1823 advanced a conceptual model of the world based on the Western Hemisphere and the 'Old World' of Europe (Rumsfeld was a mere echo in the long tradition).

The positive attributes of the new world were contrasted with negative attributes of the old, despite the diversity within both spheres. The exceptionalism of the metaphorical West could be advanced as a symbol of progress in world history. The problem was that US attitudes towards the Latin Americans were also quite demeaning: they too had been orientalised in US discourse.[21] They were at once a part of the West, they belonged to us, but they were also the 'other'. The concept of the West extended after the Second World War to incorporate 'old' Europe, the previous antithesis to US identity, and by the end of the Cold War the so-called 'clash of civilisations' had advanced its conceptual frontier to the Balkan region, where 'Islam' begins (ignoring all the Muslim people throughout Western Europe and the multicultural societies that have been built up during the period). The narratives of separation were privileged over those of integration, understanding and peaceful coexistence and moderation. The process facilitated many cultural responses to various conflicts. Dealing with the complex and heterogeneous world through categorisation allowed policy makers to cope with information overload. Neat analogies were more appealing. By the late 1950s, everyone knew that 'Egypt's Gamal Abdel Nasser is another Adolf Hitler. Guatemala's Jacobo Arbenz must be a Communist. If it looks like a duck and acts like a duck, it is a duck.' Axiomatically, during the Cold War all ducks were fed by Moscow and when it ran out of food the Hitler analogy was revived.[22] Too often this categorisation has facilitated U-turns in cultural perceptions that belie the historical relationship. The construction of Saddam Hussein as another Hitler after August 1990 obliterated the history of US engagement, deference, material assistance and its muted voice on the gassing of the Kurds in 1988. It was particularly disturbing to see British and American politicians talk with such vehemence about this episode during 2002 as they stirred emotions for the war on Iraq as if compensating for their relative silence in 1988 when Hussein was still within the fold.

Shunning complexity facilitated the crusading spirit; but similarly even though there is considerable internal and complex analysis within the various administrations, frequently some of these assumptions and ideological preferences creep into policy and contribute to difficulties the United States later encounters. If the adage, to understand one's enemy is central to effective engagement, too often such understanding has fallen short, not least in Vietnam, Nicaragua and Iraq.

If the oil crisis of 1973 led to a new rhetoric about the 'rise of Islam', the revolution in Iran in 1979 reinforced it and, by the time Saddam Hussein invaded Kuwait in 1990, the notion of an 'Islamic threat' was prevalent throughout the Western media. The bipolar view of the situation was augmented by Bernard Lewis' explanation of the 'roots of Muslim rage' derived from an Islamic irrational hatred of the Western and Judaeo-Christian civilisation, in which the United States had become 'the archenemy, the incarnation of evil' for theocracies throughout the region. For Lewis, a war against modernity in the region would ultimately lead to a 'clash of civilisations'. By 1993 Huntington used the phrase in *Foreign Affairs*, later published in book form.[23] Huntington's thesis is that 'the fundamental source of conflict in this new world will not be primarily ideological or primarily economic. The great divisions among humankind and the dominating source of conflict will be cultural.'[24] The argument is replete with selectivity and has come under considerable criticism. It contained subtitles and sections that dealt with 'the west versus the rest' and 'the Confucian-Islamic connection', anticipating another later conflation by the 43rd president on the 'axis of evil'.

Shortly after 9/11 Bush and Blair went out of their way to visit mosques and to insist that the conflict was not with Islam, that it did not represent a clash of civilisations. But of course within the wider, more popular contexts the actions of the terrorists of 9/11, the subsequent bombing of Afghanistan and the invasion of Iraq made it appear and feel all the more like one; indeed bin Laden insisted there was one. Three years after the invasion of Iraq, bin Laden, feeding off the discontent generated by the Western response to the Danish cartoon controversy, the US response to Hamas' electoral victory and the ongoing situation in Afghanistan, Iraq and Darfur, continued to maintain that the West was waging a long war against Islam. Moreover, the polarisation was reflected in the United States. Polls indicated that negative perceptions of Islam in the United States were growing. Nearly half of those polled held negative views of Islam.[25] Though there was much ink spilt on the 'Islamic threat', few commentators in the mainstream press wondered about how people in the Middle East and Muslims more generally felt about the West. Jonathan Freedland writes, 'with typical arrogance, most western thinkers assumed Huntington's thesis was all about us; we forgot about them'.[26] Washington paid little attention to anti-Americanism prior to the attacks. After 9/11 a lot of media print, academic conferences and collections addressed the issue. When

Abdu Sattar Kassem indicated that he understood the anti-American feelings, he later complained that 'the dumbest thing of all is that when I tried to talk to American colleagues and explain why they were disliked in the Middle East, they simply did not want to hear it or believe it. ... They simply believe that they are the best, and nothing can challenge that.'[27] US exceptionalism, which was evident throughout President Bush's post-9/11 rhetoric, remained intact. The failings were those of others, in either comprehension of the United States or its variation on the modernist project, or in envy and resentment. Though a very brief and closed two-day State Department seminar addressed the issue, afterwards anti-Americanism was largely treated as a PR problem. Offices were set up to disseminate 'strategic information'.[28] But by 2004, after the invasion of Iraq, Margaret Tutwiler, now in charge of public diplomacy at the State Department, admitted 'it will take us many years of hard, focused work' to restore the image of the United States. Edward Djerejian, testifying to the House Appropriations Committee, later pointed out that 'the bottom has indeed fallen out of support for the United States'.[29]

AMERICANISATION AND ANTI-AMERICANISATION

Anti-Americanism is inconceivable without Americanism, it is 'an expression of nationalism that is a product both of the United States itself and of others' expectations of it'.[30] Its virulence seems to be quite directly related to the growth and assertion of US power, especially in the Middle East. Initially, its presence was more or less confined to the corporate pursuit of oil interests, but after the Second World War it projected its power into the region, first as a by-product of the Truman Doctrine, then with its recognition and initial, hesitant support for Israel.

The United States increasingly made its presence felt after deposing the Mossadegh government and supporting the Shah of Iran. By the mid 1950s and especially after the Suez crisis the British and French influence was increasingly replaced. The Cold War ensured a US presence, to 'contain' the Soviet Union but also, as many commentators have argued, to contain radical Arab nationalism[31] and regimes that sought greater return on their oil deposits.

By the late 1950s the National Security Council recognised that the United States would have to live with the difficulty of the Middle East for a long time and treated the 'problem as hopeless of solution in the near future'. It recognised that there were a number of 'Arab beliefs' that 'cut across our existing policy guidance' and that were 'obstacles to U.S. objectives'. Amongst the Arab beliefs that the National Security Council commented on were that: Israel posed a greater threat than communism; eventually, Israel should 'disappear'; the US 'befriends the ex-"colonial" powers'; that 'Algerian "freedom" is a must for Arabs'. The National Security Council also detected further beliefs that remain pertinent. First, 'there is a mystique that ties all Arabs together – not only common religious belief. The U.S. wants to keep the Arab world disunited and thus get Arab oil for itself and allies...'. Second, 'the U.S. is identified only with archaic, status-quo, and reactionary regimes'.[32] That association remained a pertinent issue into the twenty-first century. Such relationships were vital to US strategic imperatives.

Beyond the economic necessity of maintaining access to oil in the region, several layers of conflict and war ensured a US presence. The Cold War was central to US planning, but it intersected in many ways with the other regional conflicts. US policy was primarily concerned with strategic denial; a Soviet regional presence was considered detrimental. Middle Eastern oil was not just a strategic concern in terms of the Cold War rivalry. The phenomenal economic growth of the early post-war period, the ideologies and the models of economic growth, development theories, were all dependent on access to cheap oil. Without it, the West might not have grown so fast, appeared so prosperous or been so strong. In the absence of a significant alternative fuel, Western and US dependency was acute and growing. Even the projections of US oil needs at the beginning of the twenty-first century posited US access to the Middle East, sub-Saharan Africa, Venezuela and Central Asia, amongst other areas.[33]

Given the Cold War divisions in the Middle East, Washington was caught on the horns of a dilemma, because it supported both Israel and certain Arab states and Iran. Between the Arab–Israeli wars of 1967 to 1973 both superpowers increased their presence considerably. This process was tied to the third level of conflict relating to the Palestinian problem. As the Soviets supplied their client states with arms, Israel constantly opted to enhance its security through the acquisition of more arms, primarily from the United States. As it did so, the US allies in the region also sought weapons, to 'balance' both the Soviet client states, but also the added power of Israel.[34] The bottom line was that from the late 1960s, the US presence in the region grew rapidly. They were increasingly viewed as supporters not only of Israel, but also the authoritarian regimes from Saudi

Arabia to Iran. And, of course, when the Shah was overthrown in a primarily anti-American revolution in 1979, Iraq was brought into the fray to ensure US presence and access. In time US covert and overt aid buttressed Saddam Hussein's regime as a counterbalance to the 'loss' of Iran.

The US relationship with Hussein grew. With a radical and anti-American Iran, Iraq's invasion of Kuwait and sudden alienation of the United States threatened to leave the West extremely vulnerable. Without Soviet counterforce at the end of the Cold War, Washington was free to roll back Hussein's invasion of Kuwait after August 1990. The critical decision not to move on and topple Hussein in early 1991 meant that the US presence in the region expanded further. Its presence was manifested in three evocative, emotive and potent symbols. First, the sanctions regime imposed on Iraq depicted both Washington and London, its main sponsors, as callous and cruel powers, willing to impoverish and kill the most vulnerable in Iraqi society. In a now infamous exchange, in 1996, when the then US Ambassador to the United Nations and later Secretary of State, Madeleine Albright, was asked by *60 Minutes* in a somewhat convoluted question: 'We have heard that half a million children have died. I mean, that is more children than died in Hiroshima. And, you know, is the price worth it?' Albright replied: 'I think that is a very hard choice, but the price, we think, the price is worth it.'[35] The second important symbol is of the near constant and relentless bombing of Iraq throughout the 1990s. And finally, to conduct these operations, the United States needed bases in Saudi Arabia, which drew the ire of radicals.

Osama bin Laden enumerated these issues. When Robert Fisk interviewed him, Fisk noted that history, or bin Laden's version of it, underpinned most of his reasoning and resentment. Three issues were specifically identified: the US presence in Saudi Arabia and the protest against it by the *ulema*. Saudi Arabia was regarded as a US colony, a regime that frustrates the aspirations of its people: 'the ordinary man knows that his country is the largest oil producer in the world, yet at the same time he is suffering from taxes and bad services'. Further, bin Laden cited the Palestinian issue and the deaths of Iraqi children as a result of the UN imposed sanctions against Iraq and added: 'We as Muslims do not like the Iraqi regime but we think that the Iraqi people and their children are our brothers and we care about their future.'[36] Bin Laden continued to describe the most pertinent issues in the Middle East and to voice the concerns of Muslims throughout the world in his intermittent video messages in subsequent years. His rhetoric tapped into an anger that was further fuelled by US efforts to isolate Hamas, the provocative Danish cartoons and the festering situation in Darfur.[37]

Beyond the specific issues, Professor Abdu Sattar Kassem at the University of Nablus explained shortly after 9/11 that the United States did not seem to understand that Arabs and Muslims wanted to build their own civilisation and that they 'blame the West in general – and America in particular – for subjugating that ambition by dividing the Arab world through the dictators that America supports'. He elaborated, 'America has perverted the attempts to democratise the Arab world. They are hypocrites. They preach freedom and democracy, but prevent Arabs from enjoying it and exploit their wealth.'[38] These views were very much a part of the immediate post-9/11 discourse: 'From Algeria to Egypt to Yemen, from Iraq to Pakistan, military or authoritarian governments – many of them U.S. allies – deny their citizens basic freedoms.'[39] The point can be both related to the accusations of double standards, but also to what others have referred to as a deep crisis within the Middle East, which suggests that since its encounters with the West over the last half-century, Arab states have not advanced indigenous models of development. This coupled with the dramatic rise in Arab population, and its relative youth, without any substantial improvements in living conditions, has led to a gap between expectations and fulfilment. It is no wonder that Islamists focus their attention and recruitment methods on these disaffected youth and that in the words of an Egyptian diplomat, 'people like bin Laden carefully target the poor and illiterate, people they know are suffering, and present their vision as a kind of revolutionary Islam that will magically solve all their ills'.[40]

Tracing 200 years of interaction, Ussama Makdisi contends, 'Anti-Americanism is a recent phenomenon fuelled by American foreign policy, not an epochal confrontation of civilizations. While there are certainly those in both the United States and the Arab world who believe in a clash of civilizations and who invest politically in such beliefs, history belies them.' Anti-Americanism 'stems less from a blind hatred of the United States or American values' than from a deep and profound 'ambivalence about America'. The United States is admired on a range of levels, not least for its affluence, films, technology, secularism, law and order, but also it is a 'source of deep disappointment given the ongoing role of the United States in shaping a repressive Middle Eastern status quo'. Moreover, anti-

Americanism is not ideologically consistent or coherent, it varies across the Arab world.[41]

The discrepancy between US promise and performance has produced widespread disappointment. At the broad conceptual level it is galvanised by three issues. First, there is enmity because of US support for Israel. Second, there is the politics of oil and secular Arab nationalism. And finally, there is radical Islamism and the political expression of it.

Initially there was considerable admiration for the United States and its stated principles on democracy and self-determination. Such ideas could undermine the authority of the Ottoman Empire. Then in 1917, Washington supported the British and the Balfour Declaration, which pledged British support for the establishment of a Jewish homeland. Makdisi explains, 'no account of anti-Americanism in the Arab world that does not squarely address the Arab understanding of Israel can even begin to convey the nature, the depth, and the sheer intensity of Arab anger at the United States'. The anger focuses on particular areas that cause aggravation. Of course there is the *nakba* or catastrophe of 1948, when Palestinians were uprooted from their homeland and 400 villages razed. The constant displacement and violence against the Palestinians has fermented anti-Americanism. There is a huge gap in the perceptions on Palestine held between the United States and many in the Middle East: 'satellite television stations such as Al-Jazeera daily beam pictures of Palestinian *suffering* under Israeli *occupation* directly into Arab households at a time when American television represents the Palestinian–Israeli conflict largely as Arab *violence* against Israel and Israeli *retaliation* against this violence'.[42] In this sense, globalisation and its products of bringing satellite TVs and the internet into many Arab homes, has loosened the tight control on information in previous years.[43] All of this is compounded by the Israeli expansion and occupation of further lands after 1967: the West Bank, Gaza, East Jerusalem and the Golan Heights. The continued expansion of the settlements and the conduct of the Sharon and subsequent governments added further fuel to the anger. Throughout this, Israel has remained the largest recipient of US aid, running at over $3 billion a year. Finally, there is the strong perception that the United States operates a system of double standards throughout the region, not only concerning democracy and self-determination, but also directly related to their lax approach to enforcing UN Security Council Resolutions (242 and 336) against Israel, while monitoring and responding to every Iraqi transgression of UN Security Council resolutions, particularly Resolution 687 on their possession of weapons of mass destruction.

The tensions between the politics of oil and secular Arab nationalism have caused further anger, distrust and hatred. The discovery and development of oil prior to the Second World War led to the emergence of a symbiotic relationship between Washington, US corporations and authoritarian regimes. While there is a high regard for US ideas and institutions, US power compromises the principles associated with democracy, self-determination and liberty. In pursuit of regional stability, a balance of power and access to oil, the US government is more closely associated with the undemocratic status quo and the repressive regimes that maintain it. The polarity and the Cold War constructs merely enforced these tensions, ensuring that Washington moved at decisive moments against Arab nationalism and nationalists who sought greater control of their resources. There are deep cultural memories of the deposition of Mossadegh in 1953, of US opposition to Nasser and US support for the Shah of Iran. The United States was not seen as the progressive power reflected in so much of its rhetoric.[44] Ultimately, American power was identified with the forces of repression rather than liberation.

If secular Arab nationalism prevailed through the 1960s, an Islamic alternative arose from the defeat of Arab nationalists, particularly Nasser, by Israel in 1967. The success of the Iranian revolution of 1979 and Ayatollah Ruhollah Khomeini's accession to power symbolised the changes. In much of Khomeini's rhetoric, anti-Americanism was used to foster a sense of common purpose and common enmity. Khomeini identified the United States as the 'most important and painful problem' of the subjugated nations of the world. During the 1980s, the resurgence of militant anti-Americanism focused on increased US aid to Israel under Reagan, a growing sense of US hegemony throughout the Gulf states, continued US support for authoritarianism, despite the end of the Cold War, and greater US presence in Saudi Arabia after the 1991 Gulf War. Many viewed the House of Fahd as too dependent on Washington. And again, the continued and devastating sanctions on Iraq provided the focus for the renewed strain of anti-Americanism.[45] The continued US engagement further fuelled Middle Eastern antipathy. Makdisi puts it well:

Their specific political anti-Americanism is inextricably bound up with their religious defensiveness and their more general repudiation of secular culture.

Their anti-Americanism is not, however, simply a reaction against the basing of U.S. 'infidels' near Mecca and Medina; nor is it simple fury at long-lost Muslim ascendancy. Such Islamists see the United States as a leader of a new crusade, a term that in the Arab world is replete not only with religious connotations of spiritual violation but equally with political ideas of occupation and oppression, in short, of worldly *injustice*.[46]

Further, reports on the recent 'street' anti-Americanism suggest that the attacks on the West Bank, the Gaza Strip, Afghanistan and Iraq are seen as interlinked projects. US power, especially airpower, and its particular application in the early stages of the wars in Afghanistan and Iraq, is seen as overwhelming. Fahed Fanek, writing in the *Jordan Times*, captured the hopeless and helpless sentiment well: 'what can the world do to confront the overwhelming superiority of the US air force? Nothing more than face up to it with hatred of America, its policies and the Bush administration. It is possible that the weapon of hatred will prove more effective and more enduring than that of the American air force.'[47]

CONCLUSION

Orientalism and Occidentalism are symbiotic discourses that have fed and continue to feed off each other and maintain the distance between the extremes, the regimes and people that benefit from such discord and animosity. Such language does not admit to complexity or explore the real engagements and encounters between various peoples, cultures, countries and states. When examining these encounters the vital politics of identity are soon seen as thoroughly wanting.

Double standards seem to lie at the heart of much anti-Americanism. It is probably a convenient and comfortable conclusion to suggest that there is a hatred of American institutions, ideas and ideologies. As Waterbury argues, it 'is a more comforting explanation of Muslim rage than the notion that the United States has violated its own norms, elevated conflicts of interest to crusades against evil, and dismissed entire peoples as hopelessly corrupt, violent, and mired in medieval cant'.[48] The reservoir of good will towards the United States has evaporated over fifty years because of the perception that the United States has failed to act in accordance with the principles on which it was founded. It has acted contrary to those principles and betrayed them: 'In a word, power seems to have mattered more than principle. The empire has subsumed the democratic republic.'[49]

In sum, several key features are worth reflection. First, the economic structures and processes of globalisation associated with American hegemony are widely seen as contributing to much of the relative and absolute poverty in the world. The rhetoric on US 'leadership' does little to ameliorate the tensions and the beliefs that the United States is a defining power in the world order. There is a widespread resentment against the United States and the West as a result of the perception that its power and globalisation erode traditional cultures and values. Washington set the agenda. What it wanted went, so the reasoning goes. It is at once the broker of the Palestinian–Israeli conflict, though its interests are so clearly one-sided. Other major international interests and issues stand or fall depending on the US stance. The ICC or the Kyoto protocol prosper or perish depending on US inclinations.[50]

Second, the mutual perceptions of the extremes are important; no matter how inaccurate and at times ludicrous are the depictions of the 'other', these characterisations command adherence. But they do represent extreme approaches against the possibilities and potential for a rich and diverse engagement. Such polarisation is not unfamiliar, but it is important to understand that the United States and its foreign policies cannot be left out of the equation. The clash, if there has to be one, has also been more aptly referred to as *The Clash of Fundamentalisms* and *The Clash of Barbarisms* in recent works.[51] It did not begin on 9/11, 'on the timing and terms of others' and underestimating the endurance of resistance it will probably not 'end in a way, and at an hour, of our choosing', as Bush proclaimed.[52] Western 'fundamentalism' echoes its 'other'. There is a combination, as Madeleine Bunting writes, of: 'first, a sense of unquestioned superiority; second, an assertion of the universal applicability of its values; and third, a lack of will to understand what is profoundly different from us'.[53]

Third, there exists what Sardar and Davies have referred to as the ontological reasons for such enmity. If the United States vilifies the 'other', be it Nasser, Arbenz, Ortega, Noriega, Khomeini, Hussein, bin Laden, or asserts the existence of an 'evil empire' or 'axis of evil' through the Manichaean looking glass, ontologically the United States is posited as the power of good. Such narratives of US foreign policy and intervention have fostered widespread scepticism and disbelief. It is perhaps a historical irony that a list of characters from Mao Zedong, Ho Chi Minh, Gamal Abdel Nasser and Fidel Castro were great admirers of the United States until they came to power. Ho looked to the United States for support in 1919 and 1945; the CIA assisted Nasser in the overthrow of the monarchy in 1952; Castro thought that perhaps the United States would welcome his revolution at least in principle. Jeffersonian and Wilsonian rhetoric was echoed throughout speeches by these characters.[54]

Finally, the United States has become the *defining* power in the so-called 'American Century' and after. It decides what 'democracy' is, and which states are 'democratic', it decides what freedom means, of what justice comprises and so forth. No other power has such rhetorical influence. Consequently there is a widespread belief that US style universalism has left very little room for greater pluralism within the global order, that other people might have very different conceptions, traditions and practices of democracy, freedom and justice.[55] After all, a half-century of interaction has, by and large, maintained the position of disparity.

Power remains crucial. The promotion of democracy, freedom and justice would find little resistance at the periphery. But this is quite different from talking about the promotion of American style or backed democracy, US conceptions of liberty or justice. There is much ambivalence: an admiration for the ideas, products and lifestyle, and simultaneous animosity towards aspects of its foreign policy.[56]

4

War and Just War: Terrorism and Afghanistan

'Afghanistan proved that expensive precision weapons defeat the enemy and spare innocent lives, and we need more of them.'[1]

The 'war on terrorism' is not a 'clash of civilisations'. Not even in the sense of the delineation of the 'civilised' against the 'terrorists' so prevalent in official rhetoric. The neat categories do not work in history or in practice.[2] Though there is little doubt that the attacks of 9/11 were acts of terrorism, justice requires a considered response. In the haste between 9/11 and 10/7, when the bombs started to fall on Afghanistan, too much occurred to suggest that the war taken to Afghanistan ignored the requirements of justice and too little occurred to suggest that the Bush administration was really interested in establishing a just response to the atrocities in New York, Virginia and Pennsylvania. The concept of justice was never far beneath the surface, but it was defined by Washington and mostly applied to non-state actors. The presumed framework of justice exercised by the Bush administration was based on an ontological disposition. In circular arguments, the United States defined what was good and what was just, because they themselves depicted their traditions and the exercise of their power as both good and just. September 11 shaped the Bush administration and its reaction in significant ways. The US response would not merely attempt to capture the perpetrators of 9/11. Days later, Bush told his audience that 'our responsibility to history is already clear: to answer these attacks and rid the world of evil'.[3] And a week later to a Joint Session of Congress: 'Whether we bring our enemies to justice, or bring justice to our enemies, justice will be done.'[4] These dispositions were coupled with long-held traditions in which the US executive had become accustomed not only to making judgements but also, and especially, from the turn of the nineteenth into the twentieth century, acting as the world police power.

In the Manichaean construct of 'civilisation' and 'terrorism' the various admonitions by Bush administration officials, by the British

Prime Minister or members (now former members) of his cabinet, in Jack Straw and Claire Short's accusations of 'appeasement' and charges of 'emotional' argument, and Bush's warning, 'You're either with us ... or against us', were all designed to maintain consensus, adherence and clarity of purpose. Yet the assumptions of justice in the case of taking war to Afghanistan need to be questioned. The conduct and repercussions of the war in Afghanistan evolved under quite particular circumstances; it was ineffective, immoral and possibly illegal.

On 11 September 2001 Kofi Annan, the Secretary General of the United Nations, spoke of a world unity 'born of horror'. He later wrote that the terrorists 'aimed at one nation but wounded an entire world'.[5] This was a clear signal of the shared grief and outrage at the acts of 9/11. Here was an opportunity for communal response that could undercut any narratives of legitimacy and isolate these particular terrorists.

Considerable debate within the Bush cabinet on the most appropriate response was conducted. There were the obvious divisions between the Secretary of State, Colin Powell and his rivals, in the Pentagon, Paul Wolfowitz and his boss, the Secretary of Defense, Donald Rumsfeld. In the charged atmosphere there were few advocates of diplomacy. Yet, immediate military action was difficult; Bush had been highly critical of Clinton's use of $2 million missiles launched into $20 tents. Still, within three weeks the war became reality.

A war needs to address a series of criteria to be considered just. These criteria are generally divided into two categories dealing with the approach to war and the conduct of the war. *Jus ad bellum* deals with questions of competent authority, just cause and right intention. *Jus in bello* deals with the principle of proportion and discrimination. Though there was tremendous opportunity for the United States to drive the argument on justice home and to seize the moral high ground after 9/11, the choices that the Bush administration made are called into question by too many of the strictures of just war theory. Let's deal with them in turn.

COMPETENT AUTHORITY

There are two areas to consider here, jurisdiction within the United States and beyond it. Though Bush did not seek a declaration of war on Afghanistan, there is scant evidence to suggest that many opposed him. The exception of course was Congresswoman Barbara

Lee representing the 9th District of California. She was the sole member of the House to vote against the resolution on the grounds that it provided the president with a 'blank check' to pursue force 'in any country' and 'without time limit', conjuring up all the attendant cultural memories of the 1964 Gulf of Tonkin Resolution at the outset of the Vietnam War. The facts had to be ascertained to 'ensure that violence does not beget violence', she later wrote. She did not dispute the president's stated intention to rid the world of terrorism, but questioned his methods. They would likely, 'spawn further acts of terror' or would 'not address the sources of hatred' and would 'not increase our security'. Finally, she pointed out, a 'rush to launch precipitous military attacks runs too great a risk that more innocent men, women and children will be killed'.[6] On purely pragmatic grounds it was worth while for Bush to insist on a declaration of war, not least to share the burden of responsibility. Vietnam lasted eight years without a declaration, but the tragedy of that war (for Americans) was that once they were in the war they found it impossible to extract themselves from it, without suffering even more casualties or losing their credibility, personal, party and patria. In Vietnam there was the temptation to expand the war, incrementally, just to do a little bit more to avoid defeat, but not enough to win the war, as if that were possible. Of course, we now know and many suspected early on that the current 'war' would not be limited to the pursuit of bin Laden, al Qaeda, the Taliban, or Afghanistan; it too expanded, incrementally. The administration's 'vaulting ambition' was stalled and subverted in the Sunni triangle, in places like Falluja and Najaf. Congresswoman Lee's words were prescient. The killing continued, anti-Americanism developed further, security was no more enhanced and the closure of war was elusive.

There was broad support for the United States immediately after 9/11. On 12 September, the UN General Assembly condemned 'the heinous acts of terrorism'. It expressed condolence and solidarity with the United States, and urgently called 'for international cooperation to bring to justice the perpetrators, organizers, and sponsors of the outrages of 11 September 2001'. In a statement that closely mirrored Bush administration thinking that made no distinctions between the terrorists and those who harboured them, the United Nations called for international cooperation to prevent and eradicate terrorism, and stressed 'that those responsible for aiding, supporting, or harbouring the perpetrators, organizers and sponsors of such acts will be held responsible'.[7] Kofi Annan underlined the unity and solidarity of the United Nations: the 'United Nations must have the courage to recognise that just as there are common aims, there are common enemies.' He argued that the United Nations was 'uniquely positioned' to build a universal coalition that could ensure 'global legitimacy' for a long-term response to terrorism. Its legal framework provided the guidelines against extradition, prosecution of offenders, money laundering and so forth. Such legitimacy was required because, 'essential to the global response to terrorism is that it not fracture the unity of Sept. 11'. The response could not single out divisions between societies and cultures; the response would have to be broad, and 'address the ills of conflict, ignorance, poverty and disease'. The intended message was that the response should be broad in its agenda, rather than merely in geography. Rather than buying into the clash of civilisations, the world should show that if it will 'carry on, that it will persevere in creating a stronger, more just, more benevolent and more genuine international community across all lines of religion and race, then terrorism will have failed'.[8]

Initially, the United Nations Security Council passed two resolutions, Resolution 1368 on 12 September and Resolution 1373 on 28 September. Both provided broad support for the United States. The latter reflected much of Annan's thinking and presented a long list of steps that states were required to pursue in the struggle against terrorism. Though much action has been taken along these legal and economic procedures, they have not been the focus of the Bush response. The words 'readiness to take all necessary steps to respond to the terrorist attacks' has been read as providing competent authority, but the rest of point 5 in Resolution 1368, 'in accordance with its responsibilities under the Charter of the United Nations', has been largely ignored.[9]

Resolution 1373 did recognise the right to self-defence echoing both Resolution 1368 and more generally Article 51 of the UN Charter. It is largely on these grounds that the United States rests its case. But it is essential here to separate arguments of self-defence and preparations against the prospects of another attack from a war of retributive choice.

Moreover, one cannot ignore that second section cited above that the response must accord with the UN Charter. Chapter VII, Article 39, states 'The Security Council shall determine the existence of any threat to the peace, breach of the peace, or act of aggression and shall make recommendations, or decide what measures shall be taken in accordance with Articles 41 and 42, to maintain or restore international peace and security.' Article 41 indicates that the United Nations Security Council will decide what actions to take short of the use of force and Article 42 indicates that if these measures are inadequate, force may be used under the United Nations, providing that, as required under Chapter VI, Article 33, peaceful alternatives have been exhausted; negotiations have been tried and have failed. That is, war is the last resort.[10]

The haste with which war was pursued undermines the notion that war was the last resort. Moreover, the 'cause' of the Bush administration was wider than the pursuit of al Qaeda. By widening the war and dictating its pace and scope, Bush undermined the basis for a just response. Charles Knight put it well:

As a nation we have come to understand that *due process* is an essential, and perhaps defining, characteristic of the best approximation of justice in civil disputes and criminal affairs. *Why is process so central to achieving justice?* Because when passions are high it is hard for us to fairly weigh evidence. Furthermore, a process that requires judgements by juries and panels of judges makes sure that more than a few people with some meaningful degree of power to reach *independent* judgements share a common assessment of the evidence and its relevance before a verdict is rendered.

Citing Clinton's response to the 1998 bombings of Afghanistan and the Sudan, the decision to use deadly force,

violates nearly all of our notions of due process of justice. In this case the injured party takes it upon itself to be prosecutor, judge, and jury and allows the accused no opportunity for testimony or witnesses.[11]

JUST CAUSE

Likelihood of success

Pursuit of the terrorists was and is just; there is little argument on that. However, the issue of 'cause' in the 'war on terrorism' raises some concern. First, on methods, that is: war. Second, proportion and comparative justice need to be considered. An addendum to this point is that of the various consequentialist arguments: do the consequences bring about a safer, more just outcome, or do they destabilise and fuel the cycle of hatred. Third, how one defines and addresses terrorism is important because it in part defines the scope of action to be taken. Obviously this relates to the point on methods. And finally, it is important that if war is pursued, it is a war of last resort.

In August 2004 Bush induced another flap at the Republican Party convention when he indicated that the war on terrorism could not be won, apart from successfully stigmatising terrorism.[12] Terrorism is not something that can be defeated. It is a tool, a method. The most one might expect is to alter conditions so that the terrorists lack legitimacy and are perceived as criminals rather than heroic freedom fighters, or symbols of resistance to what appears to be and often is a state of tyranny. Propaganda and public diplomacy are obvious tools in this struggle.

The comment was somewhat surprising coming from Bush. After all, had the policies that he had already implemented made it less attractive to resort to methods of terrorism? It is not inconceivable that the US air strikes in Afghanistan or Iraq or the use of overwhelming power in combat fuels further violence: a violence that will necessarily be asymmetric and therefore through some official perception be seen as terrorist. The US response did little to break the cycle of violence. Shortly after 9/11 Vice President Richard Cheney understood that al Qaeda was not a conventional enemy, there was no territory to be recaptured or conquered. He stated, 'It's not like a state or a country. The notion of deterrence doesn't really apply here. ... The only way you can deal with them is to destroy them.'[13] And so, as is well known, the United States led others into war in Afghanistan, to capture bin Laden, dead or alive, and destroy the terrorists. Their four objectives were to bring bin Laden and al Qaeda to justice; to incapacitate al Qaeda and prevent it from posing a threat to US interests; to end Afghanistan's ability to harbour terrorists; and to break the relationship between the Taliban and international terrorism, by changing the regime if necessary. After a year, the Washington-based Center for Defense Information concluded that while there were some successes, 'not one of the original objectives has been conclusively realised'.[14] Bin Laden has not been captured, terrorism continues and has indeed stepped up a pace, sometimes with assumed connections to al Qaeda. Many operatives escaped to Pakistan and remain free due to the military tactics of aerial bombing and dependence on Northern Alliance ground forces. Those brought to Guantanamo in Cuba have hardly been brought to 'justice', which has created its own backlash in critical and anti-American sentiment. Certainly the training camps in Afghanistan were destroyed, but the results remain problematic. The Taliban has been overthrown, but has regrouped and continues to exert pressure and to fight in Afghanistan. The results are mixed.

The problem was one of definition and labelling from the outset. In one of the most comprehensive studies of al Qaeda, Jason Burke writes, 'the good news is that al-Qaeda does not exist. The bad news is that the threat now facing the world is far more dangerous than any single terrorist leader with an army, however large, of loyal cadres.'[15] Al Qaeda was and is a disparate group, if the term can be used accurately at all. It was a mistake to assume that it was a coordinated and hierarchical entity. Even amongst the core, Burke contends, it was a mistake to think of it as monolithic. There was a diverse and disparate set of views and opinions even amongst the dozen or so men closest to bin Laden. Bin Laden should be considered as one of several influential figures in this form of radical politics, and again it is largely a mistake to suggest that there is an international network of militant groups that are obedient to bin Laden. In the wake of Afghanistan al Qaeda was dispersed. Probably its most organised period was between 1996 and 2001. After Afghanistan, 'new groups, barely allied to bin Laden, have sprung up'. They look to bin Laden as a symbolic leader; they might act like al Qaeda and follow some of its methods, but they 'are not controlled in any meaningful way by "al-Qaeda"'. The phenomenon has become 'the precept, the maxim, the formula, not "the base"—[and] is more powerful than ever'. It cannot be fought by traditional counterterrorism, let alone by the instruments of war.[16] Overuse of the term creates its own problems. An array of terrorist groups now might look to al Qaeda methods and as a symbol of what is possible, but they harbour particular motivations derived from very different life experiences, local contexts and local ambitions. In that very real sense their grievances, though often expressed through the language of religion, are rooted in reality, in pursuit of a better form of life, as they understand it.[17] Labelling all the terrorism that we have witnessed since 9/11 as the work of al Qaeda, Burke concludes, is 'sloppy and possibly counterproductive'. Accurately it only describes a small group of men that came together after the Afghan War against the Soviets and dispersed after 9/11.[18]

The bombs that were dropped on Afghanistan were counterproductive. Many have been killed, wounded and detained, carted off half way around the world. Considered as an attitude, an outlook, a method, al Qaeda cannot be defeated by military means. And yet this is what Washington attempted. Defined too widely, the war was un-winnable. Defined too narrowly, and it would have appeared as if the President was doing nothing to avenge the deaths of 9/11. The response was stale and predictable; lacking imagination and ultimately counterproductive, the 'war' did not address the pertinent issues; the costs, in terms of lives, casualties, dollars and reputation, were far too high.

Certainly, given the mood of America, it would have been a political liability to do nothing. But one must separate the moral argument from the political argument. Bush prepared the country for a prolonged war. He did indicate that it would not be short, that it would require sustained resolve and patience. Cheney spoke of a war that 'may never end ... at least, not in our lifetime'.[19] They were serious. In October 2001 we were told new fronts would be open; Iraq would have its moment.[20] The parameters of the cause were being stretched beyond credulity.

One could accept the 'war' on terror as a metaphor, 'But instead of being a harmless linguistic exaggeration to describe a broad campaign encompassing a range of political, economic and police counter-measures, it was narrowed down to real war at the top echelons. The slippery slope that began with Afghanistan quickly led to the invasion of Iraq, a symbolic and political enormity whose psychological impact Bush and Blair have not yet grasped.'[21] Archbishop Rowan Williams argued that as soon as the word was employed, and the momentum towards action accelerated, 'clarity disappeared'. Vengeance and ambitious agendas came into play. The attraction of such a discharge is that it 'has a beginning and an end'. The territorial war in Afghanistan provided that. The fall of the Taliban compensated subliminally for the elusiveness of bin Laden; the fall of Saddam Hussein, perhaps even more the orchestrated fall of his statue, provided symbols of progress in an otherwise ineffective strategy. The attraction of the discharge fades, Williams wrote, 'when we cannot see the end; and here lies the risk and frustration of the conflict that began in October [2001]'.[22]

Within a year of 9/11 there was increasing realisation that the war, defined in its present terms, could not be won. The instruments, methods and targets were inappropriate. Supporters of the strategy continued to argue in monolithic terms, much as their forbears had done during the Cold War until the realities of Vietnam stemmed their ambition and global outlook. They took succour from the fight in Afghanistan; by destroying the bases they had 'ripped the heart out of the beast'. But soon, CIA director, George Tenet, confirmed that al Qaeda had reconstituted itself, and purportedly 'they are coming after us'. The former Head of British Intelligence, Dame Stella Rimington, argued that the war could not be won unless 'the causes of terrorism are eradicated' by removing the genuine grievances around the world, which 'will not happen'. The response had to be simultaneously political and economic. Using intelligence, the military and security forces could attempt to 'contain' terrorism, but ultimately reducing the causes of terrorism, the grievances rooted in real deprivation, had to be addressed. Though this was recognised in the September 2002 US National Security Strategy, it advanced a market solution as opposed to a Marshall Plan. It might be pertinent to remember that the 'Washington consensus' and the market solutions have not alleviated relative poverty, recognised as a pertinent context for terrorist action, for decades. On the other hand, the confrontational approach, much to the delight of extremists on both sides, would perpetuate the problem and deepen the divide. There was early warning by high-level US military personnel about the tactics. Wesley Clark argued that an 'effective response is likely to be something unfamiliar. For the US the weapons of war should be information, law enforcement and rarely, active military force.' Airpower did not suit the endgame of enhancing security.[23] On the first anniversary of 9/11, *Guardian* editorial ran a stinging indictment of the strategy, which concluded:

Like Bin Laden's al-Qaida, George Bush has much (privately) to celebrate this day. A weak, second-rate president with no mandate and less *nous* has since September 11 gained unprecedented levels of voter support. Only an increasingly self-induced sense of an American state of siege, characterised opportunistically by the Republican right as a state of war, could have produced such a result. Only Mr Bush's progressively higher-handed, unilateral and exaggerated responses to September 11 could have made of Bin Laden, and now Saddam Hussein, such potent and (to some) heroic bogeymen. Perhaps only Mr Bush could have squandered the almost universal goodwill offered the US a year ago.[24]

A part of considering just cause is to weigh in the factors of comparative justice and the consequences of any action taken. The arguments for comparative justice suggest that in deciding to take action, one must be assured that for the war to be just, the injustice suffered by one party must *significantly* outweigh the suffering of others. Before making the decision to go to war the calculation must account for its impact on all concerned within Afghanistan, regional neighbours and the stability of the international community.

Consequences

Finally, the consequentialist arguments cut both ways. On the one hand, the argument runs that if the United States waited, another attack could occur, therefore time was a crucial factor. On the other hand, another consequentialist argument suggests that the air attacks will invoke or provoke further action, accelerating the cycle of violence. This was one of the outcomes. By late 2002 US officials had already started talking about the reconstitution of al Qaeda, and picked up on a message from one of bin Laden's associates, Ayman al-Zawahiri, which linked US plans to attack Iraq with the al Qaeda attacks on American interests and their allies.[25] Washington did attack Iraq and not only has the resistance been a long and a bitter experience, but the attacks have continued around the world, and anti-American sentiments have increased.

It seemed that there would be no US revisions despite the disastrous course pursued. A favourite claim was that al Qaeda was 'on the run' but it did not exactly appear that way. By 2004 a senior US intelligence official published a book that damned the Bush strategy. His central claim was that Washington was losing the 'war' against al Qaeda and that the 'avaricious, premeditated, unprovoked war against a foe [in Iraq] who posed no immediate threat but whose defeat did offer economic advantages' played right into the hands of bin Laden. The official, writing anonymously, suggested the potential of another attack against the United States might not be aimed at removing Bush from power as was the case in Spain, but at keeping him there. There was no better administration to fuel the motivations of those who sought to either join or act under the broad label of al Qaeda. His arguments represented a growing consensus in the US intelligence community. The choice of timing for the war in Iraq showed 'an abject, even wilful failure to recognise the ideological power, lethality and growth potential of the threat personified by Osama bin Laden, as well as the impetus that threat has been given by the US-led invasion and occupation of Muslim Iraq'.[26]

Terrorism: state and non-state

Bush's original injunction, 'either you are with us or with the terrorists', advanced a stark distinction that does not reflect the messy reality of the use of force in international affairs. The US understanding and use of the word 'terrorism' is in practice confined to non-state actors, even though many of its allies, both state and non-state, have engaged in acts of terrorism and, semantics aside, many US actions are considered to employ terror as a method. The *US Code* indicates that an act of terrorism can be understood as intending to 'intimidate or coerce a civilian population' or to 'influence the policy of a government by intimidation or coercion' or to 'affect the conduct of a government by assassination or kidnapping'.[27] Though this is quite explicit, the normal polite language used for actions of this sort conducted by states is 'coercive diplomacy'.[28] Richard Falk argues that if it is ethically unacceptable to kill innocent civilians, as in 9/11, states cannot be excluded from the consideration of such ethical standards. States have been 'the most persistent source of mass violence' against civilians and the United States cannot be excluded from this list of states. The media normally treats terrorism as something that non-state actors engage in, state terror is treated in a different manner, and has been 'exempted from the stigma of terrorism'. State violence is usually placed within various 'legitimising' contexts as necessary, if regrettable, action required for purposes of self-defence, deterrence or retaliation. Falk writes:

The locus of terrorism can blur considerably depending on the identity of the party responsible for recourse to violence against civilian society. In this regard, it is one thing to denounce the September 11 attacks as immoral and as massive Crimes Against Humanity, but it is quite another to treat the United States as innocent of a massive terrorist taint over the course of decades in its own pursuit of foreign policy goals. If terrorism is to be truly eliminated from human experience, then it must be done through a process that engages all relevant political actors, and above all those states that suppress their own citizenry and play exploitative geopolitical roles on the world stage.[29]

But such consideration remained outside the framework advanced by Washington. Terrorism has been employed frequently over the years. Many of the actions associated with the Reagan Doctrine, whether perpetrated by the *contras* in Nicaragua, the *mujahedin* in Afghanistan or UNITA in Angola can be characterised as terrorist.[30] The Reagan Doctrine chose non-state actors because of the limitations after Vietnam: in short, 'official America decided to harness, and even to cultivate, terrorism in the struggle against regimes it considered pro-Soviet'.[31] The Reagan Doctrine in Central America, pursued by the contras and the CIA, conducted operations that, according to a former contra leader, Edgar Chamorro, advocated '"explicit and implicit terror" against the civilian population, including assassination of government employees and sympathizers.' In an affidavit in the

District of Columbia he indicated: 'the practices advocated in the [CIA] manual were employed by FDN [contra] troops. Many civilians were killed in cold blood. Many others were tortured, mutilated, raped, robbed or otherwise abused.'[32] In the broader picture, the International Court of Justice found that by aiding the contras, the United States had violated international law on several counts.[33]

To effectively eliminate terrorism, all forms of terrorism need to be addressed. Without that, the charge of double standards will remain and will be a source of resentment and bitterness. Thus the selective pursuit of terrorism may in the long term be counterproductive, because there will always be those who point out that the emperor has no clothes and that given their power, terrorism and asymmetrical warfare are the only viable methods. Diplomatic language and semantics should not provide apparel for the emperor.[34]

Last resort

Just cause insists that the option of war should be the *last resort;* all other options must have been tried and failed; this precept is echoed in Chapter VI, Article 33 of the UN Charter. The war against Afghanistan was launched with undue haste. Apart from haste, motive also needs consideration. Though it is possible to understand the sentiment, vengeance is not condoned under just war theory. Finally, negotiations and legal procedures had not failed.

Bush decided that the United States was at war on 9/11 and began demanding military options that could be pursued in conjunction with diplomatic, economic and legal actions. Woodward writes, 'the president and his advisers started America on the road to war that night without a map. They had only a vague sense of how to respond, based largely on the visceral reactions of the president.' Bush insisted on the Taliban producing al Qaeda, negotiations were ruled out: 'Let's see them, or we'll hit them hard. We're going to hurt them bad so that everyone in the world sees, don't deal with bin Laden. I don't want to put a million-dollar missile on a five-dollar tent.'[35] Though the strategy had yet to be considered, the overall aim of hitting Afghanistan had been taken. Yet as far as justice is concerned, 'a war of vindictive justice wherein the belligerent fights against error and evil as a matter of principle and not of necessity is no longer condoned by just-war doctrine'.[36]

Afghanistan was going to be hit despite the attempts to negotiate the fate of bin Laden. On 20 September 2001, Bush delivered the Taliban four ultimatums that were not negotiable. They had to:

deliver the leaders of al Qaeda to the United States; close every terrorist training camp in Afghanistan; hand over every terrorist and persons in their support structure; and give the United States full access to terrorist training camps.[37]

These were demands and not negotiations. No sovereign government would fulfil these demands without the necessary evidence or procedures of extradition. Alternatives existed, though they were obviously not appealing. Various options were discussed in the media. Amongst them were taking the case to the International Court of Justice (ICJ) at The Hague, or to the International Criminal Court, but Washington had undermined the efficacy of these institutions, not least in 1986 when it ignored the ICJ's ruling on Nicaragua and withdrew from the court's jurisdiction. A 'Lockerbie solution' was also proposed, because it was not thought that any of the captives would get a fair trial. It was suggested that the Organization of the Islamic Conference get involved. Finally, the Taliban negotiated with Pakistan to explore ways to avert the inevitable bombing; they even contacted Jesse Jackson to intercede on their behalf and offered to discuss the situation with US officials. They requested evidence of bin Laden's involvement. As Peter Singer has pointed out, none had been presented at the time, and such a request would be a normal and reasonable request for any extradition process. By the end of September 2001, Washington had decided that the goal in Afghanistan included overthrowing the Taliban. For Singer, this was to widen the war beyond the legitimate pursuit of al Qaeda. As such, it is not clear that the cause was just, though Bush professed as much on the Sunday before the bombing began.[38] But certainly, given that negotiations had not been exhausted or even entered into in any meaningful sense and that other options had not been exhausted, the war was not one of last resort. Even after the war began the Taliban continued to search for options that could stop the bombing. They suggested turning bin Laden over to a third country, but Bush's response was swift: 'When I said no negotiations I meant no negotiations … We know he's guilty. Turn him over. There's no need to discuss innocence or guilt.' Singer concludes, even though negotiations would have been difficult after 9/11 that is 'what Bush ought to have done'. Given that, the Taliban had responded, 'such treatment of a response to an ultimatum indicates that the intention behind the ultimatum was not to find a satisfactory solution to the problem, but to provide an excuse for going to war. War was not the last resort.'[39]

Intermediaries were hardly needed, and the option of extradition and trial in third countries was not new. These options had been explored between the Taliban and Washington through 33 contacts, three of which were conducted by the Bush administration. From 1997 the Taliban clearly indicated that they wanted to improve relations with the United States and that if they could locate bin Laden that they would put a ban on his activities.[40] The negotiations picked up immediately after the United States launched 70 missiles into Afghanistan and Sudan in August 1998, hitting a chemical plant in the latter which was later found not to be involved in the alleged production of materials for chemical weapons. Two days after the US bombing of Afghanistan, 22 August 1998, Mullah Omar contacted the State Department directly. He spoke to the director for Pakistan, Afghanistan and Bangladesh Affairs, Michael Malinowski. The State Department cable reported: 'Omar warned that the U.S. strikes would prove counter-productive and arouse anti-American feelings in the Islamic world … he claimed that the strikes could spark more terrorist attacks.' Omar asked for evidence of bin Laden's involvement in terrorist attacks. He suggested that Clinton should resign and that US troops should get out of the Gulf region. The strikes 'would further increase Islamic solidarity against the US'. On bin Laden, 'Omar said that getting rid of one individual would not end the problems posed to the U.S. by the Islamic world.' The document ended with the comment: Omar's contact 'is indicative of the seriousness of how the Tall Ban [sic] view the U.S. strikes and our anger over bin Laden'.[41]

In response to the contact, Washington instructed its representatives to engage an authoritative representative of the Taliban, specifying the 'need for the Taliban to expel Saudi terrorist Osama bin Laden so that he can be properly brought to justice for his terrorist acts'. Washington indicated that it was interested in 'a serious dialogue with the Taliban' and that, incredulously, 'in launching the strike of August 20 against Khowst, the U.S. in no way wanted to harm the peaceful people of Afghanistan nor damage the Taliban'. The missiles were launched in self-defence! The State Department indicated that they knew bin Laden was trying to acquire weapons of mass destruction to use against US interests. They concluded: 'The world – and his victims – demand that justice be done and it looks to the Tall Ban [sic] to help see that it is done.'[42]

Later, the US embassy in Islamabad reported that Mullah Omar was upset at bin Laden, who had extensive contacts with the Taliban's enemies within Afghanistan and who continued to make threats against the United States, which were not in Taliban interests, given their search for improved relations and the negotiations on the construction of an oil pipeline. They had told bin Laden that they would deal with the United States, and that there was only one government in Afghanistan. 'Omar purportedly felt that this meant that bin Laden was setting himself up as an alternate leader in Afghanistan since the Taliban have told him many times to control his activities.' Ultimately, however, the sticking point remained. They indicated that they would not hand over bin Laden to anyone, but would try him themselves, if evidence was presented to them.[43]

But by October 1998, the Taliban made clear to the State Department that they wanted to 'rid themselves of terrorist Usama bin Laden'. They provided three options for exploration. They could not simply get rid of him because of the Pashtun tradition of providing refuge to those who seek it, but probably also because of his popularity. Should they expel him, they feared for their own power in Afghanistan. The State Department cable concluded: '[excised name] reiterated an earlier point: "the bottom-line is they (the Taliban) really want to get rid of bin Laden"'. In a precursor to Bush's line that they would make no distinctions between the terrorists and those who harboured them, the Clinton State Department also indicated that: 'As we have previously informed you, the United States will hold the Taliban responsible for any further terrorism conducted by the Usama bin Laden network, as long as the Taliban provides sanctuary to members of that network.'[44]

RIGHT INTENTION

'Right intention' is central to just war theory. Belligerents are limited to the pursuit of *the* just cause and should not widen the scope of their response. The situation should not be turned into an opportunity to pursue other causes that fall outside the immediate just cause, such as the threat to widen the war against Iraq and to numerous other locations. The logic of this expansive opportunity that 9/11 provided the Bush administration wove through the initial discussion on Iraq, through to the 'Axis of Evil' in Bush's January 2002 State of the Union Address, to the June 2002 speech at West Point in which all terrorists and tyrants were conflated, through to the National Security Strategy of September 2002. Though there were obviously significant divisions within the administration, the hard line prevailed over the more reasoned and strategic line advanced by Colin Powell. Despite the secret contact that the Bush administration maintained with the Taliban, only after 9/11 did Bush more aggressively assail them, preparing the ground for the attack. Still, Bush told Americans 'Fellow citizens, we'll meet violence with patient justice – assured of the rightness of our cause, and confident of the victories to come.'[45]

But again the scope and the speed of the response need to be considered. The choice not to make a distinction between the state that harbours terrorists and the terrorists is not supported by international law and would necessitate a re-examination of the notion of sovereignty in the international system. Though Richard Falk and others do not think that a legal, diplomatic route would have been possible or that it would have succeeded, it should have been tried. After all, the military option did not succeed in the original, primary and just cause: capturing bin Laden. Instead, given the military response, Mahmood Mamdani contends that, it 'is more likely to be remembered as a combination of blood revenge and medieval-type exorcism than as a search for a solution to terrorism'. A key distinction between terrorism and crime is that the former has a political cause and needs also to be addressed politically. Punishment or deterrence is unlikely to succeed on its own, unless the civilian casualties of US bombing in Afghanistan were popularly blamed on al Qaeda instead of on Washington. But this was not the case. Ultimately, the issues that the terrorists are concerned with will need to be addressed: the US presence in the region.[46] One of the key concerns was that US troops pull out of Saudi Arabia and the Gulf region. After 9/11, they expanded the network of bases throughout the region, in Central Asia, the former Soviet republics, Afghanistan and now also in Iraq. That presence will continue to cause angst and humiliation. Moreover, little will be solved in the short, medium or long term without squarely addressing Palestine and wider regional grievances.

US credibility was a central concern after 9/11. In many respects the target selection in Afghanistan was inappropriate. The camps were hit, but so was much else besides. Within a short period Washington had run out of targets. As one commentator put it, they ended up turning big pieces of rubble into small ones, and ending many human lives. But the war also pitted the strongest country in the world against one of the weakest; one that spends far more than its closest rival does on defence and more than the next 13 countries combined (in 2002) against one of the poorest countries on earth. Militarily there was a complete mismatch. But, seemingly, administration perceptions of

US credibility demanded a vigorous response. The immediate military operation would undoubtedly succeed, but Washington would fail politically because it harboured wider priorities elsewhere.[47]

The military response in Afghanistan appeared as though it was conducted to demonstrate US power and credibility. Widely approved of in the United States, elsewhere it was also perceived as a form of vengeance. The United States did not take the time to examine the alternatives, to try, in the words of Archbishop Rowan Williams, 'to act so that something might possibly change, as opposed to acting so as to persuade ourselves that we're not powerless'.[48] The option of choice, predictably and as we have seen, perpetuated the cycles of violence. Patient justice was not served. Washington, however, insisted that the cause was just but continued to expand its scope and therefore its intentions. Moreover, 'the goals, forms, methods, targets, scale, and duration of which are all to be determined solely by the United States ... The political scope of this claim is nothing short of breathtaking, and all in the name of fighting a selectively defined terrorism.'[49]

While the pursuit of al Qaeda was one thing, the removal of the Taliban stretches the limits of 'right intention', however desirable that outcome might have been.

PROPORTIONALITY AND DISCRIMINATION

Proportionality is central to just war theory. The principle demands that the force used should be proportionate to the ends pursued. As Singer points out, 'even if the cause of a war is inherently just, the costs of achieving justice may be so high that it would be wrong to go to war'.[50] As such this issue is directly linked to the issue of discrimination. If there is a substantial risk of killing innocent civilians, the costs and the benefits of pursuing the action must be weighed up and considered. As argued above and confirmed through various US reports, the benefits of going to war have been doubtful, given that the incidence of terror has not abated, justice has been a travesty in the prisons in Afghanistan and Cuba, and the direct objective, the capture of bin Laden, has failed. Moreover, it is probable that the region is now in a more uncertain state, less stable, and therefore more fraught with unknown dangers not only to the United States and its Western allies, but also to the populations within the regional countries.

There are two central considerations: proportionality of US force and its discrimination. That is, did the type of force used move to minimise innocent civilian casualties within the context of the objectives that were considered just: the pursuit of al Qaeda and bin Laden?

The military response first needs to be placed in its relevant context. Terrorism has been addressed through tactical bombing in 1986, when President Reagan responded to the bombing of a Berlin discothèque in which US soldiers were killed, by bombing the alleged sponsor, Colonel Qaddafi. Consequentialist arguments suggest that the action was effective; Qaddafi became more reluctant to sponsor terrorism, notwithstanding Lockerbie, and thus the deterrence worked. Justice, however, was not served.

The operations in Afghanistan were ultimately a combination of the Reagan and the Powell Doctrines: the combination of proxy force through the Northern Alliance and overwhelming US airpower. That combination had been honed across the years since the effects of the Vietnam War precluded large-scale use of ground troops except under specific conditions.

Though Bush was conscious of launching expensive missiles into tents, after he had derided Clinton's reaction in 1998, his response was not that much more imaginative, if much more lethal. Faced with the catastrophe and the opportunity of 9/11 to construct a sustained and innovative response to such terrorism, Bush chose to reply in the only manner he knew; through strategies derived from the various lessons of Vietnam. He chose not to change the language, to echo William's words again. The strategies that relied heavily on airpower were inappropriate to the task, and counterproductive in terms of consequences. Moreover, they were disproportionate in terms of the stated objectives: to capture and bring al Qaeda operatives to justice.

Though Bush intended to move beyond straightforward Clintonesque retribution, with a more prolonged and diffuse agenda, the tactics nevertheless involved retribution. Warnings against the expected US counterattack started early. A senior analyst at the Center for Defense Information argued that 'justice is a dish best served cold', but Bush needed to craft a response within the context of a domestic populace who expected military action and a Congress that called for a robust military response (abrogating their responsibility to at least play the role of checking executive power). Terrorism must be treated differently even though it seemed war was mandatory for political survival. One analyst of the CDI indicates, 'war is the use of armed force to break an enemy's will to resist'. At its conclusion, terms are accepted, the armies go home. War in this context promised only to bolster the enemy, because fighting terrorism is not the same as fighting a conventional country or regime. The terrorist organisations, al Qaeda in particular, could survive as long as its members survived. And it was widely reported that many left Afghanistan after 12 September 2001 in anticipation of what followed. Many others fought, but also escaped during the bombing. Many others died. Al Qaeda, on the other hand, 'has no incentive to accept terms and the United States has no terms to offer'. The point of this terror was not to draw the United States into discussion on certain issues, but to 'induce Washington to do something stupid, costly and counterproductive, such as killing innocent civilians'. Such acts would be victory enough and perpetuate the cycle of hatred. Military force might have a role to play, as a police action, but not as a conventional form of war. Much greater discrimination was required. Conflating the terrorists and the supporting regime was counterproductive, as civilians were killed and the bombing aroused further enmity.[51] Retired Marine General, Anthony Zinni, advanced a similar conclusion days after 9/11. Though he was the commander under Clinton who directed the operations against Sudan and Afghanistan in 1998, this time he thought such action would merely perpetuate the problem.[52]

As noted above, of the four objectives with which the United States launched the war, not one was conclusively achieved. Both the strategy and the method were inappropriate. By the end of October 2001 the United States had destroyed most of the fixed targets in Afghanistan, but enemy forces were scattered rather than destroyed. After that Washington decided to focus on the destruction of enemy operatives from early November. The strategy was fraught with problems. While the Vietnam syndrome precluded US ground troops, many of the digitally guided missiles were sent to targets identified by indigenous forces who frequently called in mistaken coordinates or deliberately targeted opponents. Despite the talk of precision weaponry, the use of carpet-bombing, daisy cutters (described as akin to a nuclear weapon without the fallout), and gun ships that could fill football fields with bullets in seconds, was devastating and counterproductive.[53] Innocent civilians were killed in the process, in action that was widely seen to be futile in terms of the objectives announced. Khalil Jan, a shepherd in Zhawar, captured the obvious point: 'Everyday, the Americans are dropping bombs. Last night there were six and this morning there were five. We are very afraid of the bombs, and we are very angry at the Americans. There is no reason for this. The camps are empty, but still the Americans are dropping their bombs.'[54]

Discrimination

In just war theory, direct intentional attacks against non-combatants and non-military targets are prohibited. There are certain circumstances under which it is understood, even if deplored, if there is an imminent threat that requires immediate action, or if a greater good is likely to result, such as the bombing of civilian centres in some operations in the Second World War to defeat Nazi Germany. These conditions were not pertinent in Afghanistan in 2001. Yet, it was clear that the Pentagon and the White House were somewhat concerned with the number of innocent civilian casualties. Their rhetoric indicated that the US authorities accepted that the norm of avoiding non-combatant casualties was operative. One might at this stage speculate about whether avoiding such casualties is a position taken out of a concern with just war and the requirements of conduct in war, or out of political expediency. That is, officials know that they will be held to account by the media for the death of innocent civilians. If the numbers can be downplayed, so much the better for tactical purposes. Speculation aside, the moral imperative remains: everything must be done to ensure that innocent civilians are not directly targeted and that they are not killed, even as 'collateral damage', if alternative methods exist.

Counterforce is central to this proposition. To avoid the unnecessary destruction of innocent life, force must be used in a proportionate manner commensurate with the objectives pursued. The evolution of the doctrine of 'overwhelming power' undermines the notion of counterforce and proportionality. One might argue that in the age of precision weaponry, the force remained proportionate and discriminate (notwithstanding consideration of the effects of carpet-bombing, daisy cutters and so forth). As a senior US navy officer, involved in the bombing assessment study indicated, 'with precision-guided weapons, you don't need to use as many bombs to achieve the desired effects, and using fewer weapons reduces the risk of collateral damage'. Six months into the bombing in Afghanistan, Rumsfeld heralded it as the most accurate ever; 60 per cent of all weapons dropped were precision weapons; 40 per cent were obviously less discriminate. Of the total number of munitions, from cruise missiles to heavy fuel air bombs, some 22,000 tons, 25 per cent missed their target, a figure far lower than either Kosovo or the 1991 Gulf War.[55] Though the figure is an improvement over previous wars, 'collateral damage', the killing of innocent civilians, was entirely predictable. Ultimately, if the Bush administration knew that innocent civilians would die as a result of the means it chose to respond, then it is required to take every precaution to minimise these deaths.

Of course al Qaeda are responsible for putting the Afghans in the context of the catastrophe, and the Taliban are also responsible for facilitating al Qaeda and tolerating its presence in the country. Indeed, Rumsfeld tried to obviate US responsibility by pointing to the culpability of the protagonists of 9/11. There are flaws with this argument. What if the Taliban were not in control of their entire territory? What if they could not get rid of bin Laden? Or what if they had made the calculation that to get rid of him would have amounted to the loss of their power, as they indicated to the State Department in their 1998 communications? Given that the innocent were caught in this context, it is still incumbent on the United States to use proportionate and discriminate force, to comply with the strictures of *jus in bello*.

This was not the case. Article 52(2) of the Geneva Conventions[56] indicates that only objects that by 'their nature, location, purpose or use make an effective contribution to military action' may be targeted. And even if the target is legitimate, Article 51(5b) prohibits action, 'which may be expected to cause incidental loss of civilian life, injury to civilians, damage to civilian objects, or a combination thereof, which would be excessive in relation to the concrete and direct military advantage'. As Wheeler argues, this required the use of alternative methods in pursuit of the war: 'A responsibility falls upon military commanders to accept greater risks to their armed forces if this protects civilians who have done nothing to deserve being placed in harm's way.'[57] Civilians are entitled to 'due care'. One could contrast the British Special Operations Executive (SOE) operation against the heavy water plant in Norway, sensationalised in the film *The Heroes of Telemark*, with the use of airpower since Vietnam, and even more frequently since 1991. Commanders, Walzer argues, 'must risk soldiers before they kill civilians'.[58] So, for instance when the Taliban took reporters to the site of bombed dwellings, Rumsfeld indicated that the people killed were in close proximity to ammunition dumps and 'were there for a good reason': they were part of the activity, 'they were not cooking cookies inside those tunnels'.[59]

This is an example of how far US strategy is from the pursuit of 'due care'. The site that photographers were taken to was a house, not caves. Had a more proportionate application of force been used, the distinction between a house and a cave would have been obvious.

Through this and several other examples, it becomes clear that due care was not exercised even if there was still a concern with collateral damage. It became obvious very quickly that there was considerable global alarm at the US tactics, that peoples around the world, while sympathetic to the struggle against terrorism, deplored the bombing in Afghanistan. By the end of October 2001 there were widespread calls for a pause to the bombing.[60] The numbers of civilian casualties proved to be controversial. Marc Herold, a professor at the University of New Hampshire, conducted early studies that identified an initially inflated figure that was subsequently adjusted downward to between 2,650 and 2,970 civilian deaths between October and December 2001. The Project for Defense Alternatives (PDA) concluded that between 3,000–4,000 Taliban coalition troops were killed, 'in battle, captivity, and by strategic bombardment' and that 1,000–1,300 civilians were killed due to aerial bombardment. Nevertheless, Conetta of the PDA reported,

Despite the adulation of Operation Enduring Freedom (OEF) as a 'finely-tuned' or 'bulls-eye' war, the campaign failed to set a new standard for precision in one important respect: the rate of civilian casualties killed per bomb dropped. In fact, this rate was far higher in the Afghanistan conflict – perhaps four times higher – than in the 1999 Balkans war. In absolute terms, too, the civilian death toll in Afghanistan surpassed that incurred by the 1999 NATO bombing campaign over Kosovo and Serbia, it may have been twice as high.

The reasons related to the wartime objectives, the operational features of the bombing campaign (relying on local intelligence) and certain characteristics of the weapons used.[61] Even if the weapons were more precise and more of them hit their target, why were larger 'dumb' bombs preferred in Afghanistan and not in Kosovo?

Certainly strategists must have been aware of the impact of civilian casualties. In this outcome alone, the choice of weapon and method became counterproductive in the long run as new acts of terror are placed into narratives of revenge for the bombing of October 2001. For these victims the narrative started that month, not the month before in New York. Terms like 'collateral damage' or 'just war' are meaningless to those who have lost their entire family, or to those who bear witness to this retributive aggression. There were widespread reports that civilian casualties were not being counted, perhaps because the will and the ability to do so systematically did not exist, but also because the numbers might inflame opinion and produce another 'Kosovo wobble'.[62] But these concerns seemed tactical rather than ethical.

It is simply not enough to justify the response in the context of 9/11, no matter how horrendous those acts were. Vengeance is not tolerated in just war theory. If one draws analogies to criminal law within domestic circumstances, it is easy to understand due process; for obvious reasons the aggrieved does not move towards revenge and execution of the law. Clearly the international context is somewhat different. While the anthrax scare in late 2001 raised tensions, nothing substantial indicated that another attack was imminent. Though President Bush drew direct parallels between the Taliban, totalitarianism and the Nazis, nothing suggested that the United States faced the type of threat that, say, France or Britain did in 1940. The imminence of the threat was not such that the Bush administration had to make a choice between deliberately killing innocent civilians and losing the war against terrorism. Alternative military strategies did exist; they were not exhausted.[63] If the Bush administration calculated that direct action was necessary to avoid a further attack on the United States, it was probably mistaken in that assumption and therefore does need to assume responsibility for the death of innocent civilians.

These days one does not hear much about the innocent Afghan casualties; other issues have replaced these corpses and their grieving families, though we remember the anniversary of 9/11 each year. For the innocent, the context of 9/11 is not enough. There can be no moral equivalent, unless one was to adopt a callous and hard-line realist perspective, concerned more with power rather than morality. Terrorists deliberately target innocent civilians. That is what happened on 9/11. Though the death of Afghans was not necessarily deliberate, the euphemism of 'collateral damage' does not sufficiently account for these fatalities because alternatives did exist.

There is a terrible irony to the cycle of events. Rowan Williams argues that 'it is possible to deplore civilian casualties and retain moral credibility when an action is clearly focused', but when the goals are so broad, the objectives not clearly defined and the war characterised as perhaps perpetual, the morality is suspect. 'From the point of view of a villager in Afghanistan whose family has died in a bombing raid, a villager who probably never heard of the World Trade

Center, the distinctions between what the U.S. forces are doing and what was done on September 11 will be academic.' The retaliation is both deplorable and counterproductive if a part of the US strategy is to break morale by 'allowing random killing *as a matter of calculated policy* become part of a military strategy'. Williams argues that we are at once open to the charge that there is no difference between 'our military action and the terror which it attacks'.[64]

The argument at the heart of the democratic peace theory suggests that democracies are less likely to go to war with each other, because the leaders remain accountable to the people, who will ultimately be sacrificed both on the battlefield and as a consequence of opting for war. What sensible person would opt for war if it meant sending a family member into war or risking the direct effects of war on your own civilian population? If there were alternatives, especially at the negotiating table, would it not be better to resolve the issues through such methods? Indeed democracies have rarely gone to war with each other in recent times. But democracies are frequently at war with other regimes. The Vietnam syndrome stayed the hands of the executive somewhat when they considered their options. But throughout the 1990s perhaps the democratic restraints had been weakened. Precision weaponry reduced the costs and risks to US personnel. Democracies may be more willing to go to war because the costs to their citizens have been removed by technology. Michael Ignatieff suggests that: 'Democracies may remain peace-loving only so long as the risks of war remain real to their citizens. If war becomes virtual – without risk – democratic electorates may be more willing to fight, especially if the cause is justified in the language of human rights and democracy itself.'[65] After 9/11 this became even more evident. However, a brutal irony arises from the disproportionate, US casualty-free, options. The tactics employed disproportionate, overwhelming force, daisy cutters and cluster bombs amongst the arsenal for 'enduring freedom'. As Wheeler concludes:

… there are good grounds for worrying that some of those innocent Afghans whose families suffered at the hands of US bombing will seek to extract revenge against the Americans. Put differently, the means employed by the Bush administration to end the threat posed by global terrorism could paradoxically serve to increase the risks facing US citizens.[66]

5

The United States and Iraq: 'One Can Do Nothing about the Past' 1983–91

The US relationship with Iraq has passed through several oscillations of amity and enmity. Prior to 1958 the Iraqi monarchy was regarded as a stable pro-Western regime, especially given its alliance with Britain in which it was the only Arab state to join the Baghdad Pact. In July 1958 Abdel Karim Qassim overthrew the monarch and its Prime Minister Nuri Said and moved the country closer to the Soviet Union. Qassim's eventual reliance on the Iraqi Communist Party incited a group of Ba'athist officers to seize power in February 1963. Qassim was executed and the country was moved out of the Soviet orbit. Led by Ahmed Hassan al-Bakr, Iraq increasingly negotiated both arms deals and economic aid with the United States. However, in November of 1963 he was isolated within the Ba'athist Party. When he regained power within the Party and the country in July 1968 he did so with the ruthless anti-Western assistance of Saddam Hussein.[1] By this stage Iraq had already broken diplomatic relations with Washington in 1967 following the Arab–Israeli War.

WASHINGTON AND BAGHDAD:
'ONE CAN DO NOTHING ABOUT THE PAST'

How ironic the photographs of Donald Rumsfeld shaking hands with Saddam Hussein in attempts to bolster the US–Iraqi relationship in 1983 seemed when they were posted to various websites in the twenty-first century. Posted perhaps as symbolic indictment early in the new millennium when there was renewed vigour and talk about democracy promotion in the Middle East. They harked back to a time prior to the Iraqi invasion of Kuwait in 1990, to the subsequent vitriol, sanctions and endless bombing raids lead by Washington against Iraq. In earlier times, many might have scoffed at the content and application of the Reagan Doctrine, supposedly concerned with promoting democracy in Nicaragua, supporting forces of liberation in Afghanistan, Angola and Cambodia, while simultaneously siding up to the likes of Saddam Hussein. Words like 'realpolitik' and phrases like the 'national interest' might have been used to describe the relationship by those not deluded by the rhetoric on democracy, liberation and self-determination. Such approaches to these regimes served very short-term 'national interests'. Though throughout the 1980s, with the shifting balance of power in the Middle East after the 1979 revolution in Iran, Iraq did of course offer Washington certain opportunities and vantage points for leverage. Iran had become especially pivotal to the US strategy in the Middle East because within the Nixon Doctrine such pillars might fill the gap between US aspirations and their redefined capabilities after the Vietnam War. These shifting alliances would obviously become problematic and cause embarrassment in the future. One can do nothing about the past, except perhaps to reinterpret it.

Iraq cut off ties with the United States for its pro-Israeli stance during the 1967 Arab–Israeli War. The Pike Committee of the US Senate, investigating the abuses of the CIA in the early 1970s, revealed that Washington supported the Kurds through Iran in their efforts to undermine the Ba'athist regime of al-Bakr in Baghdad and pressed for autonomy of the Kurdish region. Iraq was destabilising the Gulf region, providing shelter to Ayatollah Khomeini during his exile from Iran. The Kurds were encouraged and provided with material assistance, though of course neither the Shah in Tehran nor Washington wanted to see them prevail, thus even further disrupting the potential balance within not just the Gulf region but the broader Middle East, as their nation principally straddled across Iran, Iraq, Turkey and Syria. An autonomous Kurdistan made up of the lands from each of these countries would also prove disastrous for key US allies. The Pike Committee had documents that clearly indicated that the President and Dr Kissinger, 'hoped that our clients [the Kurds] would not prevail. They preferred instead that the insurgents simply continue a level of hostilities sufficient to sap the resources of our ally's [Iran] neighboring country [Iraq].' The Kurds were not informed of Washington's limited intentions.[2]

Washington clearly expected to see more of Iraq in the regional politics. As Henry Kissinger chaired a meeting on 28 April 1975, he was informed that Iraq's recent actions had been 'rather phenomenal'. Atherton reported that:

Hussein is going to Tehran tomorrow for meetings with the Shah, but also they've been patching things up on various very specific issues – border disputes and so forth – with Saudi Arabia. They've made an offer to Kuwait. They've been moving closer to the Egyptians and the Jordanians and altogether suddenly projecting the image of a country that wants to play a very dynamic and active role in the Arab World.

The United States worried that Iraq remained dedicated to the overthrow of Assad in Syria as a rival in the Ba'athist Party. They carefully watched the movements and rapprochements between Iran and Iraq and also between Iran and Afghanistan. Sisco observed that Iraq had offered 'to settle its border dispute' with Kuwait. Moreover, Atherton remarked,

Hussein is a rather remarkable person. We have to look more closely into his background. He's 38 years old and he holds no government position. He's the Vice President of the Command Council, but he is running the show; and he's a very ruthless and – very recently, obviously – pragmatic, intelligent power. I think we're going to see Iraq playing more of a role in the area than it has for many years.[3]

When Iraq found agreement with Iran over their border dispute, the Kurds were brutally cut off.

In attempts to build relations between Washington and Baghdad, Henry Kissinger met with the Iraqi Minister of Foreign Affairs, Sadun Hammadi, in the Iraqi Ambassador's residence in Paris on 17 December 1975. Kissinger did his best to overcome the two most pertinent issues that concerned the Iraqis, Israel and US support for the Kurds, in his attempts to assure the Minister that 'we do not think there is a basic clash of national interests between Iraq and the United States'. Two years after the Yom Kippur War, Kissinger was keen to convey the message that they had normalised relations with most of the 'Arabs'. Hammadi was much more reluctant and appeared the tougher interlocutor in the exchange. He pointed out that they had a different view. They had to be more careful because they were a small country. The United States was central to Israel, building it up to what it is today. Hammadi pointed out that Israel 'was established by force and is a clear-cut case of colonialism' on 'part of our homeland'. Moreover, it had now become a threat to Iraqi national security: 'We think the US is building up Israel to have the upper hand in the area.' Hammadi elaborated to Kissinger that further regional troubles could be expected because Israel would not confine itself to current borders, 'if there is an opportunity, they will expand'. Kissinger reiterated the point of the meeting, 'to move towards better relations'. He tried to allay fears of US dominance through Israel and provided a potted history of the creation of Israel. Israel, according to Kissinger, had emerged from domestic US politics, which no one understood, but it 'was not an American design to get a bastion of imperialism in the area'. Israel's existence was beyond discussion, even though Hammadi thought it a temporal phenomenon. But Kissinger indicated that its borders could be discussed and Israel could be reduced in size to 'historic proportions' and that in 'ten to fifteen years Israel will be like Lebanon – struggling for existence, with no influence in the Arab world'.[4] Hammadi eventually ended the conversation on the basis that they would have to remain in disagreement on Israel and moved on to more direct concerns: the Kurds. Kissinger defended US support for the Kurds because while Washington thought Iraq a Soviet satellite, it did not object to Iranian actions, but now that Iraq and Iran had resolved their border dispute there was nothing further to worry about: Washington would not engage in 'activity against Iraq's territorial integrity'. Hammadi pointed out that Iraq imported weapons from the Soviets and that if they chose to sign further agreements with the Soviets, Washington might revert to supporting the Kurds who, according to Hammadi, 'wanted to cut Iraq to pieces'. As the meeting drew to a close, Kissinger assured Hammadi that closer relations were possible through less formal channels and opportunities for discussion: 'You will see: Our attitude is not unsympathetic to Iraq. Don't believe; watch it.' Hammadi asserted that the Kurdish issue was of vital importance. To which Kissinger replied: 'There will be no concern. One can do nothing about the past.'[5]

And so the messages from Washington continued when the Reagan administration came to power in 1981. By then Iraq had become an even more vital interest. The Iranian revolution removed the Shah, a pillar of US strategy in the region. Ayatollah Khomeini assumed power, the Carter administration had been humiliated by the protracted hostage crisis, the Soviets had extended their presence through the invasion of Afghanistan – all within the context of a post-Vietnam malaise, soaring fuel prices and restricted supplies. Iraq, assuming that the internal turmoil in Iran would ensure a quick victory, invaded Iran in September 1980.

Secretary of State, Alexander Haig, made his first foreign trip to the Middle East in April 1981, during which he asked a deputy assistant, Morris Draper, to travel to Baghdad to share with the Iraqis, and Hammadi in particular, the results of Haig's regional tour and the US policies and attitudes on 'the issues and the threats endemic to the region'. Iraq was a secular state that now provided a good bulwark to the perceived 'Islamic threat' and explicit anti-Americanism posed by Khomeini in Iran and the Soviets in Afghanistan.[6] Draper's report clearly indicated that though normal diplomatic relations could not be resumed until 'the US altered its basic Middle East policies', nonetheless Baghdad sought closer relations and further commercial ties. Draper reiterated that Washington would observe a position of neutrality in the Iran–Iraq War and indicated it was in the world's overall 'interest that the war be concluded as soon as possible'.[7] It lasted eight years.

And so the rapprochement continued. Hammadi wrote an appreciative letter to Haig on the issue of arms sales to Iran and the contacts increased in intensity and in level. William L. Eagleton of the US Interests Section in Baghdad met with Tariq Aziz, the highest contact within the Revolutionary Command Council (RCC) on 28 May 1981. Eagleton outlined Reagan's general foreign policies on containing the Soviets in the region and US concerns on terrorism. Aziz recalled a metaphor used by Saddam Hussein in a meeting with David Rockefeller in 1975 that better relations between the two countries were dependent on two keys turning in a door. The first concerned US–Iraqi relations and the second, US–Arab relations. The first key was 'now turning'. The outcomes of Camp David and the peace process would determine the timing of the second key. Aziz took the opportunity to explain that Iraq 'embarked upon a nationalist, socialist and independent course hostile only to those who threaten Iraqi vital interests'. Iraq, in his view, was a force for stability within the region. The country was not interested in promoting Soviet influence in the Middle East and while it retained the right to maintain friendly relations with Moscow, it also recognised that Western Europe and the United States offered better opportunities for a trading relationship: 'there is an objective ground for close relations with the US and Europe'.[8] Further trade relations were facilitated with the 'de-designation' of Iraq from the list of countries supporting international terrorism in February 1982. At that point Washington still insisted it would not sell weapons to the regime during the war.

By November 1983 President Reagan signed National Security Decision Directive 114, concerning the Iran–Iraq War and intended to ensure US access to the region's oil supplies and therefore specifically to maintain and defend the 'critical oil facilities and transhipment points' because 'of the real and psychological impact of a curtailment in the flow of oil from the Persian Gulf on the international economic system.'[9] To ensure such access, discussions had already begun in October 1983 on a possible US move away from neutrality in the war to a 'tilt toward Iraq'. In the State Department analysis for Lawrence Eagleburger, US policies were described as: an attempt to avoid direct great power involvement; to contain the war within the territorial boundaries of the combatants; to contribute to the stalemate; and finally, to preserve the opportunity to develop relations with Iran while curtailing Soviet influence. However, the State Department indicated that two changes had occurred. While US–Iraqi relations had improved over the past three years, the Iranian strategy of attrition and financial strangulation was yielding results that could lead to the collapse of the regime in Iraq. The 'tilt toward Iraq' that 'we have in fact practised for over a year' since Iranian forces crossed into Iraq ranged from the provision of tactical intelligence to financial, diplomatic and military assistance. Washington was most concerned that such a policy 'balances our interest in seeing that Iraq is not defeated with our interest in avoiding an escalation which could draw us directly into the conflict'. So soon after the Vietnam War, another against Iran was inconceivable and the State Department recognised the 'domestic and international political burdens that would imply'.[10]

To facilitate the tilt Washington sent Donald Rumsfeld, an envoy of the President, to meet Saddam Hussein. Washington was keen to reiterate that the cessation of war was in everyone's interests. It also recognised Iraq's current disadvantage in the war of attrition because Iran had access to the Gulf whereas Iraq did not. In such circumstances Iraq's economy and therefore ability to wage war was obviously being affected. Moreover, the cable outlining the 'talking points' for Rumsfeld indicated that the United States 'would regard any major reversal of Iraq's fortunes as a strategic defeat for the West'.[11] The documents resulting from the meetings show both sides searching for improved relations and Iraq's search for assistance to end the war. Rumsfeld emphasised the importance of redressing the regional imbalances. Stability and access were watchwords for both, as the United States sought access to oil and Iraq to Western markets and technology.[12]

The Rumsfeld visit took place against the backdrop of improving US–Iraqi relations. This improvement was interrupted by a November démarche from Washington to Baghdad for its use of chemical weapons against Iran. Washington believed that the use of such weapons had been restricted for a period, but were resumed after the Iranian offensive of February 1984. Washington sent a severe warning, in part because it recognised the issue was receiving 'greater media attention in the United States'.[13] Rumsfeld returned to Iraq amidst further Iraqi setbacks in the war and the sharp deterioration in bilateral relations resulting from the US condemnation of the use of chemical weapons.[14] Despite this, US officials asked for Iraqi help 'in avoiding ... embarrassing situations' but assured Iraq that they did not want 'this issue to dominate our bilateral relationship'.[15] Within weeks the National Security Decision Directive 139, directed the State, Defense and CIA to prepare plans 'of action designed to avert an Iraqi collapse'.[16]

Prior to the resumption of diplomatic relations between the United States and Iraq on 26 November 1984 during which Aziz met with Secretary of State George Shultz, the Defense Intelligence Agency conducted an 'Estimative' on the prospects for Iraq in which future problems were recognised; moreover, there were few illusions on the nature of Hussein's power and capabilities. The Estimative recognised Hussein as a 'ruthless but pragmatic leader' of a 'well-organized' party who dealt with some of his Shia opponents 'by executing, jailing and deporting suspected members' of the Dawa Party. There followed analyses of Iraq's economic and military prospects in the war, which eventually continued until 1988, during which Washington provided further assistance and during which Hussein used chemical weapons against the Kurds, especially in Halabja. But presciently the Estimative recognised that while Iraq had reduced its hostilities towards certain Arab countries during the war, they were likely to resume after it.

Husayn most likely will resume fully his support toward the overthrow of Assad. Moreover, Iraq's intransigence in settling territorial claims to two islands (Bubiyan and Warbah) with Kuwait, despite Kuwaiti support during the war, suggests that Baghdad's relationship with the Arab Gulf states will continue to experience strains.

Despite a likely military occupation of one of the islands, giving Iraq access to the Gulf, military activity or subversion against the Arab moderates was considered unlikely.[17]

In 1988, after the war, an Intelligence Assessment indicated that Iraq would probably seek a UN Security Council guaranteed peace before 'resuming full-time pursuit of its international leadership ambitions'. The US tilt had certainly paid dividends. Iraq's emergence from the war in a 'position of strength' would renew Hussein's aspirations towards both Arab world leadership and leadership within the Non-Aligned Movement. It had the largest Arab armed forces and its oil reserves would 'give Saddam enormous economic leverage in pursuit of his policy goals'. The assessment concluded that a moderate stance would probably prevail and that a 'war weary Iraq probably will not undertake significant military adventures in the near to medium term'. However, it would intensify its efforts to obtain nuclear weapons following its successful use of chemical weapons, which had 'whetted its appetite for advanced technology'. It would continue to emphasise the importance of its oil in its relationship with the United States, who by 1987 had become Iraq's largest supplier of civilian goods, amounting to some $700 million in exports.[18]

Washington was well aware of the tensions between Iraq and Kuwait that prevailed throughout the war with Iran, despite Kuwaiti support for Iraq. The Intelligence Assessment concluded that:

Iraq's need to finance rearmament, reconstruction of war damage, and economic and social development to fulfil the expectations of its populace will lead it to seek maximum oil revenues. Iraqi efforts to capture a larger share of any increase in demand for OPEC oil probably will worsen present frictions with other OPEC exporters, especially Iran.

On Kuwait, it suggested that Baghdad was likely to press the country hard to obtain control of the islands and might insist on the rights to build a military base and obtain a long-term lease to Bubiyan 'as a price for formally settling the border dispute'. Iraq had rejected the solution of the border dispute with Kuwait during the war, even though it concluded agreements with Jordan and Saudi Arabia.[19]

KICKING THE VIETNAM SYNDROME: 'NO GREAT NATION CAN LONG AFFORD TO BE SUNDERED BY A MEMORY'

The United Nations reacted quickly after Iraq invaded Kuwait on 2 August 1990; it soon passed the first of twelve resolutions against Iraq. Resolution 660 condemned the invasion and called for the withdrawal of Iraqi forces, 'immediately and unconditionally' to where they 'were located on 1 August 1990'. These phrases, coupled with uncompromising attitudes in Washington, secured the path to war. The resolution asserted that UN supported negotiations should be pursued to find a solution, though negotiations of course imply a form of compromise and it soon emerged that there would be little of that. Iraq had violated international law by invading Kuwait, as it had in its invasion of Iran in 1980. This time some form of a response was considered necessary. Still the response was anomalous; international law had been violated frequently in the past, not least during the US invasion of Panama less than a year before.[20]

President Bush's response was also swift. As he announced the unilateral deployment of US forces to Saudi Arabia on 8 August 1990, he also set out US objectives. Conveniently forgetting Panama, Bush explained, 'a puppet regime imposed from outside is unacceptable'.[21] 'U.S. interests in the Persian Gulf were vital to the national security. These interests include access to oil and the security and stability of key friendly states in the region', National Security Directive 45 asserted in August 1990. Those interests would be defended with force if necessary. US policy would first seek 'the immediate, complete, and unconditional withdrawal of all Iraqi forces from Kuwait'; second, the restoration of the legitimate government of Kuwait; third, stability in the Gulf; and fourth, 'protection of the lives of American citizens abroad'.[22] US policy adopted the essence of the UN resolution. National Security Directive 45 reiterated the need for 'the immediate and unconditional withdrawal of Iraqi forces from Kuwait'. It would support the mandatory sanctions; but in time-honoured tradition it was prepared to act unilaterally to ensure compliance.[23]

There really was no mystery about US interests in the oil of the region, nor should there have been. Washington has usually been fairly blunt about its interests in oil, though they are of course couched in wider rhetorical agendas. Again National Security Directive 45 was quite straightforward: 'The United States now imports nearly half the oil it consumes and, as a result of the current crisis, could face a major threat to its economy.' Other parts of the world, especially Europe and the Japanese economy were even more dependent on oil from the region and therefore 'vulnerable to Iraqi threats'. There was an interesting circularity going on in this scenario. One of the principal reasons for Iraq's invasion was primarily to gain increased revenue from its oil sales. Iraq was unlikely to threaten the withdrawal of these supplies prior to the invasion and forego that revenue stream. Nevertheless, in response to the invasion and Iraqi control over Kuwaiti reserves, Bush would ask other oil-producing states to increase their production and urge Americans to decrease their consumption of oil products.[24] The American 'way of life' was being affected, perhaps threatened, by a tyrant in the Middle East, but now it was too late for the policies of compromise and appeasement that had served US policy during the 1980s.

Iraq's military strength was acknowledged and it was recognised that Hussein's control of oil could compromise US 'economic independence', but overall Bush stressed the action was defensive; Saudi Arabian sovereignty was vitally important. The policy was not new: the administration had indicated in National Security Directive 26 of 2 October 1989 that the 'United States remains committed to defend its vital interests in the region, if necessary and appropriate through the use of U.S. military force' against either the Soviet Union or 'other regional powers with interests inimical to our own'. But even in 1989 Washington was still pursuing a strategy of moderating and integrating Iraq. National Security Directive 26 pointed out that 'normal relations between the United States and Iraq would serve our longer-term interests and promote stability in both the Gulf and the Middle East'. Thus, 'The United States Government should propose economic and political incentives for Iraq to moderate its behaviour and to increase our influence with Iraq.' However, the Iraqi leadership must understand that the United States would not tolerate its illegal use of chemical and/or biological weapons or breach the IAEA regulations on its nuclear programme. 'Human rights considerations should continue to be an important element in our policy toward Iraq.' Nevertheless, the United States should 'consider sales of non-lethal forms of military assistance'.[25] Despite tacking on the moral high ground in this Security Directive, Washington was well aware of US corporate strategies to continue business with Iraq even if human rights abuses occurred. When the US Senate proposed invoking a genocide bill after Hussein gassed the Kurds at Halabja, US embassy officials reported on a conversation between Husayn Kamil, Hussein's son-in-law and Minister of Industry, and Bechtel officials. The embassy reported to Washington that Bechtel had signed a deal on Iraq's petrochemical project worth $2 billion: 'Bechtel representatives said that U.S. firms – including Bechtel – will resort to non-U.S. sources to carry out their respective contracts.'[26]

Between August 1990 and January 1991, Bush knitted together an international coalition, obtained UN authority to use force to expel Iraq, and secured US Congressional authorisation to go to war. Sanctions were imposed on Iraq through UN Security Council Resolution 661 on 6 August 1990. The 'Desert Shield', which Washington deployed to Saudi Arabia, was authorised on 29 November to use 'all necessary means' to expel Iraq; when Iraq did not withdraw by the imposed deadline, 15 January 1991, Desert Storm was unleashed. After an air war of six weeks, ground troops were sent in. Iraq surrendered in three days. The United States suffered 148 casualties; estimates of Iraqi casualties vary widely. The Project on Defense Alternatives estimate that about 3,500 civilians were killed and between 20,000 to 26,000 military were killed.[27]

The four US objectives were achieved; the war ended. It is, of course, the premature exit that returned to haunt subsequent administrations. But military success did not translate into political success. Saddam Hussein retained power. Had Washington pushed on into Baghdad the multilateral coalition would probably have fallen apart. Bush and Scowcroft realised that to pursue the war would be in breach of international law and would potentially destabilise the region with unknown consequences. Powell was clear that the war was limited, with a limited mandate and a limited purpose. Pushing on involved unnecessary risks, especially to US forces.[28] Moreover, the memories of urban combat from Vietnam still haunted US strategies. Political inadequacy was further compounded after Bush encouraged the revolt against Hussein, but did little to assist the rising, which Hussein crushed.

Bush tried to earn political capital. After the Cold War, he was widely criticised for failing to provide a 'vision thing'. He ultimately settled on the 'New World Order', which was brief and quite vacuous, but more to the point Washington had no interest in enforcing the gist of it elsewhere. The short-lived success of the Gulf War was that the UN could function properly; there was no automatic veto from either superpower. Attempting to gain the high moral ground, Bush explained that 'out of these troubled times, ... a new world order ... can emerge; a new era – freer from the threat of terror, stronger in the pursuit of justice, and more secure in the quest for peace, an era in which the nations of the world, East and West, North and South, can prosper and live in harmony'.[29] Optimistic, duplicitous, opportunistic perhaps, but there was a brief feeling that had the coalition not restored the situation *ante bellum*, the 'verdict of history may well have been that this was the point at which the international community gave up attempting to enforce its own norms'.[30]

But this war was not just about norms. Order and access could probably have been restored through negotiation and compromise; US credibility and hegemony required a demonstration of power. The problem with the other methods of persuading or coercing an Iraqi withdrawal was that the process required compromise or time or both. Fundamentally, those options were far less satisfactory in terms of exorcising the ghosts of Vietnam. Both sanctions and diplomacy required time. Washington refused to negotiate on any matter of substance until after Iraq had withdrawn, and Iraq refused to comply with the imposed deadline of 15 January; however, viable options for a diplomatic solution were worth exploring. For Washington the time factor was crucial because the United States population, Congress or Riyadh would not tolerate the unilateral deployment of US troops to Saudi Arabia indefinitely. Moreover, both George Bush and the US media also effectively curtailed the possibilities of compromise through the demonisation of Saddam Hussein as the new Hitler. The demonisation of Hussein was good for US morale and its public diplomacy, but inaccurate historically, and also blurred the extent to which the coalition members and the US had been involved with the regime during Hussein's rise to power and during Iraq's war with Iran. Elizabeth Drew reported that the Hitler analogy was unpopular amongst Bush's advisors, suggesting he still did not understand the essential characteristics of Hitler. Still, Bush wanted the sanction of history, and given the need to retain Soviet and Chinese support there were few other options: '... the analogy guided Bush, revealed his worldview, and adhered to the history of American militarization, so tied to World War II. With the Cold War's added layers peeled away, a return to the founding moment made sense.'[31] The West and others had armed, financed and assisted Iraq with intelligence throughout the 1980s. Some $40 billion in arms were provided, mostly on credit. If Saddam Hussein was a Hitler, Western objections were muted on his conduct prior to this war. He was encouraged to invade Iran in 1980 because at that point it made convenient sense within the Middle Eastern balance of power. Hussein's domestic record was always appalling: he was responsible for numerous atrocities throughout the 1980s, most glaringly in 1988 when over 3,000 Kurds were gassed in Halabja, with the Western response confined to the verbal, while his actions against the southern Shiite population were also oppressive. It was duplicitous to make so much of these heinous crimes in the run up to war in 2003 when the same atrocities had earlier gone unremarked. During the early stages of Saddam Hussein's trial in 2005 the journalist Robert Fisk accused the Americans of running the reporting of the trial just as Saddam Hussein had run Iraq. The television screens showed the face of the old dictator but without words; the Americans had decided to censor them. The BBC admitted the pictures were 'mute' without explanation. Fisk writes,

If Saddam was really being charged with war crimes over the killings of the Shias – which I hope he was – then why, in heaven's name, didn't we hear what he had to say? Why use the methods of Saddam himself? The silent film, the assumption of guilt? Or was Saddam telling the court that the United States was behind his regime, that Washington had given him the means to destroy the Halabja Kurds with gas? [32]

After the invasion of Kuwait, Iraqi abuse of human rights was widespread. There is no real question about the characteristics of Hussein's regime, but there never was, as recognised in US documents. Amnesty International caught the double standards well:

... violations which have been reported since 2 August are entirely consistent with abuses known to have been committed in Iraq over many years, and which have been documented by Amnesty International in its numerous reports. Iraq's policy of the brutal suppression of all forms of internal dissent continues to be implemented, and the people of Iraq remain its victims. Amnesty International has repeatedly placed such information on the public record, and regrets that until the invasion of Kuwait, the international community did not see fit to apply serious pressure in an attempt to put an end to these abuses.

But the demonisation and the constant reference to the size, if not the capability, of Iraq's army made the prospects for using 'overwhelming power' more palatable.[33]

While it was necessary to ensure the withdrawal of Iraq from Kuwait, it is by no means clear that the war was necessary. Sanctions and diplomacy might have resolved the situation. By and large, the sanctions were implemented effectively. To be sure they were breached on several occasions, but this did not undermine Iraq's overall isolation. In Congressional testimony, a range of speakers, former and current members of the US government, testified to the effectiveness of the sanctions. Admiral William Crowe suggested the US dislike of Hussein had 'crowded out many other considerations ...'. He argued sanctions should be given a 'fair chance' before being discarded. He indicated that if the sanctions would work within a year to 18 months, it would be worthwhile given the sacrifices war required. The proponents of an imminent war, according to Crowe, were selling the United States short. Referencing containment and the Cold War, he observed: 'It is curious that just as our patience in Western Europe has paid off and furnished us the most graphic example in our history of how staunchness is sometimes the better course in dealing with thorny international problems, a few armchair strategists are counselling a near-term attack on Iraq.' General David Jones echoed the sentiment. But what if war did not require too great a sacrifice on the part of the United States? Bush privately indicated his disappointment with Crowe. The following day, 29 November, the UN Security Council authorised the use of force. Within the week, CIA director William Webster testified to Congress on the general efficacy of sanctions, though it remained impossible to predict when they would produce the desired results. Former Secretary of Defense, James Schlesinger, told Congress that even the costs of maintaining sanctions over an eleven-month period would be less than the resort to war. But he indicated that it was becoming apparent there were additional US motives, which not only threatened coalition coherence, but probably limited Hussein's latitude to withdraw voluntarily. The additional objectives included removing Iraq's capacity to intimidate, its military capability and its nuclear programme, or Hussein from power. These were counterproductive to the stated objectives. Schlesinger indicated:

The general effect is to paint Iraq as a rogue or outlaw state, and that its menace to its neighbours and to the international order must be eliminated. To the extent that these additional objectives are embraced, either in appearance or reality, the prospect for a voluntary Iraqi withdrawal from Kuwait is sharply diminished. To achieve these objectives there is really no alternative but to resort to war.[34]

Diplomatic options were effectively blocked to avoid compromise. Ultimately, the resort to war represented a failure of the stated policies. Had Hussein opted for a limited annexation of some Kuwaiti territory or the acquisition of the Bubiyan islands that blocked Iraqi access to the Gulf, he might have got away with the action. His fundamental mistake was to underestimate the US response, its ability to influence the media and turn Arab countries against him, and the Soviet abandonment of their 30-year Friendship and Co-operation Treaty. The vital mistakes included annexing Kuwait entirely, claiming it as the nineteenth province, and linking the situation to the Palestinian problem. Of course it was opportunistic to co-opt the Palestinian cause in his justification, an appeal for Arab solidarity against the West and Israel. But Hiro argues the conflicts of the Middle East since 1948 have been centred on the position and existence of Israel. The radicalisation and the rise to power of the Ba'athist Party after the overthrow of the pro-Western monarchy in 1958 are by-products of the Arab–Israeli dispute. The successive wars militarised the region, assisted by Western governments and arms merchants, thus, '... the linkage between the Palestinian problem and the Gulf crisis of 1990 ... is organic and indisputable'.[35]

Oil was an important factor. During Hussein's meeting with US Ambassador April Glaspie in July 1990, Hussein claimed that Kuwait had been operating an economic war against Iraq by overproducing and consequently depressing the price of oil. Maintaining the OPEC reference price was a vital national concern to Iraq. After its eight-year war with Iran it was saddled with enormous debts and needed the finance for post-war restoration. In addition, Hussein had charged Kuwait with horizontal drilling into the Iraqi oil fields.[36] Glaspie expressed concern at the military build-up on Kuwait's border in July 1990, and explained that she understood the problem of oil hovering around the price of $12 a barrel, which reduced the Iraqi budget by $6 to $7 billion. While she sought clarification on Hussein's intentions, she indicated: 'I know you need the funds. We understand that and our opinion is that you should have the opportunity to rebuild your country. But we have no opinion on the Arab–Arab conflicts, like your border disagreement with Kuwait.' Even if Glaspie told Hussein 'We have many Americans who would like to see the price go above $25 because they come from oil-producing states', the issue was not just Western access to cheap oil. Iraqi control of such a proportion of the world's oil reserves was a crucial consideration. Oil had become a 'critical element in the global balance of power' since the First World War.[37] National Security Directive 45 stated the position clearly: 'The United States now imports nearly half the oil it consumes and, as a result of the current crisis, could face a major threat to its economy. Much of the world is even more dependent on imported oil and more vulnerable to Iraqi threats.'[38]

Throughout the pre-war period there were several attempts to mediate a diplomatic solution to the crisis. Bush's ultimate claim that Washington would go the extra mile to find a diplomatic solution should be placed within the framework of building and maintaining consensus for military action. To perfect the strategy, diplomacy had to appear to have been pursued and failed. With this result, Congress was more likely to approve the use of US force, and Congressional consent was regarded as '... one final box that had to be checked'. To that end James Baker was dispatched to Geneva to meet Iraqi Foreign Minister Tariq Aziz. Though the meeting lasted longer than expected, Baker indicated: 'I met Mr. Aziz today not to negotiate, as we had made clear we would not do, that is, negotiate backwards from UN Security Council resolutions.' Even before the talks had been conducted there was awareness that they would be fruitless. In Congressional testimony, James Schlesinger dismissed the likelihood of their success for the very reason Baker later cited: 'we will not have any direct communication with Iraq until it has left Kuwait'. Washington could not offer anything that would look as if it was appeasing aggression, and Hussein was not willing to accept the price of unconditional withdrawal, though it is also important to note that *Newsday* (a Long Island newspaper) had reported that a US Middle East specialist thought there were 'serious' possibilities for negotiation. The *New York Times* reported that the Bush administration 'intended to block the "diplomatic track," ... for fear that negotiations might "defuse the crisis"'.[39]

If Baker had the power but not the will to negotiate, the reverse appeared to be the case in the meeting between UN Secretary General, Javier Pérez de Cuéllar and Saddam Hussein in Baghdad on 13 January 1991, two days before the imposed deadline for withdrawal. Hussein referred to the UN resolutions as 'American resolutions. This is an American Age.' The resolutions reflected the US desires, not those of the Security Council. De Cuéllar, stated: 'I agree with you as much as the matter involves me.' Hussein charged Washington with complicating the situation, claiming that they were still demanding the total withdrawal of Iraq, 'although they do not say where to, irrespective of Iraq's views'. Resolution 660 demanded withdrawal to the border of 1 August 1990. With a map Hussein indicated that over time Kuwait had expanded. 'Here were Kuwait's borders when it was a protectorate ... it then expanded to here, and then to this point in a place called Mitllah. I think you should write down this name. This is the way the Kuwaitis were until 1963. Mr. Yassar Arafat's passport is stamped in Mitllah. ... so ... when someone says let Iraq withdraw, the question is where to?' De Cuéllar urged him to take his case to the International Court of Justice; he did not receive a direct reply.[40]

Hussein had miscalculated. Playing on the Vietnam syndrome he had told Glaspie, 'yours is a society which cannot accept 10,000 dead in one battle'. After the war with Iran he knew his could, and he thought Iraq could at least inflict enough damage on US forces to inhibit their range. Bush, however, was determined not to allow Vietnam to stand in the way of the Gulf. During his 1989 inauguration, he made the Orwellian statement: 'The final lesson of Vietnam is that no great nation can long afford to be sundered by a memory'; and an administration study had pointed out in February 1990 'For small countries hostile to us, bleeding our forces in protracted or indecisive conflict or embarrassing us by inflicting damage on some conspicuous element of our forces may be victory enough, and could undercut political support for US efforts against them.' Thus, in cases where the United States confronts a much weaker regional enemy, it would be necessary to 'defeat them decisively and rapidly'. The decision to use military force was taken in October 1990, long before the 'extra mile' of diplomacy, and long before Congressional or UN approval. The message was that US prestige required a spectacular victory. Not only to eliminate Iraqi military power, but to bolster the US position in the world. Bush clearly indicated:

When we win, and we will, we will have taught a dangerous dictator, and any tyrant tempted to follow in his footsteps that the U.S. has a new credibility, and that what we say goes, and that there is no place for lawless aggression in the Persian Gulf and in this new world order that we seek to create.[41]

Panama notwithstanding.

On the eve of conflict the National Security Directive set out the US reasoning. The document started with the statement that 'access to Persian Gulf oil and the security of key friendly states in the area are vital to U.S. national security'. Economic sanctions had had a 'measurable impact upon Iraq's economy but have not accomplished the intended objective of ending Iraq's occupation of Kuwait'. Moreover, 'there is no persuasive evidence that they will do so in a timely manner'. Nothing was said about the prospects for a negotiated solution around a different border to that of 1 August 1990; perhaps negotiations would have been regarded as tantamount to appeasement within the context of the Hitler analogy. Time was of the essence;

prolonging the current situation would be detrimental to the United States in that it would increase the costs of eventual military action, threaten the political cohesion of the coalition of countries arrayed against Iraq, allow for the continued brutalization of the Kuwaiti people and destruction of their country, and cause added damage to the U.S. and world economies.

Furthermore, the 'United States recognizes the territorial integrity of Iraq and will not support efforts to change current boundaries'. US actions were limited to the initial objectives, though if Iraq resorted to the use of chemical, biological or nuclear weapons, supported terrorism or attempted to destroy Kuwaiti oil fields, 'it shall become an explicit objective of the United States to replace the current leadership of Iraq'. And Bush added, 'I also want to preserve the option of authorising additional punitive actions against Iraq.'[42]

Bush's popularity rose with the beginning of war.[43] War was clearly good for presidential ratings. While there was extensive coverage of the war, it remained one of the least understood. The media were pooled into units and severely restricted from freely reporting the war.[44] For the most part, television impressed the public with the pictures of 'smart bombs'. The average person saw the successful precision bombing as 'a painless Nintendo exercise', as Edward Said put it. The tonnage of bombs dropped on Iraq was similar to the tonnage dropped in the Second World War. According to Air Force figures 93.6 per cent of tonnage were not guided bombs; there were 82,000 tons of non-precision bombs, discounting the explosives launched from missiles and battleships amounting to between 20–30,000 tons, and 7,000 tons of guided bombs. Of the guided bombs, a large percentage missed their targets. The Iraqi casualties remain estimated, because as Victoria Brittain observed, 'bulldozers scooped the uncounted bodies ... into shallow graves ... with a hasty violation of the First Geneva Convention'. Neither side had an interest in counting them: the coalition to mask the immense destruction, and Hussein, probably for the same reason. Former US military personnel from the Center for Defense Information charged Washington with going beyond the scope of UN authorisation.[45]

That no middle ground could be found to resolve the situation is further testimony of the failure of policy. The final case against Washington suggested it was trying to extend its hegemony not only in the Middle East, but also globally. In the post-Cold War the world system was experiencing a period of decentring. Power was moving away from the core, from the Washington–New York axis. Power was increasingly less reliant on the use of military force, strategies of containment and deterrence were no longer needed, and power was shifting towards other advanced industrial areas such as Europe or a Japan centred East Asia. The Gulf War mitigated these centrifugal forces.[46] The end of the Cold War contributed to the demise of US preponderance. From 1989 there had been increasing calls to pay more attention to the domestic economy, to produce a peace dividend, and finally deal with the declining health and educational standards and other infrastructural concerns. These sentiments continued up to the very last days before the actual war. Prominent opposition to the war from former Defense Secretaries,

McNamara and Schlesinger, who opted for economic sanctions, was reflected in the narrow Congressional approval for the use of force. Despite talk of the new world order, it was more, '... the perpetuation of the old order of Pax Americana that remained his purpose'. The short-term gains for Bush included improvement of his re-election possibilities and mitigating the effects of the economic recession that would have been exacerbated by the increased price of oil. In the long term, McCormick argues, Washington still believed 'the structural imperatives of global capitalism required a hegemonic center to make and enforce the international rules of liberal capitalism'. Four opportunities were too tempting to pass up. First, Washington could weld the 'special relationship' with Britain. Second, it could confirm German and Japanese dependence on US protection, not related to any Soviet threat, but to their dependence on Middle Eastern oil. Kennan earlier indicated US control of Japanese oil supplies would give Washington a 'veto' power over its military and industrial policies. Third, Washington could send a warning to potential adversaries that, despite the end of the Cold War, they could not challenge the 'rules of the game'. And finally, the Gulf War 'recreated the circumstances for renewed public support at home for American hegemony abroad'. Having failed to achieve any of these objectives Bush was ejected from the White House.[47]

There was an awareness of these systemic concerns in Washington. David Boren, Chair of the Senate Intelligence Committee, suggested:

... we've had a strange and symbiotic relationship with the Soviet Union ... the decline of the Soviet Union ... could very well lead to the decline of the United States as well ... the European countries, Japan, and others have been willing to follow the lead of the United States over the past few decades. Why? Because they needed us ... Will they be willing, in this new environment, to follow the lead of the United States as they were just a few short months ago? I don't think so.

Similarly, by the end of 1991, Undersecretary of State, Lawrence Eagleburger, indicated that 'nations will be tempted to go their own way with little regard for the common good ...'. In early 1992 a Pentagon strategy document talked about the problem explicitly. According to the now infamous planning guidance document, largely coordinated by Paul Wolfowitz, the most important matter was 'the sense that the world order is ultimately backed by the U.S., [and] the United States should be postured to act independently when collective action cannot be orchestrated'. The strategy included the following:

... the U.S. must show the leadership necessary to establish and protect a new order that holds the promise of convincing potential competitors that they need not aspire to a greater role or pursue a more aggressive posture to protect our legitimate interests. Second, in the non-defense areas, we must account sufficiently for the interests of the advanced industrial nations to discourage them from challenging our leadership or seeking to overturn the established political and economic order. Finally, we must maintain the mechanisms for deterring potential competitors from even aspiring to a larger regional or global role.

Under US hegemony, Sinatra may sing, but preferably without conviction; states could not do it their way. The document was obviously aimed at an integrated Europe, a united Germany or Japan, at the global level, and at strong countries at the regional level.[48]

The concern with the post-Cold War configuration of power and the prospects for US leadership in a post-Vietnam era that had seen the erosion of US power in terms of relative economic performance, military strength, political influence and cultural sway was augmented by the increasing confidence of a more cohesive EC/EU, the economic aspirations of the Chinese, the performance of the Japanese economy and a multitude of challenges that emerged from Third World revolutionary movements after Vietnam, coupled with the new perception of an 'Islamic threat' mirrored by vocal anti-Americanism.

An early White House review of the National Defense Strategy under the Bush administration in 1989 pointed out that since the Second World War US security interests had been served by containment of the Soviet Union, especially in Europe and East Asia. Now these areas were not so compliant, the notion of the West was not so coherent. The National Security Review 12 opined that to 'deter potential adversaries, we have to make clear that we, and our Allies, have the means and the will to respond effectively to coercion or aggression'. Faced with future uncertainties, the review called for the preservation of US strength. The review sought further enquiry on what the effects of a 'European pillar' would mean for NATO and how US interests would be affected by that prospect. It considered whether there were emerging trends in political or economic spheres that signalled sharp discontinuities that might affect allied commitments to current structures and institutions, such as trade disputes with Japan or 'popular pacifism' in Western Europe.[49]

6
Iraq and Vietnam:
The Unbearable Weight of Defeat[1]

'Many of the pronouncements made by this administration are outrageous. There is no other word. Yet this chamber is hauntingly silent. On what is possibly the eve of horrific infliction of death and destruction on the population of the nation of Iraq – a population, I might add, of which over 50 percent is under age fifteen – this chamber is silent. On what is possibly only days before we send thousands of our citizens to face unimagined horrors of chemical and biological warfare – this chamber is silent. On the eve of what could possibly be a vicious terrorist attack in retaliation for our attack on Iraq, it is business as usual in the United States Senate. We are truly "sleepwalking through history." In my heart of hearts I pray that this great nation and its good and trusting citizens are not in for a rudest of awakenings. ... I truly must question the judgement of any President who can say that a massive unprovoked military attack on a nation which is over 50 percent children is "in the highest moral traditions of our country." This war is not necessary at this time. Pressure appears to be having a good result in Iraq .... Our challenge is to now find a graceful way out of a box of our own making.'

Senator Robert Byrd[2]

So the press doesn't even hear about the American bombs that fall mistakenly on the homes of innocent civilians, wiping out entire families. We hear very little about the frequent instances of jittery soldiers opening fire indiscriminately, killing and wounding men, women and children who were never a threat in the first place. We don't hear much about the many children who, for one reason or another, are shot, burned or blown to eternity by our forces in the name of peace and freedom. Out of sight, out of mind.[3]

Saddam Hussein remained in power after the short war of 1991. The presidency in the United States would have to pass to another generation before Washington removed the regime. With the conclusion of its specific objectives in 1991, the realists in Bush's administration decided to stop the war. The ghosts of Vietnam stayed the thought on moving on to Baghdad. The war was over, period. But because of that inconclusive outcome, Iraq suffered another twelve years of sanctions and routine bombing. Hundreds of thousands were killed. Despite Bush's attempts to limit the impact of Vietnam on his foreign policies earlier, telling his inaugural audiences that 'the final lesson of Vietnam is that no great nation can long afford to be sundered by a memory'.[4] Still, those collective memories resurfaced. Throughout the 1970s and 1980s, the Vietnam syndrome hindered US strategic inclinations and tactical considerations. Casualty phobia, coupled with the search for definitive success, were central considerations for all administrations contemplating sending their troops into harm's way. The collective memories of Vietnam, half remembered, most constructed, coalesced into an undefined democratic inhibition on executive power, but those memories were slow to exert sufficient political influence. If interventions could be kept short, sharp and decisive, military power remained an instrument of choice, frequently shunning the alternative instruments, such as prolonged diplomacy. US engagement and credibility were considered vitally important. Military power could potentially dispel the notion that the United States was a wounded giant or a reluctant warrior. For some, US credibility also demanded engagement. Casualties in low numbers could be culturally tolerated if success was assured.[5]

Despite President Reagan's tough rhetoric, intervention in regional conflicts was largely confined to the use of proxy forces and the pursuit of low intensity conflict by, for example, the *contras* in Nicaragua or the *mujahedin* in Afghanistan. Notwithstanding the muscular rhetoric, others watched what the United States did rather than what it said. Both implicit and sometimes explicit narratives on US power emerged. Saddam Hussein illustrated the popular lessons to an Arab summit on 24 February 1990. He argued that the Arabs had three options in the face of Western power. They could simply capitulate; they could wait for Europe to develop and play it off the United States; or they could unite around a strong Arab leadership. Barry Rubin explains, 'Americans, he insisted, feared military confrontations and losses. It had shown "signs of fatigue, frustration, and hesitation" in Vietnam and Iran and had quickly run away from Lebanon "when some marines were killed" by suicide bombers in 1983. Experience had shown, he concluded, that if Iraq acted boldly, the United States would do nothing.'[6] He tested the waters with US Ambassador April Glaspie in that infamous meeting of August 1990. He pointed out that Iraq had resisted Iran during the 1980s. US troops would not have stood up to Iran four years after Vietnam; nuclear weapons would have been the only US option. Hussein told Glaspie that, 'I do not belittle you', but his observations of US society led him to the conclusion that they were not willing to tolerate large numbers of casualties. His society could, largely because they had no option.[7] These assumptions on US casualty phobia were repeated throughout 2002 and early 2003, and the echoes of Vietnam were frequently invoked thereafter as the Iraqi insurgencies grew in strength and effect. For instance, in March 2002, when Washington began the drumbeat on Iraq once more, Tariq Aziz warned that, 'it was not the jungle that allowed the Vietnamese to win but determination. The Iraqis will fight in every street and every house.' The looming implications and memories of urban warfare and metaphorical quagmire were intended to give US policy makers pause for thought.[8] This tactical use of Iraqi deterrent rhetoric failed in 2003. Saddam Hussein intended to draw US forces into urban battle, inflict sufficient US casualties and raise the numbers of civilian casualties to play on the Western doubts on this war of choice.[9] He did what he could rhetorically to avoid the war in the last few months before the US led invasion; but he also thought that it might be another 1991. Swift and devastating, but he could go into hiding and survive the war. The anticipated bombing campaign could be 'absorbed'.[10]

These assumptions did not account for the new determination on the part of some within the Bush administration to overcome Vietnam; properly this time. The images of a hesitant and timid United States galled such strategists, especially as they watched the hesitancy on Bosnia, the retreat from Somalia, the absence from Rwanda and the initial humiliation in Haiti, when the *USS Harlan* weighed anchor in the face of a jeering mob. Saddam Hussein's brutal treatment of the Shia uprising of 1991 and the ineffective, yet devastating, impact of the sanctions regime throughout the 1990s depicted a power without resolve, especially after the Clinton administration had made it their policy to remove Hussein from power. US technology and airpower provided a half-solution to the problem of casualty-free intervention. In Kosovo in 1999 and in Afghanistan in 2001, Clinton and then Bush demonstrated the reach of US power and technology, though political problems on the ground remained unsolved. But Kosovo and Afghanistan also confirmed certain assumptions: that since Vietnam overwhelming US airpower was the preferred tactic. However, Kosovo may have been the proverbial 'tipping point'. US power was demonstrated decisively, though the US 'will', 'stomach' and resolve were simultaneously called into question. Slaying the ghosts of Vietnam was a vital consideration in the 1991 Gulf War.[11] They remained pertinent. The Vietnam analogy has been a fluid and yet potent influence in the debate on Iraq. The point is not to make direct comparisons between the two wars or to insinuate similar conclusions. Yet, the emotional remnants, strategic and instrumental lessons have pervaded the public discourse on Iraq, just as they have pervaded the internal memoranda, minutes and policy documents, and public debate since 1975. While the analogies and lessons cannot be drawn too closely, they cannot be dismissed either. References to Vietnam, and a host of other symbolically important words and phrases, 'guerrilla warfare', 'resistance movements', 'insurgencies', credibility and credibility gap, exit strategy and 'staying the course', 'politicised intelligence', quagmire, 'tipping point' and 'Iraqification' have served to rekindle both feelings of doubt and also resolution in the culture and administration in Washington.[12]

VIETNAM LESSONS

After the disaster of Vietnam, the lessons that the policy makers could learn were numerous. For a period many just wanted to forget the war: the nightmare had ended and for some there seemed little need to dwell on it. Policy makers and, later, some historians tried to contain the 'Vietnam' analogy and the emerging 'Vietnam syndrome'.[13]

The reflections began early. On 12 May 1975, Henry Kissinger summarised for President Ford a number of studies conducted on the 'lessons of Vietnam'. The principal conclusions suggest an attempt to limit the scope of Vietnam and its impact on US foreign policy. Kissinger wrote:

It is remarkable, considering how long the war lasted and how intensely it was reported and commented, that there are really not very many lessons from our experience in Vietnam that can be usefully applied elsewhere despite the obvious temptation to try. Vietnam represents a unique situation, geographically, ethnically, politically, militarily and diplomatically. We should probably be grateful for that and should recognize it for what it is, instead of trying to apply the 'lessons of Vietnam' as universally as we once tried to apply the 'lessons of Munich'.

There was, he argued, frequent reference to the inability of the United States to stay the course, and to claims that the 'tenacity of the American people and the ultimate failure of our will' were instrumental in the US defeat. 'If one could offer any guidelines for the future about the lessons to be drawn regarding domestic support for foreign policy, it would be that American political groups will not long remain comfortable in positions that go against their traditional attitudes.'[14] In part because of these lessons, Iraq had to be placed in a positive framework. It became the symbolic icon of a US attempt to bring democracy to the Middle East. The war was not just about the weapons of mass destruction or the desire to rid Iraq of the tyrant. It was also about nation-building and democracy promotion, not just in Iraq but throughout the region! A half-century of US support for authoritarian regimes was now a potential liability.

But this more ambitious goal created a long-term problem for Bush. Overcoming Vietnam and more importantly its analogies required several steps involving military, political and cultural considerations. First, US forces demonstrated that militarily they could send significant numbers of troops into combat on the ground. The concerns about US military will and capability initially were laid to rest over the three weeks in that 'catastrophic success' of May 2003, though that success soon rang hollow in the broader context. Second, the pacification of Iraq was necessary to overcome the political analogies. By 2006, despite Bush's pledge to complete the task in Iraq, the outcome was even more far removed. Finally, the cultural analogies could only be contained through winning the 'hearts and minds' of Iraqis and the American people. That struggle was clearly lost by 2006.

Vietnam continues to be used in a loose analogical sense by the media and increasingly by US politicians. One sees the apotheosis of the 'analogy' during periods of heightened US casualties: in November 2003, during which 82 Americans were killed, in April 2004 (135), in November 2004 (137), especially during the presidential campaign, in January 2005 (107), during the 30th anniversary of the final US withdrawal from Vietnam in April 2005 and when Bush visited Vietnam in late 2006. It is clearly understood that what the United States leaves behind will be the true indication of how successful the 'exit strategy' and 'Iraqification' will be. US credibility, its ability to 'stay the course', and its ability to demonstrate resolve and commitment largely hinges on a set of outcomes of bringing stability, democracy and a degree of prosperity to the country and the region. This broader agenda stands in contrast to the pervasive lessons of Vietnam: US objectives should be limited, the mission defined, the operations supported and the outcome obtainable.

These limits were recognised by Kissinger and the Ford administration: that the American people had a more limited vision of the US role in the world. In 1975, Kissinger advocated either the total use of US power or the option of not using it at all. He described a 'control mechanism' that had evolved in the US society, which was ultimately institutionalised, that would prevent such Vietnam-like adventures.[15] When Robert Gates, who after the disastrous results of the 2006 mid-term elections for the Republicans became Secretary of Defense, previously testified in 1986 to assume the position of Deputy Director of Central Intelligence, he echoed such realist sentiments on US power. That in the post-Vietnam period, given the cultural and congressional constraints, overt intervention was impractical. US power could be used in a covert capacity or Washington would have to walk away from the situation.[16] And so from Kissinger's observations of 1975, US power was at least in this realm confined to the use of covert operations, proxy force or airpower. Direct intervention was usually counterproductive and a political liability. Still, credibility remained problematic. As Kissinger warned Ford, in words that had lasting resonance, 'I fear that we will only now begin to realize how much we need to shore up our positions elsewhere once our position in Vietnam is lost. We may be compelled to support other situations much more strongly in order to repair the damage and to take tougher stands in order to make others believe in us again.'[17]

It was clear amongst the Bush principals that the so-called lessons of Vietnam exercised a tremendous influence on strategy from Ford in 1975 to Afghanistan in 2001. Despite the opportunity of 9/11 the operations in Afghanistan were still somewhat shaped by Vietnam articulated through the Weinberger principles and the Powell Doctrine; the central concerns centred on objectives, success, domestic support and an exit strategy. After Somalia in 1993, the Clinton administration added a fifth: the United States would only intervene if national and international interests were at stake. After 9/11 the vital interests seemed clear. Most Americans made no distinction between the War on Terror and the Bush administration's fixation on Iraq, though as time wore on and casualties mounted, with little prospect of success, that distinction became ever more apparent. Since 2003 the strictures of Vietnam have been ignored.

By March 2001 Donald Rumsfeld rewrote the criteria against which the introduction of combat troops could be considered, overturning the prevailing consensus articulated in the Weinberger principles and refined by Powell over the years. Rumsfeld's memo, or at least the bits and pieces that are available, seems to reflect more the thinking that prevailed in the Ford administration, when Rumsfeld was first Secretary of Defense. In March 2001, echoing sentiment played out immediately after Vietnam when decisive force was used in response to the capture of US sailors on the *Mayaguez*, Rumsfeld argued that America must be 'willing and prepared to act decisively to use the force necessary to prevail, plus some'. America must 'act forcefully, early...'. Honesty about the potential hardships should be acknowledged and the administration should not 'dumb down' missions to gain support. Moreover, with an implicit stab at the thinking developed by Weinberger and Powell on exit strategies, Rumsfeld advised against the imposition of artificial deadlines that would provide the enemy with the ability to calculate and 'simply wait us out'. Rumsfeld's guidelines were informed by the belief in a more robust US power. Sure there were the caveats on the US national interest, the achievable mission, the requisite resources and public support, but Rumsfeld also warned about the risks of inaction. US interests needed to be calculated for the different scenarios, 'if we prevail, if we fail, or if we decide not to act. ... Just as the risks of taking action must be carefully considered, so, too, the risk of inaction needs to be weighed.'[18]

CLEAR OBJECTIVES

September 11 provided the opportunity to move against Saddam Hussein. Given the US proclivity to regard the world through a Manichaean framework, George Bush was easily able to merge two separate issues. Hussein had become a potent symbol of the inadequacy of US power in the neo-conservative mindset. With the confluence of ambition and a desire to assert US power, coupled with a relatively vulnerable regime, the injunction to pursue clear objectives was lost.

The objectives were unclear from the start. Beyond toppling Hussein, the outcomes were uncertain. Moreover, the specific military mission in Iraq stood in contradistinction to the overall mission in the War on Terror. The military mission centred on the overthrow was defined, but Bush's broader rhetoric was vague, broad, ambitious and universal: the terrorists had not only attacked the United States, but also their way of life. US ideals were also now in play and subsequently the scope of the objectives were unreachable; the so-called war endless. The war was not just on terrorism but on many things: terrorism, tyrants, rogue regimes and on that corner of the US mind that felt emasculated after Vietnam. The war would in ways provide the United States with meaning,[19] with a purpose. During the early months after 9/11, Bush took the United States down paths that had been travelled before. In 1947, when the British indicated that they could no longer 'hold their own', as the phrase went, in Greece and Turkey, the Truman administration took the opportunity of responding to a fairly localised crisis and defined the US response in universal terms that created interests, commitments and responsibilities that would ultimately lead to Vietnam, because a mindset on communism was given credence in the official US mind that privileged a universal and Manichaean outlook in favour of a more limited and particular response. That mindset seeped out into the broader culture. Within years the United States was fighting a number of nationalist movements. That confusion not only overextended the United States but ultimately exposed the limits of its power.

Colin Powell counselled a more limited response early after 9/11 but Rumsfeld and Wolfowitz ultimately prevailed. Iraq was on the agenda early.[20] Surely it was a logical conclusion that war in Iraq would not only create further difficulties for the United States, inflame opinion against the United States and provide further grist to the anti-American mill, and ferment further terrorism. Though Iraq provided a tangible and defined territorial target, the problem also rested in the American mind; coming to terms with a sense of limits.

After 9/11 such limits were elusive. There were hints and allusions, despite the evidence, on the links between Saddam Hussein and al Qaeda. Bush successfully portrayed what was going on in Iraq as a problem related to the War on Terror. And there was consistent polling evidence that the strategy was effective. Americans generally did link the two despite the evidence. The links were not seriously questioned at a popular level until things started to go badly wrong in Iraq. By that stage the prophecy had become self-fulfilling and indeed elements of the various and disparate insurgencies were connected to terrorist groups. In 2004, for instance, Americans thought: the war helped in the fight against terrorism; it illustrated the power of the US military; and revealed the United States to be trustworthy and supportive of democracy abroad. These beliefs were not generally shared elsewhere. There was much more scepticism on the links between the War on Terror and Iraq; the United States was considered less trustworthy as a consequence of the war; and 'even U.S. military prowess is not seen in a better light as a result of the war in Iraq'.[21]

The official US objectives were largely based on illusions and inconsistencies. The United States wanted to rid Iraq of weapons of mass destruction (though it was unlikely that they existed), to destroy the links between Iraq and the terrorists, and to promote democracy in Iraq. They hinted at a broader regional agenda without indicating any specifics or a timetable in case they further alienated long-time US allies such as Saudi Arabia. The ever sarcastic Maureen Dowd of the *New York Times* wrote of her initial reservations about going to war, but then she listened to a speech given by Dick Cheney to US veterans in August 2002. Cheney outlined the argument for war based on the goal of creating 'a government that is democratic and pluralistic, a nation where the human rights of every ethnic and religious group are recognised and protected'. Dowd wrote, 'OK, I'm on board. Let's declare war on Saudi Arabia.'[22]

Resources and the extension of US power and presence in the region were pertinent. Resources were vital; they had been from the 1920s and especially the 1940s. The obvious retort to such arguments was that it would have been easier for Washington to cut a deal with the dictator for access to the oil. That might have been plausible until 1990, but after all the demonisation, the characterisations of Saddam Hussein were so well entrenched in US culture that cutting deals would have been tantamount to supping with the devil or worse still might revive narratives of appeasement, after Munich! After Vietnam! But it was also clear from the combination of the 'Cheney Report', the National Energy Policy Development Group of May 2001, the September 2001 Quadrennial Defense Review and subsequent war on terrorism, that the United States was on an expansionist drive. Its dependence on foreign oil is increasing, from 52 per cent in 2001 to an estimated 66 per cent by 2020. It is anticipated that the US presence around key oil-producing areas will intensify over this period, perhaps inviting further tensions and clashes with nationalist or other groups in South East Asia, the Middle East, Central Asia, Venezuela, Colombia, Mexico and sub-Saharan Africa, especially Angola and Nigeria.[23]

STRONG LIKELIHOOD OF SUCCESS

The strong likelihood of success obviously relates to the objectives. While the conventional military operations were defined and cata-strophically successful, they stand in contradistinction to the fact that there had been little planning for the post-war order. The questions on US endurance and its political and psychological ability to sustain its commitment evoke the Vietnam analogy most potently. In turn, US resolution is closely related to the number of casualties incurred and the domestic political reactions. Following the advice contained in Rumsfeld's March 2001 memorandum, Bush prepared Americans for a broad and sustained response after 9/11: he would not settle for a token act, US patience was needed because the war would not be short or easy.[24] Still, once Americans increasingly separated 9/11 from Iraq, their patience was tested. But by then the questions that animated US politics were not concerned with generating support to go into Iraq, but with trying to figure out how, and especially when, they could get out. Moreover, they increasingly realised that Iraq was a war of choice not necessity and that the pertinence of national interests could not be sustained.

Before that the narratives on success were open to question. As already mentioned, Iraqi officials did what they could to metaphorically recall Vietnam and especially the battle for Hue after the Tet Offensive in which heavy casualties were sustained in urban battle. However, Rumsfeld pushed the arguments for a short war: 'I can't say if the use of force would last five days or five weeks or five months, but it certainly isn't going to last any longer than that. It won't be a world war three.' Because of the adjustments that Hussein had made to the Iraqi forces after 1991, they were now a much more loyal force. Should the regime fall, these forces would be caught between the Iraqi population and the foreign invaders. A fight for survival was the only viable option; and in the face of US power it could not be conventional.[25]

Insurgents' strategies played on US resolve and commitment; the United States would lose its patience and withdraw. In 2003 Iraq's defence minister, General Sultan Hashim, warned that the Americans would have to 'pay a heavy price in blood'. In mocking tones he suggested that the US forces could go to the north of Iraq, 'they can even go onto Europe. But in the end, to achieve their objective, they will have to come to the city. The city will fight them. They say a land fights with its own people.' Washington completely underestimated the real extent of the potential resistance. Talk of resistance and Iraqi nationalism was apparent throughout the region. The popular welcome Washington expected was yet another illusion fuelled no doubt by the endless benign meta-narrative of US power. In Lebanon, Iraqi exiles predicted a strong resistance: 'Iraqis are tough people. They won't accept American occupation. They have never accepted foreign occupation', Robert Fisk quoted an Iraqi exile.[26]

It is a terrible irony that the war in Iraq was only conceivable precisely because Iraq was not a threat to the United States. Had it possessed weapons of mass destruction in extensive numbers or had links to al Qaeda, Washington would surely have been much more cautious about going to war in 2003. Had weapons of mass destruction existed, the fear of a prolonged or a devastating war would have been unthinkable. Iraq was a doable operation, 'it is precisely because he [Hussein] is not now a real threat to the US, nor a real ally of al-Qaida, and nor, probably, in possession of useable weapons, that war is feasible', Woolacott wrote in 2002.[27]

DOMESTIC SUPPORT

Domestic support was considered crucial after the popular lessons of Vietnam suggested that the war was lost when the people turned against it. Containing the media was thereafter also considered vitally important to the success of US strategy. If either US or other civilian casualties were depicted, analysts understood the negative reactions and potential loss of support. Rumsfeld was wary about these concerns with casualty phobia. He wanted more bluntness on such issues, but the Bush administration still avoided the issue when possible. Critics hounded Bush for not attending funerals. Restrictions on the depiction of US coffins were enforced. The media limited coverage of Iraqi civilian casualties in contrast to Arab television coverage. These were important strategies because they protected the point of vulnerability in a democratic society, especially after Vietnam. Obviously, if public opinion turned against the war, the US commitment would be difficult to sustain. Hussein's initial strategies specifically aimed at US opinion; the insurgencies continue to do so.

The initial positive public perceptions of the US military effort declined over time. Initially 93 per cent of respondents to Pew polls indicated a positive view of operations, down to 63 per cent in January 2004, further eroded to 54 per cent in early 2005[28] with the bottom falling out in 2006. Criticism of the decision to go to war has also been rising steadily. And as the conflict drags on, opinions on Bush's handling of the war have steadily declined.

The use of the Vietnam analogy seems most potent during particular assaults on Falluja or Najaf or when US casualties become even more obvious. Moreover, the calls for an end and the transition of power became more pressing. 'Iraqification' was a double-edged sword. To the extent that it signalled a US withdrawal it might appease US opinion. Yet the word itself and a quick exit also threatened to conjure up further the ghosts of Vietnam and Vietnamisation, during which time the priority was on exit rather than strategic stability. It ostensibly provided the so-called 'decent interval' before the collapse of the South Vietnamese regime. The narratives on the decent interval before the collapse of South Vietnam supposedly exculpated Washington from some responsibility; the government was incapable of defending itself. Competing accounts of Vietnam clashed in US culture. Senators invoked Vietnam and its cultural power, Senator Edward Kennedy directly made reference to 'George Bush's Vietnam', and still, Bush repeated the now familiar mantra on resolve, strength and the US will.[29] Senator John McCain, a Vietnam veteran, pointed out as early as November 2003, 'When the United States announces a schedule for training and deploying Iraqi security officers, then announces the acceleration of that schedule, then accelerates it again, it sends a signal of desperation, not certitude.'[30] The narratives and memories of defeat lingered in US culture, even if Iraqification was supposed to signal a certain end.

Narratives of success were obviously dependent on various operational reporting. Over time this either meant limiting the coverage of the war, limiting reporter access or the use of pictures and accounts of US and civilian casualties. But this, of course, produced yet another dilemma. While US forces needed to demonstrate their prowess in military terms, they also needed to demonstrate that they had done everything in their power to avoid needless deaths, but given the propensity to use high-tech weaponry and to fight wars from a distance that would be difficult.

The decline in support was more or less steady as time went on and casualties mounted. The strategic implications were obvious. While Iraqi insurgents demonstrated their staying power, US military officials tried to belittle their impact. Lieutenant General Ricardo Sanchez, the then top commander in Iraq, described the attacks as 'strategically and operationally insignificant'. The White House reasserted its commitment; its spokesman, Trent Duffy, intimated that the violence was intended to weaken US determination and accelerate its withdrawal, but 'our will and our resolve are unshakable'. But the deeper impact was inescapable. A former US Army Colonel pointed out presciently, 'Every single one of these attacks challenges American will, and American will is the center of gravity in this campaign.' Moreover, former highly ranked US military officials further undermined Bush's position. Wesley Clark, who oversaw operations in Kosovo, outlined the desperate US position as the administration seemingly had very little response to the ongoing attacks.[31]

The Bush administration faced acute dilemmas. The psychological impact of the war was extended each time the insurgents killed more US personnel. Furthermore, they increasingly targeted Iraqi collaborators, not only for tactical reasons, but also to undermine the viability of the US project and to demonstrate that it would not be viable in the short or medium term. US doubt was a central concern. Bush too got caught up in accusations of callousness and faced another dilemma that threatened to invoke Vietnam. He was accused of avoiding the issue of US casualties. Clearly, he could not attend all funerals but even drawing attention to the rate and numbers of casualties would remind the public of the ongoing death with little positive to report. The White House was wary that the administration might get trapped into the daily body count that had haunted the Johnson presidency. The balance between expressions of sympathy and resolve remained difficult.[32]

Positive depictions of the US efforts in Iraq seemed to further enhance the 'credibility gap' and drew parallels to President Johnson's positive accounts of Vietnam in 1967. Elite opinion on Vietnam changed in early 1968 with the Tet Offensive, some time after a more general shift in opinion. In 2004 the Tet analogy returned in the media. Ultimately, Rumsfeld conceded that he had no doubts that the insurgents had learned from Tet 'and the fact that if they make a big enough splash, even though they get a lot of people killed and we pound them, they end up winning psychologically'.[33]

The psychology was imperative. Iraq was not just about a response to 9/11, or merely confined to the issue of regime change developed during the late 1990s. It also represented a symbol of a deep psychological wound after Vietnam and the limits of US power were so obviously exposed. These outcomes jarred with the narratives on US success and manifest destiny.

The Bush administration struggled with the growing culture of doubt, especially when the Vietnam analogy threatened to bring the society to the proverbial 'tipping point' in the struggle for US hearts and minds. To shore up his credibility and US resolve, Bush told a prime time audience that the commitment was firm, that there were no plans to leave Iraq in the near term. To those who had lost relatives in Iraq he pointed out, 'we will finish the work of the fallen'; that, 'if additional forces are needed, I will send them'. By late 2006 he confirmed the message to Prime Minister Nouri al-Maliki. Yet recruitment to the US forces was falling rapidly. He was committed to the security of Iraq beyond the transition of June 2004. Finally, while 'we will continue taking the greatest care to prevent harm to innocent civilians ... we will not permit the spread of chaos and violence. I have directed our military commanders to make every preparation to use decisive force, if necessary, to maintain order and to protect our troops.' The transition would proceed according to schedules. The January 2005 elections would be held and a constitution would be presented by October 2005 for national referendum. Thereafter, Iraqis would elect a government by 15 December 2005. He was acutely aware that the project was not just about Iraq. He argued:

The success of free government in Iraq is vital for many reasons. A free Iraq is vital because 25 million Iraqis have as much right to live in freedom as we do. A free Iraq will stand as an example to reformers across the Middle East. A free Iraq will show that America is on the side of Muslims who wish to live in peace, as we have already shown in Kuwait and Kosovo, Bosnia and Afghanistan. A free Iraq will confirm to a watching world that America's word, once given, can be relied upon, even in the toughest times.

And

Above all, the defeat of violence and terror in Iraq is vital to the defeat of violence and terror elsewhere; and vital, therefore, to the safety of the American people. Now is the time, and Iraq is the place, in which the enemies of the civilized world are testing the will of the civilized world. We must not waver.

Appeasement was not on the agenda.[34]

However, US tactics were counterproductive. When US authorities cracked down on Shia leader, Moqtada al-Sadr, closed his newspaper and arrested a key deputy, widespread violence broke out in the Shia dominated south and in the Sunni town of Falluja in the west. US forces used overwhelming airpower. Still, as US troops moved in, Sadr taunted: 'Iraq will be another Vietnam for America and the occupiers.' The rotation of US troops was delayed, troop morale was low and there were further reports on suicide rates amongst US troops. Ayatollah Ali al-Sistani refused to condemn Sadr, but criticised 'the methods used by occupation forces in the current escalating situation in Iraq'. The cycle of violence continued as hundreds were killed in the assault, including children. 'This behaviour of the Americans will make everyone seek revenge. Falluja has become a symbol for those who reject the occupation.' US tactics would make more people sympathetic to the resistance, argued Mohammed Hassan al-Balwa, head of Falluja's city council.[35]

Between Vietnam and Iraq domestic support was predicated on short wars, decisive use of power, especially airpower during the 1990s, leading to the eventual introduction of ground forces. If the conflict was more protracted, especially during the 1980s, proxy warfare was preferred. The Bush administration challenged these assumptions and the accumulated lessons after Vietnam; they in turn were constrained by declining levels of support, sustained resistance in Iraq and a loss of credibility globally.

EXIT STRATEGY

An exit strategy that maintained US credibility was essential, otherwise an Iraq syndrome would augment the Vietnam syndrome. Here again the Bush administration got it wrong. The United States was relatively isolated on Vietnam in the international arena; Iraq was little different in that respect. Few governments would be willing to assist in the reconstruction, having been dismissed in the initial diplomacy in 2002, cut out of lucrative contracts in 2003, they were obviously reluctant, given the cataclysmic violence and potential regional instability to assist Washington. By 2006 Washington remained fairly isolated and by that stage there was no decent outcome for Iraq or the United States on the horizon.

As pressure within Iraq and within the United States mounted, Washington became more anxious about articulating an exit strategy. It had to consider the transfer of power at the political level. The elections, constitution, referendum and the formation of government proceeded in an unsatisfactory manner, compounding indigenous problems still further. The prospects for peace and stability were and are not promising. At the military level 'Iraqification' was equally problematical as force numbers and training significantly lagged behind anticipated projections.

Finally, US credibility was crucial not just in the United States and in Iraq, but also across the world. The outcome of Iraq will have a profound impact on US power and its reputation. By May 2005 a report by the International Institute of Strategic Studies (IISS) concluded that 'best estimates suggest that it will take up to five years to create anything close to an effective indigenous force able to impose and guarantee order across the country'. Iraq has become a good environment for al Qaeda recruitment with all the attendant prospects for further international terrorism. The intervention has become 'the proverbial elephant in the living room. From al-Qaeda's point of view, Bush's Iraq policies have arguably produced a confluence of propitious circumstances: a strategically bogged down America, hated by much of the Islamic world, and regarded warily even by its allies.' These circumstances have given al Qaeda the opportunity to recruit and train another generation of its members.[36]

It was particularly odd that an administration filled with such experience, principals who served in most Republican administrations from the late 1960s, who had been through the painful process of readjustment after Vietnam, chose to ignore the lessons of that war.[37] Lessons that significantly shaped US intervention policy across subsequent decades were disregarded. Washington had no viable exit strategy. The United States had no clear idea of the endgame, its planning was paltry; the implications would be extraordinary. Its reputation and credibility was damaged by the manner in which it conducted the pre-intervention diplomacy; its determination and high-handed manner brushed aside allied advice. Ultimately, when Washington needed help of course the offers were limited. Bush's critics in the US Senate contrasted his stance with that of his father who declined to move on Baghdad. Senator Levin quoted from the memoirs of Bush Sr that he wrote with his National Security Advisor, Brent Scowcroft: 'To occupy Iraq would instantly shatter our coalition, turning the whole Arab world against us. ... It would have taken us way beyond the imprimatur of international law bestowed by the resolution of the Security Council.' US troops would be bogged down in urban warfare and the move would 'plunge that part of the world into even greater instability and destroy the credibility we were working so hard to re-establish'.[38]

Intoxicated with success in Afghanistan and illusions of a resurgent Wilsonian policy that sought to make the Middle East safe for democracy, the administration moved to war and the resort to US power without significantly considering the outcome. Their credibility was significantly damaged; they found no weapons of mass destruction, there was no widespread welcome for the US troops, the revelations at Abu Graib left indelible icons that would damage the US reputation throughout the region, the insurgencies continued, stability after the formation of the government remains elusive. The most basic questions concerning the aftermath had not been asked. What happens after they take Baghdad? What happens after Saddam Hussein? How will the country be governed and by whom?

Would they be able to foster a viable state? Would Iraq disintegrate? What were the implications for stability in the Middle East? Would a democratic Iraq necessarily comport with US strategic imperatives? The planning was a mess. As one commentator concluded, 'The failure to answer this question at the start set back US efforts in Iraq in such a way that the US has not recovered and may never do so.'[39]

US Congressional Representative, Jim McDermott, identified a series of failures as US casualties mounted. 'Iraq has been a mistake from the beginning', he noted. It was not 'a test. Iraq is not a laboratory. They are shooting real bullets, and we keep pretending we have a policy. Some say Iraq is not like Vietnam. Iraq looks more and more like Vietnam every day', he informed the House. Though Iraq could not be directly compared to Vietnam, many mistakes identified by Lyndon Johnson's Secretary of Defense, Robert McNamara, were repeated. They had not been honest with the public; the domestic debate was inadequate rushed through the slipstream of 9/11; false and fabricated intelligence was used; the tendency to exaggerate the dangers Iraq posed to the United States undermined serious strategic thinking.[40]

Still, by 2006 the exit strategy remains elusive. The 2005 elections produced a government dominated by Shia because the Sunnis mostly boycotted the process. The continued violence called the legitimacy of that process into question. Washington increasingly faced another acute dilemma. If it left they would leave behind a weak state facing what appears to be insurmountable chaos. Yet its continued presence also enhanced tensions and its military engagement further alienated many. Having shunned the international community in the run up to war, there were few it could appeal to now. There was no good option for Washington.[41] It was a disaster for Iraqis.

A viable exit strategy remains elusive. The new government and the United States continue to grapple with the violence. Iraqification has been limited from the outset. The outcomes were extraordinarily negative in Iraq, in the region and for the US reputation worldwide. US power has been sundered by a desire to overcome the limits to that power after the Vietnam War.

Washington was the latest power to fall into the age-old dilemma of empires. Without gaining legitimacy for its actions, and with the continued use of violence, there was and will be continued reaction and resistance. The dialectics of violence were not difficult to predict. The myopia of this administration brought on a situation of tragic proportions. It did not learn from its own history of regional intervention, let alone that of other empires. As US power extended across the continent in the nineteenth century, through Central America in the early twentieth century and to the Philippines there was always resistance. It is and was not only or necessarily about US power or the attendant projects associated with a traditional interpretation of that power, it is that the power is imposed and unwanted. US narratives were and are not necessarily shared by the occupied and nationalist resistance needs to be considered. Washington is the latest to fall into such a dilemma. In his magisterial survey of culture and imperialism Edward Said writes, '... it was the case nearly everywhere in the non-European world that the coming of the white man brought forth some sort of resistance'.[42]

While many initially viewed the US response in Afghanistan as legitimate, Iraq was not a part of the same process. The diplomatic resistance was most acute over the autumn and spring of 2002–3. Anti-Americanism was rife. Resistance within Iraq has remained steady. After Vietnam US strategists yearned to overcome its effects through the application of decisive military power. Their forces were rebuilt and both strategic and tactical lessons were learned. After the initial operations in Panama, Colin Powell absorbed the lessons from that intervention and resolved to counsel the use of 'all the force necessary, and do not apologise for going big if that is what it takes'. His palliative reasoning suggested that ultimately decisive force ends wars quickly and in the end saves lives.[43] Others learned that conventional resistance was pointless against such overwhelming power. There was little doubt in 2003 that Washington would not achieve its short-term objectives. But against such odds, unconventional and asymmetric counter-violence was the only viable option open to the insurgency. This was and will be difficult to defeat in the absence of a legitimising context. Moreover, after 9/11 one wonders whether an exit strategy is any longer a possibility, unless Washington works hard on the issue of legitimacy and power. Any exit at this point will enhance the maladies of Vietnam: attempts to eliminate the insurgencies will invite further resistance, or if Washington leaves without such 'victory' its self-perceived credibility will suffer. Kissinger's lesson of May 1975 remains in poignant irony on the limits of US power and the inhibiting social mechanisms, as the realists, Robert Gates and James Baker, move back into political service to salvage what can be from the mess that this adventure has become.

7
The Tipping Point:
Between Bring 'em on and Going South

The problem: 9/11 brought the calamity of death, the pain of regarding to the streets of New York, the Pentagon and the fields of Pennsylvania. The grief soon turned to narratives of resolve and a determination to seek a particular and culturally defined type of justice that the sole superpower now felt competent to define without much consultation or legitimation. Its revenge was swift and wide; initially it knew no bounds. Further casualties were surely expected as Bush prepared the nation for pain, loss and grief in his early speeches after 9/11. But Washington and Americans prepared for the inevitability of war accustomed to a quarter-century of warfare that sought to limit US casualties and in so doing inflicted widespread casualties on the 'others'. Swift and decisive victory had been a central theme in US intervention since Vietnam. The peace-keeping operations and the 'duties' of the 'reluctant sheriff' posed yet further difficulties because in such operations it was not always clear that US interests were directly involved, and if they were not central to the fight, why should US troops be put in harm's way? If national interest could be identified, swift victory buttressed by a clear understanding of success made various operations culturally acceptable. Moving the war to Iraq, enlarging the problem to solve it, exacerbated the predicament. Some US strategists were so imbued by the sense of victory that these thinkers seemed to surf the waves of assumptions that were slowly and painfully dissolved after May 2003. The fundamental lessons of Vietnam confronted the instrumental lessons that had facilitated intervention. Yet again, the admonition to know your enemy was pertinent. Yet again, one could hear the echoes of the former Secretary of Defense Robert McNamara's apology, that he had underestimated the tenacity of the Vietnamese and misunderstood the roots of their nationalism. Of course the contexts are different, but the problems share a similarity. Iraqi nationalism was seriously misunderstood. Even three and a half years into the conflict, after over 3,300 further US casualties, the Bush administration still speaks of 'the insurgency' as if it were a unified entity; it still talks of 'the terrorists' as though the Manichaean constructs of *the* enemy are so vital to social mobilisation and moral clarity in this far from just conflict. The strategies involving disproportionate power to 'liberate' peoples, involving immense further destruction and death, not only confronted the enmity of regime loyalists but also created the context for other sources of enmity. The desperate search for a viable exit strategy that maintains US credibility remains elusive. The unnecessary pain and suffering of US troops have yet again sundered the superpower. Moreover, given 9/11 and the fathomless enmity generated in Iraq, an exit strategy might be more elusive. The long-term costs to American society, in terms of the casualties, the financial and security considerations, and the implications for democracy and domestic freedom are quite profound and tragic.

'EITHER WAY, THE PRESIDENT LOSES'

With the run up to the mid-term elections of November 2006 Bush recognised the failures in Iraq. He conceded that there were parallels between Iraq and Vietnam and that they might have reached the metaphorical point of impact that the Tet Offensive had in 1968. He recognised the stepped up violence in the approach to the elections and recognised that they 'have been trying to inflict enough damage so that we leave'. Even though the White House press secretary, Tony Snow, was quick to point out that they did not think 'there has been a flip-over point' because they were 'going to continue pursuing victory aggressively'.[1] But as Election Day loomed Snow also indicated that Bush had stopped using the earlier mantra-like repetition of his intention to 'stay the course'. That phrase became dysfunctional. If earlier it was supposed to represent the resolve and seriousness of the US commitment, recognising the importance of Iraq as a symbol as well as a situation, it now suggested a tough persistence in the face of evident failure; Snow conceded 'it left the wrong impression'. Given the rising death tolls and soaring costs, staying the course implied rigidity, a lack of imagination, a determination based on a reading of character in the face of the deepening disaster in Iraq. But Bush was quick to explain: '"stay the course" means keep doing what you're doing. My attitude is, don't do what you're doing if it's not working – change. "Stay the course" also means don't leave before the job is done.' Yet metaphors represent far more than the language used to convey them. And within the political climate reflected in the 'thumping' the Republicans received in the 2006 elections, viewed largely as a referendum on Iraq, the metaphor seemed to relate more to the conservative discourse on character and moral strength, a tough though myopic persistence, 'to not stay the course', the linguist George Lakoff writes, 'evokes the same metaphors, but says you are not steadfast, not morally strong'.[2] Within that discourse the implications for Bush and US foreign policy are obvious.

The Secretary of Defense, Donald Rumsfeld, so closely associated with the war in Iraq and more broadly the short-lived use of the term 'long war', which at once both suggested the positive aspects of the US commitment and simultaneously the negative implications of long-term occupation, sustained casualties and failure, was first to go, despite Bush's indications that he would stay until the end of the term in 2009.[3] His replacement with the more moderate and realist Robert Gates, a former head of Central Intelligence in the Bush Sr administration, was supposed to signal change in US policy. But when the bipartisan Iraq Study Group (ISG), formed in March 2006 reported in December, Bush was quick to signal a rejection of their key recommendations. Chaired by James A. Baker, the former Secretary of State, and Lee H. Hamilton, an influential former Congressional representative for Indiana, the report delivered a blunt indictment. 'The situation in Iraq is grave and deteriorating. There is no path that can guarantee success, but the prospects can be improved', it began. It called for a change in the primary mission of US forces in Iraq and engagement with regional adversaries through diplomatic means to secure the situation and prevent the potential disintegration of the country and war in the Middle East. It advocated attempts to build a new consensus, to talk to Iran and Syria who had shared interests in Iraqi stability and it placed its recommendations within the overall regional context emphasising the need to directly deal with the Arab–Israeli conflict with the renewed intention to create a two state solution for Israel and Palestine. In Iraq the exit strategy it advocated centred on a shift of responsibilities to Iraqi forces with US support that should lead to the withdrawal of US combat brigades by early 2008. It noted the huge costs of the war in terms of the lives lost, the 21,000 American wounded and the financial burden of spending some $8 billion per month with total estimates running to some $2 trillion by wars end. Yet 'despite a massive effort, stability in Iraq remains elusive and the situation is deteriorating'. It drew out the consequences for the United States, Iraq and the region. Staying the course was clearly failing:

current US policy is not working, as the level of violence in Iraq is rising and the government is not advancing national reconciliation. Making no changes in policy would simply delay the day of reckoning at a high cost. Nearly 100 Americans are dying every month. The United States is spending $2 billion a week. Our ability to respond to other international crises is constrained. A majority of the American people are soured on the war.

Adding more troops, the report argued 'would not solve the fundamental cause of violence in Iraq'.[4] But Bush moved in that very direction. Despite the ISG observations on the shortcomings of the August 2006 'Operation Together Forward II' which saw US forces working together with Iraqi forces to 'clear, hold and build' – clear an area, hold it and build projects to win hearts and minds – Bush shuffled personnel and persisted with the 'surge' of US troops into 2007.[5]

The ISG report not only exposed the differences between the Democrats and the Republicans on this issue, but also the fissure within the Republican Party foreign policy elite that divided over the realism advocated by Baker and those more influenced by the neo-conservatives, who saw the report as a 'strategic muddle', 'stupid', 'absurd' and characterised its authors as 'surrender monkeys'. The more ideologically inclined neo-conservatives, at least on this issue – on others such as North Korea and China they are far more realist, anticipating the costs of engagement –[6] were seen as opposing the realism of the Baker recommendations, and advocating the tougher Bush or John McCain line of persistence through to victory.[7] As Bush pushed for further troops to be sent to Iraq, the Democrats, now in control of both House and Senate, moved to limit his options by tying further funding to a timetabled US exit. In May 2007 Bush vetoed their Bill. The Democrats were unlikely to gain sufficient votes to override the veto.

As US commanders predicted that the war could last years, as the Democrats promised to change the direction of the war, Bush persisted in the obviously failing policy, to stay the course, to pursue the elusive victories, in what the American columnist Paul Krugman characterised Iraq as 'a quagmire of the vanities – a place where America is spending blood and treasure to protect the egos of men who won't admit that they were wrong'.[8]

THE BODY AND 9/11

Shortly after 9/11 Robert Kaiser wrote in the *Washington Post*, 'not since 1968, when assassinations and the Tet Offensive left us numb, have Americans shared a trauma of this magnitude. Then we felt unhinged; this time we feel violated.'[9] The mythical narrative of isolation in US culture had been shattered, the protective barriers of the oceans that FDR even saw as diminished in 1943 were removed. Airpower, that instrument that had restored so much of America from the trauma of the Tet Offensive and the legacies of Vietnam, had been turned against it in the attack on the Twin Towers and the Pentagon. The illusion of a casualty-free war could no longer be sustained. The United States would act; few were under the illusion that it would not respond with violence.

But Washington found it difficult to generate a sustained legitimacy for its actions. In many ways it had separated itself from notions of the global community. Nicholas Rizopoulos, historian at Adelphi University, observed that 'in our triumphalism, we like to think we are the best that ever inhabited the earth. But we assume that every one else will just accept this as a given, and that we don't have to do anything but have fun.' Kaiser concluded from this, 'It's a harsh judgement, but awfully difficult to refute. We are the leading world power, but we rarely lead the world ... What great American initiative has helped solve a global problem in recent times'? Kaiser asked.[10] In many ways that leadership has been myopic, inward looking, unproductive for many others. If the twentieth century was indeed, in the words of Henry Luce, the 'American Century' it too must look at what it has contributed to the milieu. The results are mixed. Still, US exceptionalism thoroughly informs US constructs of its identity.

A central tragedy of Colombani's *Le Monde* headline on the shared experience with the United States was that it was so momentary. As Rajeev Bhargava argued, the shared sense of humanity through the recognition of pain and suffering was plain, but easily and soon forgotten.[11]

That this shared feeling was so short-lived is a tragedy of profound proportions. The suffering of the days after 9/11 was quickly politicised. The appropriate political context of the attacks was ignored as 9/11 was reduced to a potent symbol and the basis for a semiotic instruction. Contrary to the rules of visual engagement, the bodies of Americans were mostly absent. The visual destruction of the Twin Towers was repeated ad nauseam producing a banality that is crucial to the numbing effects of the modern media. That distancing was further enhanced by the choices made in the minutes and days after 9/11.

The normal guideline for tabloid coverage: 'if it bleeds, it leads'[12] and the search for the more gruesome images was missing in the media coverage of 9/11. The suffering was both present and absent in very different ways from coverage of other acts of terrorism, when the newscaster admonishes us that some scenes might offend our sensibilities. Žižek recognised the '"derealization" of the horror went on after the WTC [World Trade Center] collapse: while the number of victims – 3,000 – is repeated all the time, it is surprising how little of the actual carnage we see – no dismembered bodies, no blood, no desperate faces of dying people ... in clear contrast to reporting on Third World catastrophes, where the whole point is to produce a scoop of some gruesome detail.' For Žižek, such responses further enhanced the separation of us from them. The real horror happens elsewhere.[13]

Richard Drew, the photographer who stood close behind Robert Kennedy when he was assassinated in 1968, worked Manhattan on 11 September. Arriving at the Twin Towers shortly after the news broke, he shot sequences of pictures of the people who were jumping from the windows high in the towers. One picture stood out. 'The Falling Man' was reproduced widely across the country. The frame, one of roughly twelve, depicts the man in a vertical plunge, his body in line with the vertical lines of the tower. The frame stood out for Drew because of its verticality and symmetry. It elicited various comments on its grace, direction and even freedom. The other frames, in which the symmetry and verticality, the grace and freedom are absent, were not used. And even that initial picture was rarely seen again. Many editors were accused of exploiting a man's death, removing his dignity through the printing process, invading his privacy and turning a tragedy into a form of pornography. Drew's photograph 'became at once iconic and impermissible'.[14] Such decisions on what to show and not to show are a normal problem for editors of photo-journalism and television and are closely related to ideologies that consolidate the prevailing consensus.[15]

Though depiction of the body was largely absent from the coverage of 9/11, the US casualties were palpably there. Normally, on issues of foreign policy the problem of casualties is not immediate. US agencies have time to develop strategies and rules of engagement. In Vietnam, the body bags returned home some considerable time later, but after 9/11 they were instantly there. The freedom that the President and his advisors had previously enjoyed, Paul Braken argues, was gone. The impact was now immediate and the pressure to react was immense: 'Now we've seen body bags on the streets of New York.' There is a terrible irony to his comments and analysis, written long before the Iraqi War began, even though it was well seeded in the minds of White House strategists, when he concluded that, 'The luxury of considered action may be one of the biggest casualties of September 11.'[16]

There was something more insidious attending the death of those Americans and others of 9/11. Remember the dead; their deaths shall be avenged. But as the war was widened well beyond its legitimate scope, the exploitation of 9/11 and the multitude of death were entwined by the Bush administration in the agenda that not only related to Iraq, but also to wider agendas associated with the pursuit of victory and demonstrations that the wounds of Vietnam could be exorcised. In Bush's brief statement on the anniversary of 9/11, he asserted that the men, women and children killed at the Pentagon were killed because they were Americans, 'and because this place is a symbol to the world of our country's might and resolve'.[17] As the war in Iraq widened, and ultimately faltered, the connections between US resolve, commitment and 9/11 were invoked repeatedly. After the third anniversary, the former president, Jimmy Carter, indicated that Bush 'has been adroit at exploiting that attack and he has elevated himself, in the consciousness of many Americans, to a heroic commander-in-chief, fighting a global threat against America'.[18]

The proliferation of such iconography, 'unlike the real thing which was utterly singular, drew on past images to guide instinctive response', Schama wrote, even as the plans for taking the war to Iraq were being formulated. The country owed the dead of 9/11 a good debate, rather than reiterating the sublime words of the American past, the Gettysburg Address, the Four Freedoms and the Declaration of Independence that were read out on 11 September 2002. The Bush administration hoped for a reverential 'hush' and counted 'on just such a pious hush to bestow on its adventurism the odour of sanctity'.[19]

All memory is individual. Bush sought to exploit the collective. 'Strictly speaking, there is no such thing as collective memory – part of the same family of spurious notions as collective guilt. But there is collective instruction.' Sontag elaborates: 'what is called collective memory is not a remembering but a stipulating: that *this* is important, and this is the story about how it happened, with the pictures that lock the story in our minds. Ideologies create substantiating archives of images, representative images, which encapsulate common ideas of significance and trigger predictable thoughts, feelings.'[20] In the aftermath of 9/11 the atmosphere of nationalistic fervour, a fairly normal reaction under the circumstances, was augmented by the rhetorical framework advanced by the Bush administration and the semiotic cross-references to earlier images, instructions and imperatives for war. The collective instruction delivered by the powerful and persuasive presidency was one of calculated retribution and long-term resolve; in the US system there are few other voices that command such recognition, respect and deference in times of crisis. That the administration then stretched the evidence was an abuse of power given its commanding ability to persuade. The Iraq War was a war of choice, which in a democracy should necessitate decision based on debate and consent. Too frequently it seemed Bush relied on the 'hush' of 9/11 to pursue long-held agendas. In 2007, as the casualties in Iraq mount, the dead of 9/11 still deserve a more thorough debate rather than the manipulation of their memory.

THE RUSH TO WAR

The rush to war was unseemly and unwise, counterproductive for the United States in the long term, devastating to the Iraqis.

By mid to late 2005, President Bush was still peddling the insinuations of links between Saddam Hussein, 9/11 and al Qaeda. These were appalling uses of rhetoric, which displayed an administration bereft of ideas, with no idea articulated publicly on how to defeat the various insurgent groups and get the United States out of Iraq, if not out of trouble. A plan for victory was eventually advanced in November 2005.[21] By and large, there was growing scepticism towards Bush's policies and credibility. The persistent positive depiction of Iraq jarred with perception.[22] After thousands of deaths and increasing acts of terrorism and resistance the proverbial 'tipping point' was mentioned. The absence of weapons of mass destruction and links between al Qaeda and Hussein further eroded Bush's credibility. The conflation of 9/11 with Iraq now appeared one of desperation. In a typical speech delivered at Fort Bragg, North Carolina in mid 2005, Bush asserted: 'terrorists who kill innocents on the streets of Baghdad are followers of the same murderous ideology that took the lives of our citizens in New York, Washington and Pennsylvania'. Further developing the associations with 9/11, he asserted that the only course of action was to defeat them abroad before they returned the war to the United States: 'the only way our enemies can succeed is if we forget the lessons of September 11'.[23] While Nancy Pelosi, then minority leader in the House of Representatives, accused the administration of exploiting 'the sacred ground of 9/11, knowing that there is no connection between 9/11 and Iraq', and despite the fact that the 9/11 Commission Report confirmed the absence of such links, Bush's rhetoric still intended to have the desired effect of shoring up support by simply making the connections.[24]

Removing Saddam Hussein had been a long overdue piece of business for many within the administration; 9/11 provided the opportunity. In 1998, a letter posted on the Project for the New American Century website, written by a number of conservatives including Richard Armitage, John Bolton, Zalmay Khalilzad, Richard Perle, Elliot Abrams, Donald Rumsfeld, Paul Wolfowitz and Robert Zoellick amongst others, urged President Clinton to adopt a bolder strategy towards Iraq which 'should aim, above all, at the removal of Saddam Hussein's regime from power'.[25] After 9/11 Wolfowitz advanced the Iraq issue and Richard Clark was instructed to 'see if Saddam was involved. Just look', Bush instructed him.[26] By July 2002 the decision was taken. The diplomatic obstacles remained and the preparations for war were set in place, but Richard Haass, a policy planner in the State Department who ultimately resigned in 2003, enquired whether they really wanted to put Iraq 'front and centre at this point'? Condoleezza Rice replied, 'that that decision's been made, don't waste your breath'.[27]

The legality of the war was dubious. Sure there was a division of opinion, but the issue was far from settled. President Bush did not have the competent authority to go to war. Resolution 1441 specifically omitted the words 'all necessary means', which was intended to oblige the United States to return to the United Nations for further discussion. Pre-emptive attack was treated as a war crime at Nuremburg.[28] Despite this the practice was widespread throughout the Cold War. Regimes were removed or undermined prior to posing any significant threat to the United States; for example, the removal of Arbenz in Guatemala, Allende in Chile or the attempted removal of the Sandinistas. Some in this administration regarded the United Nations as superfluous. Rhetorical justification for war was provided by cross-references to the Kosovo war, which also did not acquire UN authorisation. That operation was a short-term success, even if the Kosovo Liberation Army (KLA) subsequently moved against the Serbs. A fundamental problem for those within the United States who besmirch the importance of the United Nations lies in the US

Constitution. The UN Charter, which precludes the resort to war, except as an act of self-defence or under UN authorisation, was ratified as a treaty by the US Senate, and the Constitution makes treaties 'the supreme law of the land'. The interpretation of self-defence could be argued, but given the absence of weapons of mass destruction and relevant terrorist ties with Iraq prior to 2003, the administration was stretching a point. Even President Kennedy considered the stringent requirements of the UN Charter as the Soviet ships sailed with missiles towards Cuba in 1962. The US Congress can of course override the United Nations in terms of US law. They could have written a narrow authorisation for war and ensured that their wording remained in line with UN strictures. Bush Sr adroitly obtained the UN resolutions in 1990, including Resolution 678 to use 'all necessary means' for a limited course of action, before obtaining authorisation to go to war from the US Congress. In 2002 and early 2003, Bush opted not to go back to the United Nations and submitted a broadly defined resolution for war to Congress in September 2002, which would allow him to use force in Iraq without the limitations imposed by the UN Charter, designed specifically to ensure that war was an option of 'last' resort.[29]

The other strictures of just war theory were similarly disregarded in the approach to Iraq. If the regime in Washington lacked competent authority, it fabricated the just cause. The narratives on the weapons of mass destruction and the links between al Qaeda and Iraq are sufficiently and obviously so flawed there is little need to re-establish them here. Increasingly one comes across the so-called post-revisionist thesis: that even if we now know that weapons of mass destruction were not found and that links were absent, the Bush administration *perceived* them to exist, which in some ways exonerates much of their culpability. That is an argument of irresponsibility that has had devastating consequences within Iraq and potentially in a much wider region and over a much longer period of time. The evidence did exist at the time and there were widespread beliefs within the administration and in London that the evidence was being cooked to fit the policy. Despite this, the President used the Veterans Day speech in November 2005 to castigate Congressional critics because they had originally provided authorisation for the war.[30] Later, months after his resignation, Colin Powell described the presentation that he had given to the United Nations on the eve of the war as 'painful' and a blot on his record. When the US Iraq Survey Group (ISG) delivered their report to the US Senate they concluded that there were no concrete plans for Saddam Hussein to rebuild his weapons programme which had been largely destroyed after the 1991 war. As a headline in the *Guardian,* as if to outline the desperation of the search for any shred of evidence, indicated: '1,625 UN and US Inspectors spent more than two years searching hundreds of sites at a cost of over $1bn. Yesterday they delivered their verdict: There were no weapons of mass destruction in Iraq.' Saddam Hussein made it clear to the ISG that he would have liked to rebuild the programme. Again, in the history of US foreign policy the differences between intention and capability were conflated and presented as a threat. As Charles Duelfer, head of the ISG, indicated to the US Senate, 'Iraq was further away in 2003 than it was in 1991. So the nuclear programme was decaying steadily.' Had it been real Washington might not have been so eager to attack.[31]

Beyond the failures of intelligence and manipulations of the public concerning weapons of mass destruction, much else on just war theory was ignored. The human rights arguments call out for a more consistent application of concern. Many regional countries have used the War on Terror to crack down on dissidents. The consequentialist arguments on the links between Iraq and al Qaeda became self-fulfilling. Moreover, in August 2002, Brent Scowcroft, a former National Security Advisor to Bush Sr and senior advisor to Reagan, Ford and Nixon before him, argued that an 'attack on Iraq at this time would seriously jeopardise, if not destroy, the global counterterrorist campaign we have undertaken'. Similarly, the British former chief of defence staff, Field Marshall Lord Bramall, warned that attacking Iraq would pour 'petrol rather than water' on the flames and provide further fertile recruitment for al Qaeda. By June 2005 the CIA reported that Iraq was creating a new arena for recruiting 'Islamic Jihadists'.[32] Finally, the war was far from the option of last resort.

By mid 2005 an exasperated editorial in the *New York Times* identified three facts that should form the basis of any sober discussion of the war. First, it had nothing to do with 9/11. 'Saddam Hussein was a sworn enemy of Washington, but there was no Iraq–Qaeda axis, no connection between Saddam Hussein and the terrorist attacks on the United States.' Second, the war has not made the world or the United States safer. And third, 'If the war is going according to plan, someone needs to rethink the plan.' The Bush administration could not seriously entertain these points. Bush offered no new policy directions 'or course corrections' and persisted in the post-Vietnam rhetoric of resolve and steadfastness, continuing to 'assert that it is an integral part of a broader struggle to protect the United States from terrorism'.[33]

There was something wider in the US wont to war. The American Founding Fathers were aware of the attraction of war for a president somewhat removed from the field; they took care to separate powers so that the president could not go to war at his own discretion, 'but', Paul Krugman presciently writes, 'after 9/11 President Bush, with obvious relish, declared himself a "war president". And he kept the nation focused on martial matters by morphing the pursuit of al Qaeda into a war against Saddam Hussein.' Helen Thomas, the veteran White House correspondent, noted that she had never covered a president who wanted to go to war as much as Bush clearly did. The 'Downing Street Memo' was pretty blunt. It stated: 'Bush wanted to remove Saddam through military action, justified by the conjunction of terrorism and WMD. But the intelligence and the facts were being fixed around the policy.' In a representative democracy *just* powers are derived from the *consent* of the governed. On matters of foreign and security policy and especially on matters relating to terrorism and war, where most agree that some form of secrecy is required, at minimum Congressional oversight is supposed to shore up the processes of accountability, and the consent of the governed largely has to be based on trust that the executive will not abuse its powers. Krugman concludes, 'leading the nation wrongfully into war strikes at the heart of democracy. It would have been an unprecedented abuse of power even if the war hadn't turned into a military and moral quagmire.'[34] To date the administration has not been subject to far-reaching accountability.

CASUALTIES OF WAR

It would be facile at this point to revert to the well-worn sayings on 'the first casualty' of war and notions of truth. The war in Iraq was a war of choice, a choice taken by the United States. Even though the executive misused and abused intelligence and capitalised on the loathing of Saddam Hussein, his demonisation began only after his invasion of Kuwait in August 1990 threatened Western interests, not before and certainly not when he committed his worst crimes in war and against his own people. Given the consequences of the choices made in Washington, it bears a heavy responsibility for the casualties of war and post-war Iraq: US, Iraqi and the many other nationals that have suffered as a result of this adventure.

How wide does one draw the circle in the discussion of casualties? Certainly the philosopher, Ted Honderich, stirred up a storm of controversy with his argument that we in part were also responsible for the conditions that led to 9/11 through 'our omissions with the bad lives':

> ... the atrocity at the Twin Towers did have a human necessary condition in what preceded it: our deadly treatment of those outside our circle of comfort, those with bad lives. Without that deadly treatment by us, the atrocity at the Twin Towers would not have happened. ... our omissions were a necessary context for the particular intentions on the part of the killers having to do with Palestine, Iraq and Saudi Arabia.[35]

More particularly, Iraq has become the focus of a spiral of casualties that did not start with 9/11 and will not be limited to Iraq, the region or confined necessarily in time. The consequences of the atrocities and the animosities are difficult to fathom. Especially during periods of extreme violence and a political context that is attracted to facile rhetorical extremes and polarisation, there is a tendency to reduce, to move towards, descriptions of them and us.[36] A range of considerations is obvious. In Iraq there are Saddam Hussein's victims, the victims of the Iraqi insurgencies and suicide bombers, the Iraqi troops, police, US troops, adult civilians and children. There are the dead of New York, the Pentagon and Pennsylvania. There are the dead of Bali, Madrid, Istanbul, Jakarta, Casablanca, Riyadh, London, Amman and many other places. The circle concentrates and then widens geographically. The relationship of these acts is not always a part of the same narrative and frequently of tangential connection. The thousands that have been killed and wounded will harbour grief and anger for generations with untold consequences. In that respect the war option was based on a callous strategy.

As Saddam Hussein's trial began with the initial case on the 1982 Dujail atrocity during which 150 men and boys were killed following an assassination attempt, prosecutors indicated that the selection of this case was based on its discrete nature and the availability of a clear documentary record. This selection would allow the process to proceed rather than waiting until the 500 or so separate cases were assembled. Though the judge assured Iraqis that the far worse crimes of later dates would be prosecuted, including the killing of tens of thousands of Kurds in the Anfal campaign when many victims were killed with poison gas, shot and dumped into mass graves, this one would be completed first. Hussein would be held accountable for killing the Shiites who rose, with the encouragement of former President Bush in 1991, resulting in 150,000 killed and similarly bulldozed into mass graves. It is imperative that these crimes are prosecuted. But the wider circles of responsibility also need acknowledgement.[37] These were enormous crimes against humanity that need to be prosecuted with a clear case established against Saddam Hussein, his deputies and a clear record established on the external support for his regime. The United States favoured narrowing the circle to focus on Hussein, arguing that moving to prosecute his subordinates would establish a chain of command and identify the focus of culpability. No doubt, but there are wider lessons to be learned on the consequences of supporting repressive regimes and the impact that that has not only in terms of long-term stability and strategy, but also in terms of the crimes against humanity that such support might have facilitated. The continued support of regional and other repressive regimes suggests that Western powers are not interested in some of the consequences of their foreign policies, intended or not.

The early decision on de-Ba'athification after the war in 2003 might have been inspired by an attempt to morally isolate these forces, but these very forces might have maintained some order in Iraq; the programme presumably also moved many of the security forces to join or initiate the resistance with their training, finance and weapon caches. The decision was strategically catastrophic and historically myopic. But where can the line of culpability be drawn? Paul Bremer's righteous decision to disband the Iraqi army and to de-Ba'athify it was quickly recognised as counterproductive. Many Iraqis had joined the Party for careerist reasons. By early 2004 the policy was beginning to be reversed as the new regime accepted the return of Ba'ath Party members recognising that the country needed teachers and engineers, for instance. How ironic that just as the insurgents increasingly targeted Iraqi security forces, the policy of reversal was finally announced in late 2005, recognising a process that began in early 2004. Reversing the US directive of 2003, the Iraqi government invited 'junior officers' up to the rank of 'major' to return to their positions. Disbanding the army and de-Ba'athification are widely seen as major policy errors in the early occupation period. That the processes fed the insurgencies, there is little doubt.[38]

The removal of Iraqi forces that might have been used to maintain order was compounded by the US decision to go to war with insufficient troops for the post-war occupation. That immediate period of lawlessness set the atmosphere and the conditions for the future, moreover it signalled clearly to the insurgent groups and others that the US forces were incapable of policing the territory and asserting their hegemony and rule on the country.[39] After Powell's resignation he admitted that, 'What we didn't do in the immediate aftermath of the war was to impose our will on the whole country with enough troops of our own, with enough troops from coalition forces or by re-creating the Iraqi forces, armed forces, more quickly than we are doing now.'[40]

By late 2006 estimates of Iraqi casualties stood at a low of 50,291 and a high of 55,774.[41] These numbers must be added to the hundreds of thousands killed by Hussein during his 24-year rule, and the estimated 500,000 who died as a result of the sanctions regime in the 1990s. Iraqis were increasingly the targets of attack by the insurgents for their cooperation with the regime. And vast numbers of Iraqi civilians were killed in US directed operations against insurgent 'strongholds' and on the various offensives, most symbolically but not by any means exclusively, on Falluja. The communal violence showed no signs of abating in 2006.

The US conduct during the war, and its offensive operations after it, killed and devastated thousands of civilians. It was critically covered by the regional media and is counterproductive in the short and long term, in terms of generating enmity, providing a focus for recruitment to the insurgencies and to al Qaeda, generating further, deeper Arab opposition and anti-Americanism, and enhancing the narratives of humiliation. Even as the war for the liberation of Iraq proceeded, the *New York Times* reported that the Arab media had already been depicting US troops as 'callous killers' and that 'only resistance to the United States can redeem Arab pride ... the Iraqis are fighting a pan-Arab battle for self-respect'. Widespread headlines accused US soldiers of deliberate killing of civilians and ironic reportage juxtaposed Rumsfeld's depictions of US weapons as the most precise in the history of warfare against the bodies of dead children; an estimated 7,000 civilians were killed in the initial stage of the war.[42]

Such reporting continued throughout the period of occupation. Sometimes sensational perhaps, but it is important to note that US troops' tactics were disproportionate and frequently indiscriminate. Even though US troops were now on the ground in this war, the very tactics of war, developed to mitigate the influence of the Vietnam syndrome, involved disproportion. Under such conditions discrimination in battle was sacrificed. In operations, most symbolically represented by Falluja, but starting with Operation Peninsula Strike in June 2003, the preference was to use tactics of 'great lethality', as Lieutenant General David McKiernan described it.[43]

That lethality became a fairly consistent pattern over the years. Rumsfeld indicated early that the United States would not be recording the Iraqi casualties, in an apparent attempt to reverse the Vietnam era proclivity to judge progress on the numbers of dead or the body count. But in that atmosphere of unaccountability, unreported and unrecorded atrocity too frequently became the norm in US-led attacks against targets that were not always clearly insurgent bases. For instance, Peter Beaumont of the *Observer* reported the death of Farah Fadhil:

[She] was only 18 when she was killed. An American soldier threw a grenade through the window of her apartment. Her death, early last Monday, was slow and agonising. Her legs had been shredded, her hands burnt and punctured by splinters of metal, suggesting that the bright high-school student had covered her face to shield it from the explosion.

But it was not only this particular death; there were contradictory accounts provided by local residents and official sources which indicated that US forces had come under fire and replied with lethal force. But, for Beaumont, 'whatever happened here was one sided, a wall of fire unleashed at a building packed with sleeping families'. The troops failed to report the details to the coalition military press office. 'What happened in Mahmudiya last week should not be forgotten, for the story of this raid is also the story of the dark side of the US-led occupation of Iraq, of the violent and sometimes lethal raids carried out apparently beyond accountability.'[44]

Falluja: 'this is our Guernica'. The city, the symbolic stronghold of Sunni resistance, was twice the focus of devastating US offensives to eliminate defiance. In April 2004 the operation ended after Iraqi politicians, who had supported the war, 'condemned the use of air strikes to terrorise an entire city'. Hundreds were killed. In November 2004 warnings of another attack caused over 300,000 to flee the city after which the remaining occupants were assumed to be 'terrorists' and therefore legitimate targets before the area was declared a free-fire zone. US reports indicated about 1,300 dead, while the BBC reported 2,000. Falluja acquired the status of symbolic resistance and defiance, a place that demonstrated that US forces had little control over the territory that they occupied. Shiite leaders were informed that it was necessary to bring the area under control to prevent a Sunni inspired civil war. When Robert Zoellick, the Deputy Secretary of State, visited Iraq, he became one of the few Western politicians to request a visit to Falluja. Even though he did not express his impressions, he probably understood something of the reality. 'Remember Falluja' would join the list of those injunctions, across history and geography, for resistance to occupation; a resistance that would no doubt be buttressed by the bitterness and extremity of violence. Steele concluded:

In the 1930s the Spanish city of Guernica became a symbol of wonton murder and destruction. In the 1990s Grozny was cruelly flattened by the Russians; it still lies in ruins. This decade's unforgettable monument to brutality and overkill is Falluja, a textbook case of how not to handle an insurgency, and a reminder that unpopular occupations will always degenerate into desperation and atrocity.

By late 2005 US forces increasingly reverted to the body count in an attempt to demonstrate progress. But the body count that really mattered in US politics was obviously that of American soldiers. By October 2005 the US casualties passed the watershed of 2,000 and the analogies to Vietnam, often misleading though still potent, exercised minds in the United States as the numbers grew, an exit strategy seemed elusive and any criteria for success seemed ill defined. President Bush's speeches were filled with pathos, as they revealed nothing that could change the situation beyond the standard exit strategy that would take place after the job was done, when Iraqi security forces would be sufficiently trained to take over. By April 2007 it was over 3,000. The purpose of these casualties was increasingly subject to political questioning with dramatic results in the November 2006 mid-term elections.

Bush largely remained defiant and seemed immune to the criticism and closed to a dialogue on the future. This war of choice had to be concluded on the terms that the Bush administration had advanced. Anything short of that would appear disastrous, with devastating consequences for Iraq, its integrity, the stability of the Middle East and security around the world. Yet maintaining the course also proved disastrous.

For many painful months Bush did not attend funerals of the US deceased, he did not directly address the suffering, depicting the return of coffins from Iraq was proscribed; the death could hardly bear to speak its name. But by mid 2005, with violence intensifying and the insurgents' attacks becoming more frequent and more lethal, the issue had to be confronted directly. In a major speech on Iraq delivered at Fort Bragg, North Carolina, Bush persisted in the failing strategic framework. He asserted that the troops were 'fighting a global war on terror ... the war reached our shores on September the 11th, 2001. The terrorist who attacked us – and the terrorists we face – murder in the name of a totalitarian ideology that hates freedom, rejects tolerance, and despises all dissent.' And with piquant irony, 'their aim is to remake the Middle East in their own grim image of tyranny and oppression – by toppling governments, by driving us out of the region, and by exporting terror'. Washington would deal with the issues in Iraq before it had to deal with them on the shores of the United States again. Its objectives were clear, if myopic and open-ended. They were 'hunting down the terrorists', building a free nation, advancing regional freedom, excising the sources of violence, and 'laying the foundation of peace for our children and our grandchildren.' To these ends Bush then described the US casualties as 'worth it'. Their work was vital for US security. The outcome of this struggle in Iraq would be decisive. It would leave the terrorists 'emboldened, or defeated'. The example of freedom in Iraq would spread through the region.[45]

'GOING SOUTH': LOSING AT HOME

Bush consistently pledged to stay the course.[46] Yet US critics were concerned with the levels of violence, the apparent lack of progress and the absence of a closely defined set of objectives, let alone a set of closely defined criteria for success, that could be identified as the yardstick for US withdrawal. The casualties were deemed too costly in the absence of these clear objectives. The US tolerance of casualties since Vietnam not only had a close relationship to the defined and perceived national interests but also to the likelihood of success. It was far from clear that the assault on Iraq and the subsequent morass had enhanced US security: the measures of success were often expressed in abstract terms, and there were frequent contradictory signals. As Rumsfeld and Bush reported progress, citing the Iraqi elections, the assembly and the constitution, these contrasted with increasing attacks using even more lethal 'improvised explosives devices' (IEDs). As Bush identified progress, US generals indicated that they saw no ebb in the fight. As Cheney asserted that the insurgency was in the 'last throes', General John Abizaid pointed out in testimony that the insurgents' 'overall strength is about the same'. He also identified another concern. He had recently toured Iraq, Afghanistan and the

Horn of Africa, and was surprised at the number of questions from US troops on whether they were losing support at home. Senator Lindsay Graham told Rumsfeld at the Senate Committee that he was worried that the United States might be forced to leave too soon, because the US public might be 'going south'.[47]

Generally, the US support for their troops in Iraq remained strong, but the polls clearly indicated that the public were indeed thinking of 'going south'. Bush had no apparent strategy beyond the political process towards a constitutional democracy that in itself threw up all sorts of problems regarding the regional and federal system and the long-term integrity of the country, the position of women under the constitution, the disproportionate influence of Shia groups, now supported by thousands of advisors from Iran, and the seemingly obvious Kurdish disregard for long-term membership of the federal entity: Iraq. Besides this, his strategy rested on the fairly abstract notion that the Americans would stand down as the Iraqis stood up. These conditions were set against the barrage of criticism that was quite specific and resonated widely. Writing in the *New York Times* on the day Bush delivered his speech, Senator Kerry blasted the President's strategy:

Our mission in Iraq is harder because the administration ignored the advice of others, went in largely alone, underestimated the likelihood and power of the insurgency, sent in too few troops to secure the country, destroyed the Iraqi army through de-Baathification, failed to secure ammunition dumps, refused to recognize the urgency of training Iraqi security forces and did no postwar planning. A little humility would go a long way – coupled with a strategy to succeed.

Moreover, he argued that the United States needed to send a clear signal that it did not intend to maintain any permanent presence in the country.[48]

The issue of the American presence in Iraq cut both ways. While some argued that with Iraq's vast oil fields, its pivotal regional position and its vital importance to the international economy, the United States, while not envisaging a permanent occupation, certainly wanted to maintain bases, access and influence over the country. It had no intention of leaving. More were concerned with the proverbial Q-word: quagmire. Even if the United States wanted to leave Iraq, its ability to extricate itself, credibility intact, was limited. The bravado of Bush's injunction of July 2003, 'bring 'em on', was increasingly juxtaposed with the insurgents' deadly attacks and the suspicion that

US troops were now in a 'murderous quagmire'. A scathing *New York Times* editorialised that it was far from clear that the war was winnable and having heard the President's speech, they had

... hoped he would resist the temptation to raise the bloody flag of 9/11 over and over again to justify a war in a country that had nothing whatsoever to do with the terrorist attacks. We had hoped that he would seize the moment to tell the nation how we will define victory, and give Americans a specific sense of how he intends to reach that goal – beyond repeating the same wishful scenario that he has been describing since the invasion.

The administration needed to state clearly that it would be years before the Iraqi forces could take over. The regime in Iraq was utterly dependent on the United States; it was crucial for them that the United States remained, if they were to stay in power. But the *New York Times* argued that the American presence might in fact be 'making a terrible situation worse' and the administration had to judge when that 'tipping point' would arrive.[49]

US casualties were still comparatively few compared to either the Second World War or to Vietnam where the average death rate was more than 6,400 per year. The crucial differences in US attitude relate to the comparative strength of the justificatory narratives. If the Second World War was imperative, Vietnam initially important, Iraq, a war of choice, seemed pointless. By the end of 2006, 66 per cent of Americans disapproved of the way Bush was handling the war, 60 per cent believed he was wrong to invade, and 73 per cent indicated that the level of casualties was unacceptable, while over half, 55 per cent, thought the United States was not making significant progress. Over half of the country thought they had been misled into the war, a conflict that even more indicated was not worth the cost.[50]

The proverbial 'tipping point' at home was feared to arrive sooner than expected because of the disproportionate use of the National Guard in Iraq and the impact their deaths have across the country, especially since many indicated that they never really expected to be sent to Iraq. Far fewer National Guards were deployed in Vietnam, but since 9/11 250,000 National Guard troops have been mobilised, with tens of thousands sent to Iraq. Recruitment obviously suffered. Over 90 per cent of US casualties have occurred since Bush declared an end to 'major combat operations' on 1 May 2003. 'Unique to the war in Iraq ... is the way in which the combat deaths are hitting home, with the Guard and reserves paying a high price because of their unprecedented involvement overseas.' They accounted for about a quarter of the fatalities, which has sent 'the shock of death throughout cities and towns in most every state'.[51]

This was a turn away from US trends of intervention over recent years. While the democratic peace theory suggests that democracies do not go to war with each other, democracies frequently went to war and intervention has been a consistent practice in US foreign policy. For a period after Vietnam an effective cultural check was placed on the executive. The positive side of the Vietnam syndrome indicated that large segments of society were not willing to bear the burden of war and intervention, especially when national interests were not clearly identified, or the objectives not clearly set, or the exit strategy and likelihood for success not clearly defined. After the Vietnam War the use of US ground troops was limited. The 1991 Gulf War stands out as an exception. The depiction of high technology weaponry and airpower were crucial to assuaging public opinion. Given the relative impunity with which the US forces, especially the Air Force, could wage war, and given the removal of this social cost, after Kosovo in 1999, in which there were no US casualties directly related to the combat as the planes bombed from on high, Michael Ignatieff suggested that with such technology one of the democratic constraints on going to war might be removed.[52]

Kosovo also became a tipping point. If that war demonstrated that the US could fight with impunity, it also demonstrated a lack of will and ability to fight in conventional symmetric warfare; Iraq would be different. Given that regime change was on the agenda, which necessitated continued political engagement, US troops would have to stay on the ground. Given US firepower, it was always unlikely that the insurgents would opt for symmetric engagement. There were major disagreements between the top US generals and Tommy Franks and Rumsfeld on the strength of the insurgents. While Franks and Rumsfeld 'saw them as little more than speed bumps on the way to Baghdad', other top commanders realised they were a 'dogged foe', numerous, well armed and dispersed through the country.[53]

Moreover, the US rules of engagement and the heavy-handed occupation increasingly looked as if they were contributing to the problems. The stories of US force and civilian casualties are well known; lesser known is a reckoning by the Iraqi Health Ministry that suggests that perhaps twice as many civilian casualties 'have been killed by US military action as by terrorist bombs', as the late Robin Cook wrote in mid 2005. Such tactics are counterproductive and serve insurgent recruitment strategies. Cook argued, 'It is an inexorable law of foreign occupations that the greater the repression, the stronger the resistance.'[54] Months later, without any change in operations, US officers recognised that winning the hearts and minds was essential to draining support for the insurgents. It was essential to deprive them of resting places, recruiting grounds, training facilities and so forth, to alienate the Iraqi people from the insurgents. General Sattler argued: 'We don't want to take out one enemy and create five more.'[55]

Ultimately, the insurgents and the tactics that they opt for can only be ameliorated, if not entirely defeated, when they lose popular legitimacy and Iraqis become increasingly revolted by the continued violence of Iraqis against Iraqis. It could well be that at that point the insurgents would lose legitimacy and become increasingly isolated. Stanley Hoffman observed presciently that even if US training of the Iraq forces has been stepped up to advance the exit strategy, so long as those troops stand beside the US troops the efforts could be counterproductive. As the *Financial Times* observed, they cannot 'stand alongside a US military that daily rains thousands of tons of projectiles and high explosives on their compatriots'. Iraqi hostility is only exacerbated and the insurgents show few signs of isolation in Iraq. US withdrawal could present the insurgents and terrorists with certain difficulties. The impact of their arguments that the government in Baghdad is a puppet of US imperial policy would not be convincing. As Hoffman argues, 'successful counterinsurgency requires popular support, and foreign occupation inhibits such support'. Moreover, as Washington prolongs its occupation, it risks greater embroilment in the political system, evident in the process of writing the constitution, and its subsequent pressure on the Maliki government.[56]

Secretary of State Condoleezza Rice, in testimony to the Senate Committee on Foreign Relations, remained confident of US strategy. Quoting from a letter from Zawahiri to Zarqawi, she claimed that there were indications that the insurgency leaders were 'extremely concerned' that without popular support they would 'be crushed in the shadows'. The insurgents specifically noted that they did not want to repeat the mistakes of the Taliban who, 'collapsed in days, because the people were either passive or hostile'. Yet Rice maintained the tough approach. The US objectives remained to 'break the back of the insurgency', to prevent 'Iraq from becoming a safe haven from which Islamic extremists could terrorise the region and the world', to continue to use Iraq as a positive model for democratic change and free expression, and to 'turn the corner' economically to restore faith and generate self-reliance. The strategy included clearing the 'toughest places', depriving the enemy of sanctuaries and disrupting their foreign support lines, holding and securing areas, integrating political and economic strategies, and building 'truly national institutions' that could sustain the security forces, maintain law, deliver the services and offer hope for a better economic future.[57]

Without substantial change in objectives and strategy there was little reason for US confidence in the administration's approach. The insurgents continued to demonstrate a capacity to inflict severe damage. As early as January 2005, Iraq expert, Toby Dodge, in discussions with senior US officials, indicated that there was awareness that the situation was untenable and that both US and British officials wanted an exit, but did not know how to effect it. Iraqification remained the catchword for phased US withdrawal. But Dodge wondered how US officials thought that a new Iraqi army, only two years old, could bring about a situation that a superpower had failed to achieve. If Saddam Hussein needed 400,000 in his army to maintain control, how could the new Iraqi National Guard and army, with recruitment figures of just one-quarter that amount, and facing an insurgency estimated at 20,000, organised into 60 fairly autonomous groups, succeed?[58] The shift suggested that while the US commitment remained important, the objectives had been scaled back. Rather than transforming the region through democracy promotion, the administration might have to settle for trying to maintain the viability of this regime through arms and finance, even if it left the forces to fight out a civil war that could last years. Barring a hasty US withdrawal presaged by an event resulting in mass casualties, the US withdrawal might be left to that point when the administration in Washington changes in 2009. A new administration could cast the war as a Republican misadventure and seek withdrawal. Senior officials indicated to Dodge that 'damage limitation' was the best that could be hoped for at this stage. It was unlikely that US troops would remain until they achieved their promises and Iraq might become, instead of a 'beacon of democracy', 'the centre of sustained instability, a breeding ground for violence and radicalism'.[59]

Withdrawal would require abandoning the goals of the administration. The myopic dreams of imposing a democracy by force would need to be acknowledged; change in the area will be gradual and on Iraqi terms. It might be necessary to abandon hopes of transforming Iraq into a regional US satellite, with US bases, its oil facilities dominated by US corporations and contractors. For Hoffman it was not just about Iraq, but also about the region and US foreign policy and credibility. While the traditional post-Vietnam narratives on credibility suggest sustaining the effort, remaining until the job was done, withdrawal, accompanied by a recognition of the limits of US power, might do a lot to restore US credibility and its traditional soft power: 'recognizing the limits of America's vast military power might, paradoxically, do more than anything else to increase American influence in the world'.[60]

However, the ethics of an exit strategy are imperative. Whether the Iraqis will be better off in the long run without Saddam Hussein will of course depend on what the United States leaves behind and the viability of the regime, government and system in Iraq in the years ahead. Given the far-reaching impact of this invasion it is also about regional politics and world order.[61]

8
Imperial Frustrations

THE EMPIRE FOR 'LIBERTY'

The United States, since its inception, since it declared independence in 1776, has been an imperial power. One may argue about the characterisation of the empire, and the different forms that it took at different stages in its history. One might think about the differences between formal empire and an informal sphere of influence. One might consider the issue of the consent of the governed in various spheres of influence and in various empires. One would caution that if the words imperialism and empire are defined too narrowly, if one ignores the 'outcomes and the coercion' involved in much US foreign policy, only then can the narratives of innocence and exceptionalism be sustained.[1] Attempts to exonerate US power from the traditional taint of empire have argued that apart from its imperial outburst of the 1890s it has rarely tried directly to rule others. First, one must think about distinctions between colonisation and empire, and between both those concepts and an imperial mindset or attitude. Those distinctions made, it is important to remember the nineteenth century, during which, like other countries, the United States engaged in extensive 'border colonisation', pushing its frontier to the west, acquiring vast swathes of land from various European powers: the British, the Russians, the French and the Spanish, as well as half of Mexican territory. It should also be remembered, before accepting the benign meta-narrative advanced through the sites of US collective memory, that the United States ruled the Philippines until 1946. But the word empire is important and needs to be utilised through a broader understanding; direct rule over territory is not enough. Michael Cox rightly points out that the British Empire operated through formal control, 'informal domination, direct political rule and indirect economic control', and centrally: 'what mattered most for the imperial British was not the means they employed to secure the outcomes they wanted, but the outcomes themselves'.[2] Debates continue on how one characterises this power: imperial, influential, hegemonic, benign or exceptional? But it is futile to suggest the empire does not exist.[3] At most points of US expansion, or periods of disproportionate power, the discourse of empire and imperialism resurfaces, be it the 1820s, 1840s, 1890s, 1950s or in recent years.[4] If anything, the use of the term 'empire' facilitates comparison with the other great powers of history and pulls the United States back into history and away from that exceptionalist claim that buttresses so much traditional historiography and cultural commentary.[5] Moreover, few in mainstream America used any such pejorative terms until relatively recently. Euphemisms that elide the history of intervention and imperial engagement, such as leadership, or more recently 'soft power', that both deny and affirm dominance, are used to exert disproportionate influence and reshape the world towards US preferences.[6] It was crucial that these particular preferences were shared and thus expressed in universal terms.

The attacks of 9/11 were immediately presented as an attack on freedom. Bush asserted, 'this is not ... just America's fight. And what is at stake is not just America's freedom. This is the world's fight. This is civilization's fight. This is the fight of all who believe in progress and pluralism, tolerance and freedom. We ask every nation to join us.'[7] Few objected to the renewed efforts against terrorism. But it was far from clear that this struggle was about freedom. And very quickly, wider US agendas were incorporated into the post-9/11 ambitions. Bush's National Security Advisor, Condoleezza Rice, went further, likening the post-9/11 period to those formative days of the post-Second World War period. The United States, she argued, had a unique opportunity to reshape a part of the world. Just as it had democratised Germany and Japan after the war, it would now, echoing Bush's inaugural, 'create a new balance of power that favored freedom'.[8] After the Second World War, the United States similarly stood alone as a superpower, strong and resolute. Now, as then, opposition and enemies, the constructed 'other' was important. Few would object to the promotion of freedom, then or now, but crucial to these considerations was what exactly that freedom entailed. Certainly the Cold War freedom, closely associated with another constructed concept, the West,[9] did not bring freedom to vast numbers of people, even those who lived in that conceptual West. One need not look very far to question the type of freedom in many Latin American 'national security states' or the freedom that was enjoyed by many citizens and subjects of authoritarian US allies in the Middle East and throughout the Third World. The word 'freedom' had sometimes become a vacuous signifier and a benign identity tag for US power. That abstract noun was appended to a familiar strategy. After 9/11

Bush asserted that there was no middle ground in this struggle, that other countries were either 'with us or against us'. Such conceptual harmony was attractive and also exhibited at the time of the Monroe Doctrine of 1823 and the Truman Doctrine of 1947; conceptually, the world was divided in two. Defining choices in world history had to be made.

Yet the options in the choices often denigrated global pluralism and advanced a military, economic and ideological agenda that undermined local alternatives. The US symbols of empire were obvious. How else would you describe a power that has bases throughout the world and frequently polices regional problems, prepares to fight two and a half wars of global reach simultaneously, operates through five global military commands, keeps more than a million forces on four continents, has battle groups in all oceans, acts as the centre of the world economic system, claims to lead the world politically, and seeks as no other has to win hearts and minds across the world.[10]

There is a balance to be struck between leadership and hegemony. In Bush's reading of world history, he told Americans: 'we have a place, all of us, in a long story – a story we continue, but whose end we will not see. It is the story of a new world that became a friend and liberator of the old, a story of a slave-holding society that became a servant of freedom, the story of a power that went into the world to protect but not possess, to defend but not to conquer.'[11] While this rhetoric might go unquestioned in parts of US culture, elsewhere it is difficult to reconcile with experience.

If the attacks of 9/11 were indeed attacks on the shared values of the West, especially democracy, freedom and consent, it is pertinent to seek greater engagement, accountability and consultation on issues of decision-making, tactics, strategies and 'leadership'. The advocates of US unilateralism need to address these issues squarely.

In a different context Anders Stephanson developed a key distinction, by asking the question whether the United States was interested in creating an 'empire *for* liberty' or an 'empire *of* liberty'.[12] The distinction goes to the heart of US foreign relations. In the first, the word liberty is used as a synonym for US power, influence and hegemony. Liberty and self-determination are more closely associated with negatives and freedom from various 'others'. The empire *of* liberty guarantees negative liberty and promotes pluralism and self-determination, and seeks the consent of the governed.

There is this fundamental and irreducible contradiction at the heart of US foreign policy, between particularism and universalism.[13] Hendrickson writes, 'eighteenth century Americans were not alone in treating universal empire as inconsistent with the preservation of the international system and the liberties of states. Montesquieu, Vattel, Hume, Robertson, Burke, and Gibbon had all considered the theme and were as one in regarding universal empire as, in Alexander Hamilton's words, a "hideous project".' It would ultimately rebound on itself.[14] The early 1980s began with Reagan pledging to consign Marxism to the ash heap of history; the decade closed with a promise of the 'end of History'. Such hubris was bound to blow back. The tragic irony is that some of the same people were involved in opposing both imperial projects: Soviet and American.

The characterisation of the United States as a hyperpower by the French Foreign Minister, Hubert Védrine, tapped into a widespread concern, as revealed by the Pew Global Attitudes survey. Timothy Garton Ash rightly posits, 'contrary to what many Europeans think, the problem with American power is not that it is American. The problem is simply the power.' Unchecked power is dangerous even if held by an archangel. The system of 'checks and balances' might also be appropriate to global politics.[15]

Yet within the United States there was little inclination to accept such checks on its power. Especially after 9/11, the convergence of forces – a strong tradition of American exceptionalism, the 'immensity' of American power – 'hinted at the dangers of being a nation so strong that others could not check it, and so self-righteous that it could not check itself'.[16] In 2001 there was near unanimity in Congress on the rapid expansion of the defence budget and the move to action abroad.

In terms of conventional military[17] power the United States is far ahead of its allies and rivals combined, reflecting the aspirations of the Defense Planning Guidance documents of 1992, which foreshadowed the National Security Strategy of 2002. Still, towards the end of the Clinton administration the US Commission on National Security in the Twenty-first Century, the so called Hart-Rudman Commission, cautioned that the United States would be increasingly constrained by 'emerging powers' acting either alone or in coalition, which 'will increasingly constrain US options regionally and limit its strategic influence'. The US ability to 'impose our will' would as a consequence be limited.[18] Cooperation and multilateralism were advised, because the United States could not 'advance its own interests in isolation'.

But such cooperation would necessitate compromise. The so-called 'institutional bargain' would reduce US autonomy, but most figured the gains were worth the price paid. Constraints on all parties reflected the kind of negative liberties associated with various agreements in the putative 'empire *of* liberty'. Nye strongly argues in favour of such an arrangement:

Seen in the light of a constitutional bargain, the multilateralism of American pre-eminence is a key to its longevity, because it reduces the incentives for constructing alliances against us. And to the extent that the EU is the major potential challenger in terms of capacity, the idea of a loose constitutional framework between the United States and the societies with which we share the most values makes sense.[19]

Despite these limitations on US power and its desire to 'lead', Washington continues to ignore or disregard the needs, interests and influence of its key allies. It was in a clear minority on the International Criminal Court (ICC), the 1997 Kyoto Protocol on climate, the ban on land mines, the biodiversity treaty, and the mechanism for the verification of the Biological Weapons Control Treaty. Washington unilaterally withdrew from the Anti-Ballistic Missile Treaty in 2001. Washington was isolated: 'The vote on the land mine ban was 142 to 0, with 18 abstentions; on the ICC it was 120 to 7, with 21 abstentions; and on Kyoto in 2001 it was 178 to 1, with only the United States opposed.'[20] The signs of US leadership were not good even before 9/11. According to several authors, Cox, Nye and Mathews, for instance, if the United States expects to maintain its leadership, and the extensive reservoir of 'soft power' that it enjoys, it needs to listen more, negotiate more effectively, and, for Nye, to 'define [its] national interest in a broad and farsighted way that incorporates global interests'. Sustaining an international system in the long run requires greater multilateralism, but as Cox noted in 2002 US 'hubris can easily lead to its own nemesis, and an America that is dizzy with success might find that the very scale of its achievements could easily sow the seeds of future problems'.[21]

The pursuit of empire is a long-term delusion. The unique aspect of the current period is that unlike previous periods in which empires sought to expand, the United States is the only world power pursuing such a project. In all earlier periods of history, even as an empire expanded, it would eventually encounter resistance. Its power would be limited, checked, balanced. In the post-Cold War world there were few restraints on Washington. Many have pursued empire for self-interested reasons and advanced universal platitudes to justify their efforts, though those narratives have rarely been regarded through the same lenses outside the metropolitan centres. Despite what appears as both moral certainty and conviction, when the Bush administration speaks, its words largely ring hollow outside the cultural sphere within which it operates, and that sphere was increasingly circumscribed. Growing numbers of Americans who are not interested in the pursuit of empire and would rather those tax dollars were spent on their domestic facilities, schools, hospitals, infrastructure, much in the way that President Eisenhower decried the social and domestic opportunity costs of US military expenditure, are questioning the costs of such expansive visions. The invasion of Iraq has clearly demonstrated the limits of US power, in that its superiority in military terms can still be stayed through unconventional methods. More broadly, while there were misgivings about US action in Afghanistan, there was widespread condemnation of the war in Iraq. Hobsbawm writes, the 'US government is reacting to the fact that the US empire and its goals are no longer genuinely accepted'. Hegemony has lost the element of *consent,* a concept so vital and central to any theory of Western democratic politics. Without the consent of the governed or those who are not governed, but still subordinate to US power, Washington will find it increasingly difficult to lead in the future.[22]

The Vietnamese inflicted enough damage to inhibit US ambition and to some extent that sore has been revisited in Iraq. Washington will pay the price in terms of diplomatic credibility for years to come. It takes a long time to earn respect, trust and credibility. It can be lost quickly. Its saving grace is that much is made of presidential transitions as nations and governments around the world either seek closer relations or realise their dependence and move to improve relationships after the naked emperor has left the building.

IMPERIAL TEMPTATIONS

Despite President Bush's protestations, there is a clear, if contradictory, imperial gist to his foreign policy. He assured us in his 2002 State of the Union Address that 'Americans will lead by defending liberty and justice because they are right and true and unchanging for all people everywhere.' Nations were not exempt from these aspirations, but Bush added, 'We have no intention of imposing our culture.'[23] He later assured his audience at West Point that 'America has no empire to extend or utopia to establish', but this simple claim does not comport with the belief also held by the administration that the '20th century ended with a single surviving model of human progress'.[24] The contradictions were all too obvious. The room for alternatives was limited. The point is that one view of freedom, progress, development or democracy, to paraphrase Isaiah Berlin, still robs others of their freedom. It cannot be assumed that the US system is the best in the world and that all others will want to strive towards that end in history. Pluralism, the empire *of* liberty, as opposed to the empire *for* liberty has been and remains an alternative vision to the dominance of American power.

The combination of 'unilateralism, arrogance and parochialism', as Nye writes, is dangerous.[25] But as the documents and strategies of the Bush administration clearly demonstrate, there is this clear attempt to put US power beyond reach and to ensure that Washington 'leads'. But it is a curious leadership, out of step with the world, stoking hatreds around the globe and resentment amongst its allies. After Vietnam the struggle to regain respect and its position of leadership were central White House considerations. President Clinton's tenure probably did more to restore US foundations in the long run; squandered so quickly by Bush. That it soon became, in Wallerstein's words, 'a lone superpower that lacks true power, a world leader nobody follows and few respect'.[26]

Previous world leaders, US presidents, have thought hard about post-war situations. Winning the battle is one thing, creating an environment conducive to US interests, establishing a pattern of relationships and multilateral institutions that states are willing to sign up to, were central elements in the thinking of both Presidents Woodrow Wilson and Franklin Roosevelt. Many of the institutions that they either aspired to develop after 1918 or actually developed after 1945 served US interests, by and large, until the end of the Cold War and beyond.

The United States cannot entertain the option of a retreat into isolation, despite the strong political sentiment and nostalgic fantasy evident in some rhetoric. The real options for the state and country are between internationalism and imperialism: 'between a model of consensual leadership and a pattern of hegemonic dictatorship'. The latter might prove attractive in the short term, but in the longer term US legitimacy, its attraction, its 'soft power' will fade, because others will see, more quickly than Americans, 'that the outsized and unbound power of the United States constitutes a threat to the foundations of international order'.[27] The problem with such a vision for the present and possibly for the post-war on terrorism 'peace' is that in a sense it returns the world to a more Hobbesian condition, without the appeal to or framework of the current order, flawed though it is. Ultimately, the hawks in Washington will realise that there is a cost to alienating so much of the world. That while they are far superior to their nearest rivals in military terms, not all issues are resolved by the military; indeed, Iraq is currently demonstrating that even incredible military strength is not being translated into influence. As the death toll rises, Washington loses more friends, and al Qaeda gains more recruits. Washington will ultimately realise that it cannot expect business as usual in any other sphere if it chooses not to listen to others. Though it dominates in conventional military power, elsewhere, there will be competition. The imperial project is myopic, 'it steps into the oldest trap of powerful imperial states: self-encirclement. When the most powerful state in the world throws its weight around, unconstrained by rules or norms of legitimacy, it risks a backlash.'[28] European leaders have warned of these prospects: 'do your own thing and everything seems clear and purposeful; but there is a cost in terms of legitimacy and long-term effectiveness. That cost accumulates over time', Chris Patten argued.[29] Moreover, just as in the Cold War, while the United States concentrates on amassing vast military resources, its long-term successor concentrates on the economy.[30]

One wonders about the extent to which US officials are blind to the resentment and resistance to its agenda, or whether indifference characterises their thoughts. Of course there are various degrees of conviction within the administration on the new project. There is no doubt a conviction amongst many on the benefits of US empire and its values. Without necessarily trying to identify an irony, one could cite Charles Krauthammer from June 2001 when he argued: 'we run a uniquely benign imperium. ... This is not mere self-congratulation; it is a fact manifest in the way others welcome our power.'[31] But of course there is a hard side to US power, delusions notwithstanding. What is really worrying is the disjuncture between their perceptions and that of many others.

In *Temptations of a Superpower* Ronald Steel wrote of the Victorians:

... to protect their investments in India they had to guard the Himalayas and the frontiers of Central Asia. To ensure safe transit for their ships they had also to control the Suez Canal. This meant policing Egypt, on whose soil the Canal was located, and the nearby countries of the Middle East, which could pose potential problems for the Canal. Ultimately, as the concentric rings grew ever-larger, this drew them as far afield as the east coast and even the interior of Africa.[32]

As in the wake of most wars that the United States has fought and won, there arise new military bases and increased presence in the region. Bases were set up throughout Iraq, across Central Asia, from the Red Sea to the Pacific; in Afghanistan, the Suez Canal, in the Philippines, deep into former Soviet territory, now right up to the Chinese border. Lebanon in 1983 and Mogadishu in 1993 *appear* distant memories.[33] But the strategy was much wider than that. General Martin told the *Stars and Stripes* that the basing arrangements would provide Washington with new political relationships and of course situate US power right around the Middle East, 'that some day will allow us the access we need'. Moreover, according to Wolfowitz, the bases 'send a message to everyone'; American power was not cowed after 9/11.[34] But this presence might also provoke reaction. Kolko concludes, 'at this point we can realistically dread the worst-case scenarios. There are many seeds here for future conflicts over the course of the next decades.'[35]

MODERNITY AND ENDS AND MEANS OF US FOREIGN POLICY

The theoretical underpinning to the US domestic balance of power, affirmed in the Constitution, defined in the *Federalist Papers*, instituted a system of checks and balances to ensure the viability of liberty, democracy and a tolerance of other interests. James Madison understood that enlightened people would not always guide the ship of state. It was imperative that the system safeguarded against the excesses of partial factions or interests, the excesses of particular groups of individuals. Liberty was thus preserved in the Union, at least in theory.[36] The Founders did not believe in the altruism of 'man'. They recognised selfish inclinations, but designed the Constitution to control and place limits on them.[37] Negative liberty was a key conceptual foundation to US political theory; individuals were free to do what they chose within certain accepted constraints, especially the law.[38] Of course the international system has never developed such effective constraints, though the UN Charter epitomises the furthest such thinking has developed to respect the sovereignty of states and promote rules and ideologies of non-intervention, except in cases of multilateral concurrence. In practice, the United Nations developed through a period of the Cold War in which much of its potential was compromised by the veto powers that either superpower exercised in the Security Council. In practice too, US foreign policy developed through a history that did not recognise the same theoretical inclination to limit power, but pursued an inconsistent yet still activist and expansionist foreign policy; Bush's early inclination towards unilateral action is merely the latest manifestation of the pursuit of US opportunity. It was essentially up to others to check and to balance the United States. Many did throughout the nineteenth century, as the United States also assisted in the maintenance of the European balance of power, eventually and especially in the two European wars of the twentieth century. After that the Soviet Union presented the most effective state-organised check on US power, just as Washington sought to contain Moscow.

Various currents of thought permeate US foreign policy. The Jeffersonian idealists posited the application of the values associated with US history and foreign policy as universally applicable. Wilsonianism tried and failed to ditch 'realism' through the creation of a system of collective security exercised through the League of Nations. After the United States obtained a 'second chance' to significantly influence the shape of world order, the United Nations not only combined the ideals of collective security, but compromised with 'realistic' power by providing the permanent five of the Security Council with decisive powers.

But these inclinations towards the universal ideals of US philosophies were buttressed by the influence of the so-called Hamiltonians: those who pursued the opportunity that the international economic system provided and aspired to create systems to promote US opportunity. Their success can be seen culminating in the Open Door notes of the late nineteenth century, punctured by the autarchy of the Depression, but then combining the pursuit of limited integration wherever possible. Globalisation accelerated the process and advanced integration in time and space.

The Jacksonians, 'the warriors of American society', represented the militant tendency in US foreign policy. The militarisation of US policy has advanced apace since the 1930s, and commentators, such as Michael Sherry, Andrew Bacevich and Chris Hedges, have recognised an intensification of the trend recently. And finally, James Rubin, the Assistant Secretary of State for Clinton from 1997 to 2000, identifies a fifth school in US diplomacy, led by Rumsfeld, Wolfowitz and Perle. Identified as the Pax Americanists, this school combines the visions of Wilsonian universalism, the spread of democracy and liberty with the inclination to use force to obtain such outcomes.[39] Their influence has been detrimental. In much of their thinking, the notion of checks and balances, especially in the international arena, certainly through the United Nations, is anathema.

The vision of a universal set of values, unbound and unchecked has ironically emerged from the combination of US founding myths of Puritanism, Jeffersonian and Wilsonian inclinations and the enlightenment. The limits to US power would be reached with the overactive application of the Hamiltonian inclination on the pursuit of prosperity and the Jacksonian inclinations on force. How one managed the combination of these influences was crucial.

In many ways the US strategy of preponderance[40] adopted by the Truman administration after 1945 laid the groundwork for acquiring this end. But at that point there were vast disparities of power that facilitated such visions of dominance. George Kennan at Policy Planning in the State Department clearly recognised and articulated these disparities between US wealth and the relative poverty of others, made more acute because of the limited size of the US population. Realistically, he also recognised that such a position would produce 'envy and resentment'. Still, maintaining that uneven situation was a key objective. But Kennan, unlike the current influential strategists, recognised the limits of US idealism, and explicitly urged a greater concentration on a realistic approach to the world: the less the United States was hampered by idealistic slogans, the better.[41] Moreover, Kennan objected to the use of universalistic language because it created expectations of and within the United States. In his Policy Planning Studies, he argued that this 'universalistic approach has a strong appeal to U.S. public opinion; for it appears to obviate the necessity of dealing with the national peculiarities and diverging political philosophies of foreign peoples; which many of our people find confusing and irritating'. He argued against US inclinations to force other nations onto the Procrustean bed; the attitude 'assumes ... all countries could be induced to subscribe to certain standard rules of behavior ... [and] instead of being compelled to make the sordid and involved political choices inherent in traditional diplomacy, we could make decisions on the lofty but simple plane of moral principle'.[42] Instead, the simplified outlook led to complications when such attitudes and resulting policies were applied to a complex and heterogeneous world. Still others within the Truman administration were much more ambitious and recognised the utility of such universal and idealistic language, especially when combined with powerful narratives of an external threat.

The so-called Cold War consensus departed from Kennan's more limited vision of US engagement and through the subsequent strategic document, NSC 68 of 1950, US interests were seen as universal, requiring extensive US engagement, not least to shore up its credibility. Later still, President Kennedy, imbued with the so-called lessons of Munich on appeasement, commitment and resolve, promised that the United States would bear the burden and pay the price to ensure the survival and success of liberty. Ironically, one of the fundamental and long-term lessons of Vietnam relates to the dialectics, often asymmetric in scope and power, between universalism and resistance. Despite the vast disparities in military might, US power and its economic base were chastened by the wars in South East Asia.

Despite significant attempts to stem the malaise that set in after Vietnam, a part of which involved rebuilding US military might throughout the 1980s, and despite the economic boom of the 1990s, the United States has slipped from that position of disparity of power and preponderance that it once enjoyed. Despite the victory of the Cold War and the discourse on the unipolar moment, augmented by the crushing victory over Iraq in 1991, the fears of economic slippage, industrial challenge, and a humbling of the military hegemon, most significantly in Vietnam, Lebanon, Somalia and Iraq, could not be allayed. John Gray pertinently suggested that Pax Americana 'presupposes that the US has the economic strength to support the imperial role it entails. ... it assumes that the US has the will to sustain it. [And] it requires that the rest of the world be ready to accept it.' All three propositions are open to question.[43]

Certainly the global economic balance of power changed in the late 1950s and the Vietnam War accelerated the relative US decline. Iraq threatens a similar fate. In 2002 Immanuel Wallerstein wondered whether the United States would accept the rise of multi-polarity and its relative decline with grace or whether activist conservatives would resist such trends and engage in war that would ultimately accentuate relative US decline. Vietnam undermined the US ability to remain the dominant power in the world and the revolutions of 1968, the fall of the Berlin Wall and 9/11 left the United States in the 'situation in which [it] currently finds itself – a lone superpower that lacks true power, ... a nation drifting dangerously amidst a global chaos it cannot control'. Given the international disparity, the use of military power and the inclination to solve issues through force are obvious but myopic attractions. Still, for Wallerstein, the 'hawks believe the United States should act as an imperial power for two reasons: First, the United States can get away with it. And second, if Washington doesn't exert its force, the United States will become increasingly marginalized.' Yet the approach will not avert the relative decline, the trend, despite enormous military and political power, has continued since 1945.[44]

After the stinging humiliation of Vietnam some within the National Security Council and the White House realised the impact of that war on US capabilities and reflected on the lessons of the war, albeit often with a view to containing those lessons, mitigating their impact and limiting the democratic impulse to avoid war. They clearly understood the US reticence to 'stay the course' in protracted conflict and that the 'tenacity' of the American people had been pivotal to defeat in Vietnam. After Vietnam, the American people held a more limited view of the US role in the world and its ability to influence events. Moreover, US society developed control mechanisms that might stem executive martial ambitions.[45] For some strategists these limits were too restrictive. The realpolitik and the limits recognised by Henry Kissinger and Richard Nixon as a necessary antidote to US decline, simultaneously facilitated an opening in the global system epitomised in the rise of the more cohesive and integrated EEC, Japan and China, with challenges from OPEC, and the spread of Third World revolution and greater assertions of autonomy. While the realists recognised these essential changing contexts, it was precisely these limitations that irritated the neo-conservatives who found in Nixon's variety of foreign policy a too willing acceptance of the changes and challenges. The conservatives of the Reagan administration reinjected the Wilsonian sentiment and reinserted the traditional narratives for US intervention, focusing especially and hypocritically on democracy in Nicaragua while tolerating the most nefarious violence in US supported El Salvador. This supposed 'democratic imperative' shifted to Iraq with the neo-conservative visions and many of the personnel that served Reagan.

For a period in 2001 these people foundered about in Washington. September 11 provided the opportunity and Afghanistan rekindled the urge for victory. As Charles Krauthammer, one of the leading neo-conservative commentators, acutely observed:

The elementary truth that seems to elude the experts again and again – Gulf War, Afghan War, next war – is that power is its own reward. Victory changes everything, psychology above all. The psychology in the region is now one of fear and deep respect for American power. Now is the time to deter, defeat or destroy other regimes in the area that are host to radical Islamic terrorism.[46]

Iraq called out as a location for US victory after 9/11 and removed many of the inhibitions that had been in place since Vietnam. Iraq was not only about US ambition, opportunity and a projection of its power into the Middle East. It was certainly not about those official fears of terrorists and tyrants, weapons of mass destruction or democracy in the Middle East. The confluence of three separate but related influences has in part produced the current tragedy in Iraq. After Vietnam, a yearning for victory was prevalent amongst key strategists who also happened to be imbued with idealistic and universal ambitions. Second, Iraq was regarded by these characters as unfinished business, a remnant from the realist decisions taken at the conclusion of the Gulf War in 1991. It was time to move on from such constraints. And third, this time Kosovo style airpower would not be adequate because such removed applications of power were also regarded as a sign of weakness; this time boots had to be on the ground. Yet that very presence and the terms of engagement, hitherto so brutal, have been counterproductive. The resistance has expanded, the insurgents have continued to recruit for the fight, while US recruitment has faltered and some allied troops have withdrawn. Afghanistan and the swell of arrogance associated with victory infused US strategists. The psychology was important. Iraq would supposedly provide the example of US might, resolution and commitment. Others, contemplating challenge, would be deterred. The demonstration of power was always attractive.

Implicit and explicit in US strategic documents over the past three decades linger fears of its position in the world. It is interesting to trace this seeming lack of confidence across three decades and through three Republican administrations. The 2002 *National Security Strategy of the United States* somewhat contradictorily identified itself with a 'balance of power that favors human freedom' with the illusion that there remained 'a single sustainable model for national success: freedom, democracy, and free enterprise'. That end would be supported by 'forces ... strong enough to dissuade potential adversaries from pursuing a military build-up in hopes of surpassing, or equalling, the power of the United States'. US defences must remain 'beyond challenge'. It was deemed necessary to 'dissuade future military competition' and 'decisively defeat any adversary if deterrence fails'.[47] Much of this language echoes the Defense Planning Guidance document of 1992, closely associated with Wolfowitz. That report warned that 'we must account sufficiently for the interests of the advanced industrial nations to discourage them from challenging our leadership or seeking to overturn the established political and economic order'. Regional competitors must also be deterred 'from even aspiring to a larger regional or global role'.[48] Ten years earlier, in 1982, Reagan's National Security Council considered the 'loss of U.S. strategic superiority' after Vietnam and worried about the loss of hegemony brought on by Soviet advances and 'the increased political and economic strength of the industrial democracies'.[49] These attitudes reveal a profound insecurity and a lack of confidence that the American model could stand out and compete amongst other viable options, without reliance on such military power and ideological conformity.

Of course there was the fundamental contradiction in liberalism between its aspirations for tolerance and its inclination towards universal values.[50] While Bush's second inaugural demonstrated little development in thought by suggesting that there

is only one force of history that can break the reign of hatred and resentment, and expose the pretensions of tyrants ... and that is the force of human freedom. ... The survival of liberty in our land increasingly depends on the success of liberty in other lands. ... America's vital interests and our deepest beliefs are now one.[51]

In attempts to wed his policies to traditional attitudes and promote greater consensus on Iraq, Bush passed over the complexity of freedom in US culture or its foreign policy. The concept of freedom has a contested history in different periods of the American past, and the 'clash between dominant and dissenting views has constantly reshaped the idea's meaning', as Eric Foner has amply demonstrated.[52] Indeed, David Hackett Fischer's *Liberty and Freedom: A Visual History of America's Founding Ideas*[53] clearly demonstrated that these multitudes of meaning are often reduced through iconic representation to reinforce the singular narrative of nationhood. Bush's own rhetorical deployment of the word moved from the more 'particular idea of personal liberty, private property, individual responsibility and minimal government' of his first inaugural to a vision that preserved these initial inclinations, yet added FDR's 'broader definition of liberty' and 'greater freedom from want and fear' in his second. Moreover, it alluded to Martin Luther King's 'freedom now', echoed the Quaker vision of 'liberty throughout all the land' and expanded it to 'liberty throughout all the world'.[54] This shift to a more inclusive understanding may be the result of a chastening of US power.[55] Of course great powers have the means of manipulating meaning and influence on the means of cultural production to maintain stable narratives, usually through processes of reduction and cultural iconography, but a great deal, especially in matters of interpretation, depends on whether the story is told from the top down or the much more amorphous bottom up.[56] The potential for scepticism based on experience and resistance is strong when one 'moves the centre'[57] and regards the narratives from afar. Carolyn Eisenberg reminds us that 'diplomatic historians can well recognise the compelling power of words on paper and the temptation to assign them weight. Nevertheless, deeds matter more.' Her words recalled the devastation in Iraq, especially Falluja, and the innocent dead and wounded. 'During the past week', she wrote, 'American troops have seized one hospital and levelled another in the declared effort to promote freedom through democratic elections.'[58] Let's understand what this abstract word, freedom, means in practice! And though there will be debates on US intentions and objectives, there is also a need to understand cause and effect; and it is most likely that these effects will contest and question the narratives advanced in Washington. Freedom has in many ways become a signifier for the United States; in such rhetoric, especially deployed under such circumstances, the word has little positive meaning left in it. It is not about pluralism and a respect for difference and the wider implications of negative liberty writ large. The Cold War polarised such words associated with the formal constructions of East and West, but it also significantly informed cultural understandings of the word freedom and its reception. Freedom throughout the history of US foreign policy has been invested with meaning. It has become closely associated with the positive freedoms of the United States and its inclination to act abroad as opposed to the use of freedom in the international setting associated with negative liberty, the social contract, the Constitution within the United States, multilateral agreements and conventions abroad.

Of course the early swagger of the Bush administration has made matters worse, but the unilateral inclination is not confined to this period. There has been much discussion of unilateralism as though it was a novel feature in US policy. 'Independent internationalism', to use Joan Hoff's term, or unilateralism has been a key feature of US foreign policy as a diverse range of historians, from Melvyn Leffler, John Gaddis and Lloyd Gardner[59] have argued. George Bush is far from exceptional. The aspects of continuity are more far reaching.[60]

The hubristic attitude, the United States at the core of the world system, the visions of exceptionalism and universalism, culminating in the myopic idea that America is the only viable model for human progress, coupled with the militarisation of US foreign policy and the will to victory, have pushed the United States to an incoherent position. It now seems the United States is incapable of leading an acceptable world order, given the disparate interests and oppositions. Currently, there is too much scepticism of US policy. For too long in its history and even recently in Central Asia, as the United States speaks the soft words of democracy and liberty, it continues to wield the big stick and support authoritarianism throughout the region.[61]

The utility and caricature of Saddam Hussein in much Western media or the rhetoric of other 'fanatics' is that they can be dismissed as psychopathic tyrants and therefore questions of their motivations, purposes and former connections with the West can be elided. With such depiction, the West and the United States can avoid the difficult questions about its former engagement with that particular tyrant, but more pertinently its continued engagement with others, eliding issues of 'blowback', those unintended consequences of former foreign policies. Ahdaf Soueif, the Egyptian novelist, aptly suggested that

America needs to look at its foreign policy, its stance on the international court of justice and the Kyoto agreement, its contribution to the suffering of the Iraqi people, its bombing of Libya and Sudan, its long-standing position on the Arab–Israeli conflict, and ask itself why 16 [sic] men were prepared to kill and die to bring down the symbols of American commercial and military might.[62]

There is a curious cultural proclivity to restore the old narratives, even if the loss of such pertinent and recent historical lessons demands such a high price in casualties. One positive aspect was that an intellectual discourse began on what it was in the socio-economic conditions and the political environment that would drive people to such action beyond the vacuous discourse on 'evil'. Khalil Shikaki, director of the Palestinian Centre for Policy and Survey Research, identified a widespread perception that despite the Western rhetoric, from the Arab perspective this war was largely seen as one against

Islam. The shared horror of 9/11 soon turned to anger, because the United States did not re-examine its long-standing policies in the region and its role in stifling democracy by 'helping consolidate Arab political authoritarianism'.[63]

There has been so much made of the sense of Arab humiliation and the assertions of nationalism that faded with the crushing defeat of 1967. If in many ways the grievances that fuelled the former nationalism shifted to the politics of Islamism and for a time coalesced in the anti-Western Iranian rhetoric, Iraq has become another such defining moment. There is a terrible stand-off of broader interests in the outcome of the Iraq situation greater than exclusively the stability and viability of a democratic civil society. Bush clearly recognised that US failure in Iraq would embolden what he conveniently termed 'the terrorist'. The term in such rhetoric represents a catch-all for a diverse range of opposition. But it is precisely that opposition that in some ways has provided succour to those imbued with that narrative of Arab humiliation. The resistance obviously resonates around the region, according to David Hirst, the long-term Middle East correspondent: 'they wonder, … whether this extraordinary, neo-conservative ambition will provoke what amounts to a second Arab struggle for independence'.[64] The further irony is that there is widespread opinion that in effect the ultra-nationalist and Islamist regimes have had a symbiotic relationship with the Western colonial powers and neo-colonial adventurers, and that many in the region would welcome greater democratisation and liberty. The polarisation of the political culture, coupled with intensified militarisation, resulting in part by the superpower stand-off during the Cold War, compounded by the Arab–Israeli wars, has largely undermined the middle ground and excluded democratic opportunities in the region. So while greater democratisation might well be welcomed, it cannot be imported and imposed by the United States or its provisional authorities. There is far too much scepticism on US intentions and objectives, borne out of long and bitter experiences of living under repressive regimes supported by Washington. Professor Hanan Hassan of Damascus University, eager for democracy, was quick to rule out a US imposed solution: 'The moment the Americans turn on the regime we'll support it.'[65]

Iraqi resistance will also resonate. Certainly within the region, perhaps further afield. Hani Shukrallah, editor of the Cairo-based *Al-Ahram Weekly*, in an inversion of Colombani's 2001 headline declared at the origins of war: 'We are all Iraqis Now.' The point of course referred to the rejection and opposition, in whatever form, of the aggression. As millions took to the streets of the world's capitals, Robert Fisk brutally pointed out that the Arabs were like 'mice' even in the face of disaster. Shukrallah concluded as the resistance mounted:

Yet for the Arabs, as galling and bitter as the sense of injured dignity has been and continues to be, it has also been disabling, creating a situation and mindset in which their choices seemed to be limited to either suicidal vengeance or abject and bitter hopelessness. It remains to be seen whether the war in Iraq will put the Arab masses on a new trajectory, one in which they fight to win, rather than just to die while maintaining some sense of their basic human dignity. .... for the moment the Arab masses have two things going for them: they are not mice, and they are not alone.[66]

The war, supposed to demonstrate US power, has served as an example of its weakness.[67] Again, as after the Vietnam War, Washington has to reconcile itself to the limits of its power first as the American people conveyed their lack of confidence in Bush at the 2006 mid-term elections and as the Iraq Study Group urged a more realistic appraisal, a phased withdrawal and widespread regional negotiations, repudiating the devastating and reckless militaristic proclivities resulting in over 660,000 casualties to date. ...

Notes

CHAPTER 1   BROAD CONTEXTS

1. President George W. Bush, Remarks at National Day of Prayer and Remembrance, the National Cathedral, the White House, <www.whitehouse.gov/news/releases/2001/09/20010914-21.htm>, 14 September 2001.
2. Carolyn Eisenberg, 'The New Cold War', *Diplomatic History* 29, no. 3 (June 2005), 425; David Ryan, 'Vietnam, Victory Culture and Iraq: Struggling with Lessons, Constraints and Credibility from Saigon to Falluja', in John Dumbrell and David Ryan (eds), *Vietnam in Iraq: Tactics, Lessons, Legacies, Ghosts* (London: Routledge, 2007, 111–38). See also, Andrew J. Bacevich, *The New American Militarism: How Americans are Seduced by War* (Oxford: Oxford University Press, 2005), 9–33; Bruce Kuklick, *Blind Oracles: Intellectuals and War from Kennan to Kissinger* (Princeton, NJ: Princeton University Press, 2006); Alex Callinicos, *The New Mandarins of American Power: The Bush Administration's Plans for the World* (Cambridge: Polity Press, 2003).
3. President George W. Bush, Graduation Speech at West Point, the White House, <www.whitehouse.gov/news/releases/2002/06/print/20020601-3.html>, 1 June 2002.
4. Julian Borger, 'President admits war on terror cannot be won', *Guardian* (London), 31 August 2004.
5. See Stephen M. Walt, *Taming American Power: The Global Response to U.S. Primacy* (New York: W. W. Norton, 2005).
6. William Appleman Williams, *The Tragedy of American Diplomacy* (New York: Delta, 1961).
7. National Security Council, Top Secret, 'Long-Range U.S. Policy toward the Near East', NSC 5801, 10 January 1958, RG 273, the National Archives and Records Administration (NARA).
8. NSC 5801, 1958.
9. Toby Dodge, *Iraq's Future: The Aftermath of Regime Change*, Adelphi Paper 372 (London: Routledge, 2005), 58.
10. NSC 5801, 1958.
11. Ibid.
12. Francis Fukuyama, *The End of History and the Last Man* (London: Penguin, 1992), xi. See also Lloyd C. Gardner, 'The Final Chapter: The Iraq War and the End of History', in Dumbrell and Ryan, *Vietnam in Iraq*, 8–30.
13. Odd Arne Westad, *The Global Cold War: Third World Interventions and the Making of Our Times* (Cambridge: Cambridge University Press, 2005).
14. Robert J. McMahon, 'The Challenges of the Third World', in Peter L. Hahn and Mary Ann Heiss (eds), *Empire and Revolution: The United States and the Third World since 1945* (Columbus: Ohio State University Press, 2001), 1. Nehru quoted by McMahon.

15. Amartya Sen, *Development as Freedom* (Oxford: Oxford University Press, 1999), 11.

16. 'The [US] Declaration of Independence, 4 July 1776', in Henry Steele Commager (ed.), *Documents of American History* (New York: Appleton Century Crofts, 1963), 100.

17. Warren F. Kimball, 'Foreword', in David Ryan and Victor Pungong (eds), *The United States and Decolonization: Power and* Freedom (London: Macmillan, 2000), xiii.

18. Jürgen Osterhammel, *Colonialism: A Theoretical Overview* (Princeton: Markus Wiener, 1997), 5.

19. Walter LaFeber, 'The American View of Decolonization, 1776–1920: an Ironic Legacy', in Ryan and Pungong, *United States and Decolonization*, 25.

20. Melvyn P. Leffler, *A Preponderance of Power: National Security, the Truman Administration, and the Cold War* (Stanford, CA: Stanford University Press, 1992).

21. David Ryan, 'By Way of Introduction: The United States, Decolonization and the World System', in Ryan and Pungong, *United States and Decolonization*, 13–16. See also, Robert J. McMahon, 'Toward a Post-colonial Order: Truman Administration Policies toward South and Southeast Asia', in Michael J. Lacey (ed.), *The Truman Presidency* (Cambridge: Cambridge University Press, 1989), 364.

22. Lloyd C. Gardner, 'How we "Lost" Vietnam, 1940–54', in Ryan and Pungong, *United States and Decolonization*, 133–4.

23. National Security Council, 'US Policy toward Africa South of the Sahara Prior to Calendar Year 1960', NSC 5719, 31 July 1957, RG 273, NARA, pp. 9–10.

24. Cary Fraser, 'Understanding American Policy towards the Decolonization of European Empires, 1945–64', *Diplomacy and Statecraft* 3, no. 1 (1992), 105–7.

25. Ngaire Woods, 'Order, Globalization, and Inequality in World Politics', in Andrew Hurrell and Ngaire Woods (eds), *Inequality, Globalization, and World Politics* (Oxford: Oxford University Press, 1999), 12.

26. Pew Global Attitudes Project, *Views of a Changing World,* Washington, DC: Pew Research Center for the People and the Press (June 2003), 6.

27. Pew Global Attitudes Project, *What the World Thinks in 2002* (Washington, DC: Pew Research Center for the People and the Press, 2002), <http://people-press.org/reports>, (accessed 13 February 2003).

28. David Clark, 'Mr Blair Must be Prepared to Stand up to President Bush', *Independent* (London), 14 September 2001.

29. Ted Honderich, *After the Terror* (Edinburgh: Edinburgh University Press, 2002), 17.

30. White House, *The National Security Strategy of the United States of America* (Washington, DC: The White House, September 2002), 21, 23.

31. Report by the Policy Planning Staff, PPS/23, Review of Current Trends in US Foreign Policy (24 February 1948), *Foreign Relations of the United States* (FRUS), vol. 1, 1948, 510–29.

32. United Nations Development Programme (UNDP), *Human Development Report 1992* (New York: Oxford University Press, 1992), 34–8.

33. Sen, *Development as Freedom*, 3–4.

34. Larry Eliot, 'The Lost Decade', *Guardian* (London), 9 July 2003.

35. United Nations Development Programme (UNDP), *Human Development Report 2000* (New York: Oxford University Press, 2000), 38.

36. David Ryan, 'US Foreign Policy and the Guatemalan Revolution in World History', Conference on Guatemala 1954, US Department of State, 15 May 2003.

37. David Ryan, *US Foreign Policy in World History* (London: Routledge, 2000), 126.

38. Theodore Draper, *A Present of Things Past* (New York: Hilland Wang, 1990), 73–5.

39. The NSC Planning Board, 'United States Policy Towards Iran', Report to the National Security Council, 21 December 1953, document 00375, fiche 93, Presidential Directives on National Security, the National Security Archive, Washington, DC.

40. James F. Siekmeier, *Aid, Nationalism and Inter-American relations – Guatemala, Bolivia, and the United States 1945–1961* (Lewiston, NY: Edwin Mellen Press, 1999), 9, 19.

41. Louis Halle Jr, Determination of U.S. Course of action in Case the Communists take over in Guatemala, 1 February 1954, RG 59, Lot 65D 101, Box 79, NARA.

42. Ibid.

43. Edward J. Sparks, 12 December 1956, cited in Siekmeier, *Aid, Nationalism*, 328. I am grateful to James Siekmeier for bringing this to my attention.

44. NSC 144/1, 'United States Objectives and Courses of Action with respect to Latin America', 18 March 1953, *FRUS* 1952–54, vol. IV, 6–7.

45. Draft Policy Paper prepared in the Bureau of Inter-American Affairs, NSC Guatemala, 19 August 1953, *FRUS* 1952–54, vol. IV, 1083.

46. Allen W. Dulles, Memorandum for the record re: P. B. Fortune, 8 March 1953, *FRUS* Guatemala, 2003, 79.

47. Telegram, the Ambassador in Guatemala (Peurifoy) to the Department of State, 17 December 1953, *FRUS* 1952–54, vol. IV, 1091–3.

48. Louise J. Halle to Robert Bowie, Policy Planning Staff, 28 May 1954, RG 59, Lot 65 D101, Box 79, NARA.

49. Ibid.

50. Louis J. Halle to Robert Bowie, Policy Planning Staff, Department of State, 23 June 1954, Records of the Policy Planning Staff, RG 59 Lot 65 D101, Box 79, NARA.

51. Anthony Lake, 'Confronting Backlash States', *Foreign Affairs* 73, no. 2 (March/April 1994), 45.

CHAPTER 2   FRAMING SEPTEMBER 11:
RHETORICAL DEVICE AND PHOTOGRAPHIC OPINION

1. I would like to thank Gary Levy, Scott Lucas, Liam Kennedy, Heidi Storeheier and Susan Ryan for comments on an earlier version. This chapter was first published in the *European Journal of American Culture* 23, no. 1 (2004). Reproduced with kind permission.

2. Eric R. Wolf, *Envisioning Power: Ideologies of Dominance and Crisis* (Berkeley, CA: University of California Press, 1999), 54–5.

3. Rowan Williams, 'End of War', *The South Atlantic Quarterly* 101, no. 2 (Spring 2002), 267; see also his *Writing in the Dust: Reflections on 11th September and its Aftermath* (London: Hodder and Stoughton, 2002).

4. W. R. Smyser memorandum to Secretary Kissinger, Lessons of Vietnam, 12 May 1975, NSA, Presidential Country Files for East Asia and the Pacific. Country File: Vietnam, Vietnam (23), Box 20, Gerald R. Ford Library; Trevor McCrisken, 'The Korean Tree Incident', paper delivered at the British Association of American Studies, Keele University, England, April 2001.

5. President George Bush, 12 September 2001, 'Bush Remarks to Cabinet and Advisors', *New York Times*, 13 September 2001.

6. Williams, 'End of War', 270.

7. Douglas Little, *American Orientalism: The United States and the Middle East since 1945* (London: I. B. Tauris, 2003), 316.

8. Indeed the Daniel Libeskind reconstruction of the World Trade Center will be infused with a range of symbolic references to the nation and its narratives of freedom. Graphic notes from diagrams indicate that the building will incorporate a section down to the bedrock foundations, 'revealing the heroic foundations of democracy for all to see'. The 'freedom tower' at 1776 feet will be 'reasserting the skyline'. Libeskind is highly conscious of his work following in the traditions of the Sydney Opera House or Gehry's Bilbao Guggenheim, infused with narrative echoes and structural metaphor. Libeskind echoed the patriotic line in speeches; he argued 'architecture has to give a new horizon to view, a freedom. The only way it can do this is to be rich with meaning, but rooted in life' (Dominic Lutyens, 'Ground Hero' interview with Daniel Libeskind, *Observer Magazine* (London), 22 June 2003).

9. The White House, *The National Security Strategy of the United States of America* (Washington, DC: September 2002); President George Bush, Graduation Speech at West Point, the White House, <www.whitehouse. gov/news/releases/2002/06/print/20020601-3.html>, 1 June 2002.

10. Michel Foucault, *The Archaeology of Knowledge* (London: Routledge, 1991 [1969]), 59–60.

11. I am indebted to Gary Levy for the suggestion of this theme.

12. *The Economist*, 22 September 2001. See also, Joan Didion, 'Fixed Opinions, or The Hinge of History', *The New York Review of Books* 50, no. 1 (16 January 2003), 54.

13. David Usborne, 'True Story of an Image being used to Boost American Morale at Home and at War', *Independent* (London), 22 October 2001; Susan Willis, 'Old Glory', *The South Atlantic Quarterly* 101, no. 2 (Spring 2002), 376.

14. Jean-Marie Colombani, headlines of *Le Monde* (Paris) on 12 September 2001, World Press Review, <www.worldpress.org/1101we_are_all_ americans.htm>, 5 April 2003.

15. Benedict Anderson, *Imagined Communities: Reflections on the Origin and Spread of Nationalism,* (London: Verso, 2002), 175.

16. David Ryan, 'Ten Days in September: The Creeping Irrelevance of Transatlantic Allies', *Journal of Transatlantic Studies* 1, special edition, (Spring 2003), 26.

17. Michael S. Sherry, *In the Shadow of War: The United States since the 1930s* (New Haven: Yale University Press, 1995), 498–504; Gabriel Kolko, *Another Century of War?* (New York: The New Press, 2002).

18. John Burnside, 'Standards of Belief,' *Guardian* (London), 25 January 2003.

19. Willis, 'Old Glory', 376.

20. Edward W. Said, *Culture and Imperialism* (London: Chatto and Windus, 1993), xxviii.

21. X [George Kennan], 'The Sources of Soviet Conduct', *Foreign Affairs* 25 (July 1947).

22. Francis Fukuyama, *The End of History and the Last Man* (London: Penguin, 1992); Samuel P. Huntington, 'Clash of Civilizations', *Foreign Affairs* 72, no. 3 (Summer 1993); Samuel P. Huntington, *The Clash of Civilizations and the Remaking of World Order* (New York: Simon and Schuster, 1996).

23. President George Bush, Address to a Joint Session of Congress and the American People, the White House, <www.whitehouse.gov/news/releas es/2001/09/20010920-8.html>, 20 September 2001.

24. Edward Said, 'The Clash of Ignorance', in Don Hazen et al. (eds), *After 9/11: Solutions for a Saner World* (San Francisco: AlterNet, 2001), 84.

25. Frances Fitzgerald, 'George Bush and the World', *The New York Review of Books* 49, no. 14 (26 September 2002), 84.

26. Wolfgang Schivelbusch, *The Culture of Defeat: On National Trauma, Mourning, and Recovery* (New York: Henry Holt, 2001), 294.

27. David Held, 'Violence, Law, and Justice in a Global Age', in Craig Calhoun, Paul Price and Ashley Timmer (eds), *Understanding September 11* (New York: The New Press, 2002), 100.

28. Eric Schmitt and Thom Shanker, 'Administration Considers Broader, More Powerful Options for Potential Retaliation', *New York Times*, 13 September 2001.

29. Ryan, 'Ten Days in September', 27.

30. See, for instance, Julian Borger, 'War About to Enter New Phase', *Guardian* (London), 10 October 2001; Julian Borger, 'Week of Bombing Leaves US further from Peace, but No Nearer to Victory', *Guardian* (London), 15 October 2001; Julian Borger, 'Devastating Gunship Targets Troops', *Guardian* (London), 17 October 2001; Paul Beaver, 'Old-fashioned Raids Pave Way for New Kind of Fighting', *Observer* (London), 21 October 2001; Ewen MacAskill, 'Bombs Go Astray, the Casualties Mount ... and the Doubts Set In', *Guardian* (London), 29 October 2001 (talks of Kosovo moment); Kim Sengupta, 'First US Ground Attack "Could Have Ended in Disaster"', *Independent* (London), 26 October 2001; Richard Norton-Taylor, 'Confusion Over War's Next Phase as Ground Attack Stalls', *Guardian* (London), 31 October 2001; 'Bombing Casualties Causes Concern Around the World', *Guardian* (London), 31 October 2001; US document explicitly ruled out the option of widening the war to Iraq, seen as a necessary message to keep the allies together (Donald Macintyre and

Rupert Cornwell, 'US Discloses Plan to Widen War on Terror', *Independent* (London), 11 October 2001.

31. Maria Ryan, 'Inventing the "Axis of Evil": The Myth and Reality of Intelligence and Policy Making after 9/11', *49th Parallel: An Interdisciplinary Journal of North American Studies*, no. 10, <http://artsweb.bham.ac.uk/49thparallel/currentissue/coll_mariaryan.htm>, 5 April 2003.

32. Anderson, *Imagined Communities*, 170–8.

33. Louis Hartz, *The Liberal Tradition in America* (New York: Harcourt, Brace, 1955), 289.

34. President George Bush, Remarks at National Day of Prayer and Remembrance, the National Cathedral, the White House, <www.whitehouse.gov/news/releases/2001/09/20010914-21.html>, 14 September 2001.

35. Bush, Address, Joint Session of Congress, 20 September 2001.

36. Sandra Silberstein, *War of Words: Language, Politics and 9/11* (London: Routledge, 2002), 6–7.

37. Ibid., 4–9.

38. Ibid., 14–15.

39. Williams, 'End of War', 267.

40. Eric Schmitt and Thom Shanker, *New York Times*, 13 September 2001.

41. Wolf, *Envisioning Power*, 55.

42. Susan Sontag, *Where the Stress Falls* (New York: Farrar, Strauss and Giroux, 2001), 220.

43. Edgar Roskis, 'Nothing to Say, Nothing to See', *Le Monde Diplomatique*, January 2003.

44. Frank Van Riper, 'September 11th: The Impact of Photography One Year Later', <www.allworth.com/Samples/9-11--The%20Impact%20of%20Photography%20One%20Year%20Later,%20by%20Frank%20Van%20Riper.pdf>, 4 April 2003.

45. Joel Meyerowitz, 'After September 11: Images from Ground Zero', US Department of State, <www.911exhibit.state.gov/gallery/full_image.cfm?photo_id=25>, 5 April 2003.

46. Edward W. Said, *Reflections on Exile* (London: Granta Books, 2000), 151. As John Berger explains, '... in life, meaning is not instantaneous. Meaning is discovered in what connects, and cannot exist without development. Without a story, without an unfolding, there is no meaning. Facts, information, do not in themselves constitute meaning. ... An instant photographed can only acquire meaning insofar as the viewer can read into it a duration extending beyond itself. When we find a photograph meaningful, we are lending it a past and a future' (John Berger and Jean Mohr, *Another Way of Telling* (London: Writers and Readers Publishers Co-operative Society, 1982), 89.

47. Susan Sontag, 'Looking at War: Photography's View of Devastation and Death', *The New Yorker* (9 December 2002), 94.

48. Cover photograph, Doug Mills, AP, *Time*, 24 September 2001.

49. David Usborne, *Independent* (London), 22 October 2001. 'All photographs are ambiguous', John Berger explains. 'All photographs have been taken out of a continuity. If the event is a public event, this continuity is history; ... Discontinuity always produces ambiguity. Yet often this

ambiguity is not obvious, for as soon as photographs are used with words, they produce together an effect of certainty, even of dogmatic assertion' (Berger and Mohr, *Another Way of Telling*, 91).

50. George Bush, 7 November 2001, in Little, *American Orientalism*, 307.
51. Van Riper, 'September 11th'.
52. Liam Kennedy, 'Remembering September 11: Photography as Cultural Diplomacy', *International Affairs* 79, no. 2 (March 2003), 317–8.
53. Ibid., 320.
54. Ibid., 324.
55. Sontag, 'Looking at War', 90.
56. Marc Howard Ross, 'The Political Psychology of Competing Narratives: September 11 and Beyond', in Craig Calhoun, Paul Price and Ashley Timmer (eds), *Understanding September 11* (New York: The New Press, 2002), 303.
57. Remarks by the President to Police, Firemen and Rescue Workers, Murray and West Streets, New York, the White House, <www.whitehouse.gov/news/releases/2001/09/20010914-9.html>, 14 September 2001.
58. Ross, *Understanding September*, 304.
59. Ryan, 'Ten Days in September', 27; Ted Honderich, *After the Terror* (Edinburgh: Edingburgh University Press, 2002).
60. Lewis A. Coser , 'Introduction' to Halbwachs, *On Collective Memory*, 1–3; Peter Novik, *That Noble Dream: The Objectivity Question and the American Historical Profession* (Cambridge: Cambridge University Press, 1988), 4–5.
61. Michael H. Hunt, *Ideology and US Foreign Policy* (New Haven: Yale University Press, 1987), 12.
62. Renan cited by Eric Hobsbawm, *Nations and Nationalism since 1780: Programme, Myth, Reality* (Cambridge: Canto, 1990), 12.

CHAPTER 3   ORIENTALISM AND THE ANTI-AMERICAN SENTIMENT

1. Editorial, 'The Roots of the rage', *Guardian* (London), 11 October 2001.
2. Rajeev Bhargava, 'Ordinary Feelings, Extraordinary Events: Moral Complexity in 9/11', in Craig Calhoun, Paul Price and Ashley Timmer (eds), *Understanding September 11* (New York: The New Press, 2002), 321.
3. Hani Shukrallah, 'We are all Iraqis now', *Guardian* (London), 27 March 2003.
4. Lewis Lapham, *Theater of War* (New York: The New Press, 2002), 150.
5. President George W. Bush, Address to a Joint Session of Congress and the American People, <www.whitehouse.gov/news/releases/2001/09/20010920-8.html>, 20 September 2001.
6. President George Bush, Remarks at National Day of Prayer and Remembrance, the National Cathedral, the White House, <www.whitehouse.gov/news/releases/2001/09/20010914-21.html>, 14 September 2001.
7. Bush, Address, Joint Session of Congress, 20 September 2001.

8. Bernard Lewis, 'The Roots of Muslim Rage', *The Atlantic Online*, <www.theatlantic.com/issues/90sep/rage.htm>, September 1990.

9. Samuel P. Huntington, *The Clash of Civilizations and the Remaking of World Order* (New York: Simon and Schuster, 1996), 307.

10. Huntington writes, 'The clash between the multiculturalists and the defenders of Western civilization and the American creed is ... "the *real* clash" within the American segment of Western civilization. Americans cannot avoid the issue: Are we a Western people or are we something else? The futures of the United States and the West depend upon Americans reaffirming their commitment to Western civilization. Domestically this means ejecting the divisive siren calls of multiculturalism.' Huntington, *Clash of Civilizations*, 307. For a history of the evolution of the West see, David Gress, *From Plato to NATO: The Idea of the West and its Opponents* (New York: The Free Press, 1998).

11. Edward W. Said, *Orientalism* (London: Penguin, 1995), 333.

12. Melani McAlister, *Epic Encounters: Culture, Media, and U.S. Interests in the Middle East, 1945–2000* (Berkeley, CA: University of California Press, 2001), 273.

13. Fred Halliday, *Two Hours that Shook the World: September 11, 2001: Causes and Consequences* (London: Saqi Books, 2002), 193–211.

14. See Michael H. Hunt, *Ideology and US Foreign Policy* (New Haven: Yale University Press, 1987), 46–91.

15. Douglas Little, *American Orientalism: The United States and the Middle East since 1945* (London: I.B. Tauris), 3–4.

16. Ibid., 10–11.

17. Ibid., 26–7.

18. United States Senate, The Pike Report, reprinted as *CIA The Pike Report* (Nottingham: Spokesman Books, 1977), 142–3.

19. Little, *American Orientalism*, 35; see also Edward W. Said, *Covering Islam: How the Media and the Experts Determine How We See the Rest of the World* (London: Vintage, 1997); Edward W. Said, *Culture and Imperialism* (London: Chatto and Windus, 1993).

20. Fred Halliday, *Islam and the Myth of Confrontation: Religion and Politics in the Middle East* (London: I.B. Tauris, 1995), 199–200; Said, *Covering Islam*, 36.

21. See James William Park, *Latin American Underdevelopment: A History of Perspectives in the United States 1870–1965* (Baton Rouge: Louisiana State University, 1995).

22. Richard H. Immerman, 'Psychology', in Michael J. Hogan and Thomas G. Paterson (eds), *Explaining the History of American Foreign Relations* (Cambridge: Cambridge University Press, 1991), 160; David Ryan, *US Foreign Policy in World History* (London: Routledge, 2000), 12.

23. Little, *American Orientalism*, 36; Lewis, 'The Roots of Muslim Rage'; Samuel P. Huntington, 'The Clash of Civilizations?', *Foreign Affairs* 72, no. 3 (Summer 1993).

24. Huntington, 'The Clash of Civilizations' 22.

25. Michael Slackman, 'Bin Laden Says West is Waging War against Islam', *New York Times*, 24 April 2006; Craig Whitlock, 'On Tape, Bin Laden Warns of Long War', *Washington Post*, 24 April 2006; Claudia Deane and

Darryl Fears, 'Negative Perception of Islam Increasing,' *The Washington Post*, 9 March 2006.

26. Jonathan Freedland, 'The war Bin Laden has already won', *Guardian* (London), 10 October 2001.

27. Abdu Sattar Kassem quoted in Peter Beaumont, 'The roots of Islamic anger', *Observer* (London), 14 October 2001.

28. Liam Kennedy and Scott Lucas, 'Enduring Freedom: Public Diplomacy and U.S. Foreign Policy', *American Quarterly* 57, no. 2 (June 2005).

29. Christopher Marquis, 'U.S. Image Abroad Will Take Years to Repair, Official Testifies', *New York Times*, 5 February 2004.

30. Richard Crockatt, *America Embattled: September 11, Anti-Americanism and the Global Order* (London: Routledge, 2003), 47.

31. Scott Lucas, 'The Limits of Ideology: US Foreign Policy and Arab Nationalism in the Early Cold War', in Ryan and Pungong (eds), *United States and Decolonization*, 140–60.

32. Marion W. Boggs, 'Long Range U.S. Policy towards the Near East', memorandum for the NSC Planning Board, National Security Council, 8 November 1957, NSC 5801, RG 273, NARA.

33. Michael Klare, 'United States: Energy and Strategy', *Le Monde Diplomatique* (Paris), November 2002.

34. See H. W. Brands, *Into the Labyrinth: The United States and the Middle East 1945–1993* (New York: McGraw-Hill, 1994), 102–35.

35. Richard Sheldon, 'Iraqi Sanctions: Were They Worth It?', Freedom Daily, The Future of Freedom Foundation, <www.fff.org/freedom/fd0401b.asp>, January 2004; Anup Shah, The Iraq Crisis, The Middle East, <www.globalissues.org/Geopolitics/MiddleEast/Iraq.asp>, 21 April 2003.

36. Bin Laden interviewed by Robert Fisk, 'The hatred that drives a zealot', *The Sydney Morning Herald*, 15–16 September 2001. Robert Fisk, *The Great War for Civilization: The Conquest of the Middle* East (London: Fourth Estate, 2005).

37. Michael Slackman, *New York Times*, 24 April 2006.

38. Abdu Sattar Kassem quoted in Peter Beaumont, *Observer* (London), 14 October 2001.

39. Caryle Murphy, 'A Hatred Rooted In Failings', *Washington Post*, 16 September 2001.

40. Cited in Beaumont, *Observer* (London), 14 October 2001.

41. Ussama Makdisi, '"Anti-Americanism" in the Arab World: An Interpretation of a Brief History', in Joanne Meyerowitz (ed.), *History and September 11th* (Philadelphia: Temple University Press, 2003), 132.

42. Makdisi, '"Anti-Americanism" in the Arab World', 148–52.

43. Daoud Kuttab, 'Why Anti-Americanism?', in Don Hazen et al., *After 9/11: Solutions for a Saner World* (San Francicso: AlterNet, 2001), 80.

44. Makdisi, '"Anti-Americanism" in the Arab World', 144.

45. Joy Gordon, 'Cool War: Economic Sanctions as a Weapon of Mass Destruction', *Harper's Magazine* 305, no. 1830 (November 2002), 43–9; Anthony Arnove (ed.), *Iraq Under Siege: The Deadly Impact of Sanctions and War* (London: Pluto Press, 2000).

46. Makdisi, '"Anti-Americanism" in the Arab World', 147.

47. Cited in Jonathan Raban, 'The Greatest Gulf', *Guardian* (London), 19 April 2003.
48. John Waterbury, 'Hate Your Policies, Love Your Institutions', *Foreign Affairs* 82, no. 1 (January/February 2003), 59.
49. Crockatt, *America Embattled*, 70.
50. Ziauddin Sardar and Meryl Wyn Davies, *Why Do People Hate America* (Cambridge: Icon Books, 2002), 195–9.
51. Tariq Ali, *The Clash of Fundamentalisms: Crusades, Jihads and Modernity* (London: Verso, 2002); Gilbert Achar, *The Clash of Barbarisms: Sept 11 and the Making of the New World Disorder* (New York: Monthly Review Press, 2002).
52. Bush, Remarks at National Day of Prayer and Remembrance, 14 September 2001.
53. Madeleine Bunting, 'Intolerant liberalism', *Guardian* (London) 8 October 2001.
54. Mushahid Hussain, '"Anti-Americanism" Has Roots in US Foreign Policy', *Common Dreams News Center*, <www.commondreams.org/views01/1019-05.htm>, 9 April 2003.
55. Sardar and Davies, *Why Do People Hate America?*, 198–201.
56. Mark Hertsgaard, *The Eagle's Shadow: Why America Fascinates and Infuriates the World* (London: Bloomsbury, 2002).

CHAPTER 4   WAR AND JUST WAR: TERRORISM AND AFGHANISTAN

1. President George W. Bush, State of the Union Address, United States Capitol, Washington, DC, the White House, <www.whitehouse.gov/news/releases/2002/01/print/20020129-11.html>, 29 January 2002.
2. Amartya Sen, *Identity and Violence: The Illusion of Destiny* (New York: W. W. Norton, 2006).
3. President George Bush, Remarks at National Day of Prayer and Remembrance, the National Cathedral, the White House, <www.whitehouse.gov/news/releases/2001/09/20010914-21.html>, 14 September 2001.
4. President George Bush, Address to a Joint Session of Congress and the American People, 20 September 2001, <www.whitehouse.gov/news/release/2001/09/20010920-8.html>.
5. Kofi A. Annan, 'Fighting Terrorism on a Global Front', *New York Times*, 21 September 2001.
6. Barbara Lee, 'I Will Not Put More Innocent Lives at Risk', in Don Hazen et al. (eds), *After 9/11: Solutions for a Saner World* (San Francisco: AlterNet, 2001), 16–17.
7. United Nations, General Assembly, Condemnation of Terrorist Attacks in the United States of America, <www.un.org/documents/ga/docs/56/agresolution.htm>, 12 September 2001.
8. Annan, *New York Times*, 21 September 2001.
9. United Nations Security Council, Resolution 1368, 12 September 2001, S/res/1368 (2001); United Nations Security Council, Resolution 1373, 28 September 2001, S/res/1373 (2001).

10. The Charter of the United Nations.

11. Charles Knight, 'What Justifies Military Intervention', Project on Defense Alternatives, <www.comw.org/pda/0109intervention.html>, 27 September 2001.

12. Julian Borger, 'President admits war on terror cannot be won', *Guardian* (London), 31 August 2004.

13. Dick Cheney cited in editorial, 'The "war without end" must be a political rather than a military struggle', *Independent* (London), 22 October 2001.

14. Center for Defense Information, 'The U.S. Military Campaign in Afghanistan: The Year in Review', <www.cdi.org/terrorism/afghanistan-one-year-later-pr.cfm>, 10 October 2002.

15. Jason Burke, *Al-Qaeda: The True Story of Radical Islam* (London: Penguin, 2003), 1.

16. Ibid., 10–14.

17. Ibid., 24.

18. Jason Burke, 'Where terror begins', *Observer* (London), 23 November 2003.

19. Gabriel Kolko, *Another Century of War?* (New York: The New Press, 2002), 2.

20. Donald Macintyre and Rupert Cornwall, 'US discloses plan to widen war on terror', *Independent* (London), 11 October 2001.

21. Jonathan Steele, 'A war that can never be won', *Guardian* (London), 22 November 2003.

22. Rowan Williams, 'For God's sake, stop this talk of war', *Guardian* (London), 21 January 2002.

23. Seumas Milne, 'A war that can't be won', *Guardian* (London), 21 November 2002; Richard Norton-Taylor, 'Rimington: US can't win terror battle', *Guardian* (London), 4 September 2002; Wesley Clark, 'Decisive Force' *Guardian* (London), 15 September 2001; Eric Schmitt and Thom Shanker, 'Administration Considers Broader, More Powerful Options for Potential Retaliation', *New York Times*, 13 September 2001. See also Stella Rimington, 'Why the war on terrorism can't be won', *Guardian* (London), 4 September 2002; Peter Beaumont, 'Why we are losing the war', *Observer* (London), 1 December 2002.

24. Editorial, 'A world and its losses: One year on, lessons remain unlearned', *Guardian* (London), 11 September 2002.

25. Don van Natta and David Johnston, 'Officials see Signs of a Revived Al Qaeda', *New York Times*, 13 October 2002.

26. Julian Borger, 'Bush told he is playing into Bin Laden's hands', *Guardian* (London), 19 June 2004.

27. United States Code Congressional and Administrative news, 98th Congress, 2nd sess., 19 October 1984, vol. 2, 3077, 98 Stat. 2707.

28. See Noam Chomsky, *9/11* (New York: Seven Stories Press, 2001), 16.

29. Richard Falk, *The Great Terror War* (Gloucestershire: Arris, 2003), 74–7. See also Alexander George (ed.), *Western State Terrorism* (Cambridge: Polity Press, 1991).

30. Andrew Buncombe, 'World must come to aid of America, says Bush', *Independent on Sunday* (London), 11 November 2001; Jan McGirk,

'Bush's cool cold warrior goes to UN', *Independent on Sunday* (London), 16 September 2001; George Monbiot, 'Backyard Terrorism', *Guardian* (London), 30 October 2001; Bianca Jagger, 'Selective Justice', *Guardian* (London), 8 December 2001; Duncan Campbell, 'Friends of terrorism', *Guardian* (London), 8 February 2002; Duncan Campbell, 'State terror is finally called to account', *Guardian* (London), 3 September 2003. See also, Noam Chomsky, *The Culture of Terrorism* (London: Pluto Press, 1988).

31. Mahmood Mamdani, 'Good Muslim, Bad Muslim: A Political Perspective on Culture and Terrorism', in Eric Hershberg and Kevin W. Moore (eds), *Critical Views of September 11: Analyses from Around the World* (New York: The New York Press, 2002), 49. Halliday contends: 'the *mujahedin* in Afghanistan, UNITA in Angola and the Nicaraguan *contras* were all responsible for abominable actions in their pursuit of "freedom" – massacring civilians, torturing and raping captives, destroying schools, hospitals and economic installations, killing and mutilating prisoners. In his eight years in the White House Reagan was responsible for the deaths of tens of thousands of people through terrorism, many times more than the PLO or other favourite targets of his righteous wrath' (Fred Halliday, *Cold War, Third World: An Essay on Soviet – American Relations* (London: Hutchinson Radius, 1989) 87.

32. Edgar Chamorro, affidavit, City of Washington, District of Columbia, 5 September 1985, 21–2.

33. Judgement of the International Court of Justice, *Nicaragua* v. *U.S.A.*, The Hague, 27 June 1986.

34. Achin Vanaik, 'The Ethics and Efficacy of Political Terrorism', in Hershberg and Moore, *Critical Views of September 11*, 41.

35. Dan Balz and Bob Woodward, 'America's Chaotic Road to War', *Washington Post*, 26 January 2002; Bob Woodward, *Bush at War* (New York: Simon and Schuster, 2002), 63; Peter Singer, *The President of Good and Evil: The Ethics of George W. Bush* (New York: Dutton, 2004), 150.

36. William V. O'Brien, 'Just-War Theory' in James P. Sterba (ed.), *The Ethics of War and Nuclear Deterrence* (Belmost, CA:Wadsworth, 1985), 34.

37. Bush, Address, Joint Session of Congress 20 September 2001.

38. Singer, *President of Good and Evil*, 143–53.

39. Rory McCarthy, 'Taliban order Bin Laden to leave', *Guardian* (London), 28 September 2001; Rupert Cornwell, 'Taliban want me to mediate, says Jesse Jackson', *Independent* (London), 28 September 2001; Andrew Buncombe, 'Bush rejects Taliban offer to surrender bin Laden', *Independent* (London), 15 October 2001; Singer, *The President of Good and Evil*, 151–53.

40. US Department of State, cable, Afghanistan: Raising bin Laden with the Taliban, 4 March 1997, the Taliban file IV, the National Security Archive (NSA), Washington, DC.

41. US Department of State, cable, Afghanistan: Taliban's Mullah Omar's 8/22 contact with State Department, 22 August 1998, the Taliban file IV, NSA.

42. Secretary of State to US Embassy in Islamabad, cable, message to the Taliban on bin Laden, 23 August 1998, the Taliban file IV, NSA.

43. American Embassy Islamabad to Secretary of State, cable, Pakistan/ Afghanistan reaction to US strikes, 25 August 1998, the Taliban file IV, NSA.

44. American Embassy Islamabad to Secretary of State, cable, Usama bin Laden: GOP Official – claiming Taliban want to get rid of bin Laden – Reviews three options, 7 October 1998, the Taliban file IV, NSA.

45. Bush, Address, Joint Session of Congress 20 September 2001.

46. Mamdani, 'Good Muslim, Bad Muslim', 59.

47. Kolko, *Another Century of War?*, 71.

48. Rowan Williams, 'End of War', *The South Atlantic Quarterly* 101, no. 2 (Spring 2002), 270.

49. Vanaik, 'Ethics and Efficacy of Political Terrorism', 43.

50. Singer, *President of Good and Evil*, 149.

51. Nicholas Berry, 'Justice is a Dish Best Served Cold', Center for Defense Information, <www.cdi.org/terrorism/dish-pr.html>, 14 September 2001; Robert Fisk, 'Watching the war from Kabul's rooftops', *Independent* (London), 18 October 2001.

52. Dana Priest, 'Zinni Urges Economic, Diplomatic Moves', Center for Defense Information, <www.cdi.org/terrorism/zinni-pr.html>, 14 September 2001.

53. Sofia Aldape, 'The U.S. Military Campaign in Afghanistan: The Year in Review', Center for Defense Information, <www.cdi.org/terrorism/ afghanistan-one-year-later-pr.cfm>, 10 October 2002; Kim Sengupta, '"Daisy Cutter" bombs dropped on Taliban caves', *Independent* (London), 7 November 2001; Julian Borger, 'Week of bombing leaves US further from peace, but nearer to victory', *Guardian* (London), 15 October 2001; Richard Norton-Taylor, 'Devastating gunship targets troops', *Guardian* (London), 17 October 2001; Natasha Walter, 'This war is not a moral enterprise', *Independent* (London), 19 October 2001; Editorial, 'Carpet bombing is losing us the propaganda war and may prove to be futile', *Independent* (London), 2 November 2001.

54. Suzanne Goldenberg, 'Day 100: another raid in the bombing war without end', *Guardian* (London), 15 January 2002.

55. Richard Norton-Taylor, 'A quarter of US bombs missed target in Afghan conflict', *Guardian* (London), 10 April 2002.

56. See Articles 52(2) of Protocol 1 and 51(5b), the Geneva Conventions, 1949 and 1977, <www.genevaconventions.org/>.

57. Nicholas J. Wheeler, 'Dying for "Enduring Freedom": Accepting Responsibility for Civilian Casualties in the War against Terrorism', *International Affairs* 16, no. 2 (August 2002), 209.

58. Michael Walzer, *Just and Unjust Wars: A Moral Argument with Historical Illustrations* (New York: HarperCollins, 1992), 157.

59. Julian Borger, 'Rumsfeld blames Taliban for civilian deaths', *Guardian* (London), 16 October 2001.

60. Staff reporters, 'Bombing casualties cause concern around the world', *Guardian* (London), 31 October 2001.

61. Marc Herold, 'Counting the Dead', *Guardian* (London), 8 August 2002; see his estimates at <www.cursor.org>; Carl Conetta, 'Strange Victory: A critical appraisal of Operation Enduring Freedom and the Afghanistan War',

Project on Defense Alternatives, <www.comw.org/pda/0201strangevic. html>, 30 January 2002; Carl Conetta, 'Operation Enduring Freedom: Why a Higher Rate of Civilian Bombing Casualties', Project on Defense Alternatives, <www.comw.org/pda/0201oef.html>, 18 January 2002. See also, Dexter Filkins, 'Flaws in U.S. Air War Left Hundreds of Civilians Dead', *New York Times*, 21 July 2002.

62. Ewen MacAskill, Michael White and Luke Harding, 'Bombs go astray, the casualties mount ... and the doubts set in', *Guardian* (London), 29 October 2001; Kathy Gannon, 'Kabul awakes to the aftermath of another night's heavy bombing', *Guardian* (London), 27 October 2001; Richard Lloyd Parry, 'Families blown apart, infants dying. The Terrible images of this "just war"', *Independent* (London), 25 October 2001; Rory McCarthy, 'US planes rain death on the innocent', *Guardian* (London), 1 December 2001; Jill Treanor, 'US raids "killed 800 Afghan civilians"', *Guardian* (London), 22 July 2002; Ian Traynor, 'Storm over Afghan civilian victims', *Guardian* (London), 12 February 2002.

63. Wheeler, 'Dying for "Enduring Freedom"', 215–16.

64. Williams, 'End of War', 272–3.

65. Michael Ignatieff, 'Virtual War', *Prospect* (London) April 2000, 21.

66. Wheeler, 'Dying for "Enduring Freedom"', 220.

CHAPTER 5   THE UNITED STATES AND IRAQ: 'ONE CAN DO NOTHING ABOUT THE PAST' 1983–91

1. Douglas Little, *American Orientalism: The United States and the Middle East since 1945*. London: I.B. Tauris, 2003, 198–206.

2. United States Senate, The Pike Report, reprinted as *CIA The Pike Report* (Nottingham: Spokesman Books, 1977), 212–18; Christopher Hitchens, 'Realpolitik in the Gulf: A Game Gone Tilt', in Micah L. Sifry and Christopher Cerf (eds), *The Gulf War Reader: History, Documents, Opinions* (New York: Random House, 1991), 110.

3. Meeting chaired by Henry Kissinger, 28 April 1975, declassified 7 June 2001, National Security Archive Briefing Book, no. 82 (25 February 2003).

4. Memorandum of conversation, Sadun Hammadi, Minister of Foreign Affairs of Iraq, and Henry Kissinger, Secretary of State, Iraqi Ambassador's residence, 17 December 1975, NSA, Book 82.

5. Ibid.

6. Alexander Haig, Secretary of State, Department of State telegram to USINT Baghdad, 8 April 1981, document 5, NSA, Book 82.

7. USINT Baghdad to Secstate, Department of State telegram, Morris Draper meeting with Foreign Minister Hammadi, 12 April 1981, document 6, NSA, Book 82.

8. William L. Eagleton to Department of State, telegram, 'Meeting with Tariq Aziz', 28 May 1981, document 10, NSA, Book 82.

9. President Ronald Reagan, National Security Decision Directive 114, 'US Policy toward the Iran-Iraq War', 26 November 1983.

10. Nicholas A. Veliotes and Jonathan Howe, information memorandum to Lawrence Eagleburger, 'Iran-Iraq War: Analysis of Possible US Shift from Position of Strict Neutrality', 7 October 1983, NSA, Book 82.

11. USINT Baghdad to American Embassy Amman, 'Talking points for Amb Rumsfeld's meeting with Tariq Aziz and Saddam Hussein', December 1983, NSA, Book 82.

12. American Embassy Rome to Secretary of State, Washington DC, telegram, Rumsfeld's larger meeting with Iraqi Deputy, December 1983, NSA, Book 82.

13. Secretary of State, Shultz to USINT Baghdad, telegram, US Chemical Shipment to Iraq, 3 March 1984, document 42, NSA, Book 82.

14. Secretary of State to American Embassy Khartoum, telegram, briefing notes for Rumsfeld visit to Baghdad, March 1984, NSA, Book 82.

15. Joyce Battle, 'Shaking Hands with Saddam Hussein: The U.S. Tilts towards Iraq, 1980–1984', National Security Archive Briefing Book, no. 82 (25 February 2003).

16. President Ronald Reagan, National Security Decision Directive 139, 'Measures to Improve U.S. Posture and Readiness to Respond to Developments in the Iran-Iraq War', document 53, NSA, Book 82.

17. Defense Estimative Brief, 'Prospects for Iraq', DEB-85-84, 25 September 1984, NSA, Book 82.

18. An Intelligence Estimate, 'Iraq's National Security Goals', Central Intelligence Agency, December 1988, NSA, Book 82.

19. Ibid.

20. UNSC Resolution 660, 2 August 1990, in E. Lauterpacht et al. (eds), *Kuwait Crisis: Basic Documents*, (Cambridge: Grotius, 1991), 88.

21. George Bush, 'In Defense of Saudi Arabia', 8 August 1990, in Sifry and Cerf, *Gulf War Reader*, 197–9.

22. President George Bush, memorandum to the principals, 'U.S. Policy in Response to the Iraqi Invasion of Kuwait', National Security Directive 45, 20 August 1990.

23. Ibid.

24. Ibid.

25. George Bush, U.S. Policy Toward the Persian Gulf, National Security Directive 26, 2 October 1989.

26. American Embassy Baghdad to Secretary of State, Washington DC, telegram, 0 131142Z, September 1988, National Security Archive.

27. Carl Conetta, The Wages of War: Iraqi Combatant and Noncombatant Fatalities in the 2003 Conflict Project on Defense Alternatives Research Monograph no. 8, <www.comw.org/pda/0310rm8ap2.html#1.%20Iraq i%20civilian%20fatalities%20in%20the%201991%20Gulf> 20 October 2003.

28. Colin L. Powell, *A Soldier's Way: An Autobiography* (London: Hutchinson, 1995), 519.

29. George H. W. Bush, The Persian Gulf Crisis and the Federal Budget Deficit, Address before a Joint Session of Congress, public papers, <http://bushlibrary.tamu.edu/research/papers/1990/90091101.html> 11 September 1990.

30. Lawrence Freedman and Efraim Karsh, *The Gulf Conflict 1990–1991: Diplomacy and War in the New World Order* (London: Faber and Faber, 1993), 438.

31. Michael S. Sherry, *In the Shadow of War: The United States since the 1930s* (New Haven: Yale University Press, 1995), 465.

32. Robert Fisk, 'Saddam interrogation screened – in silence. The Question is: Why?', *Independent* (London), 14 June 2005.

33. LaFeber, *America, Russia, and the Cold War* (7th edn) (New York: McGraw-Hill, 1991), 340; Amnesty International, 'Iraq's Occupation of Kuwait', 19 December 1990, in Sifry and Cerf, *Gulf War Reader*, 157.

34. Crowe cited in Bob Woodward, *The Commanders*, (New York: Simon and Schuster, 1991), 331–2; DCI William Webster, Statement to House Armed Services Committee, 5 December 1990, in James Ridgeway (ed.), *The March to War* (New York: Four Walls Eight Windows, 1991), 154–7; James Schlesinger, 'Crisis in the Persian Gulf Region: U.S. Policy Options and Implications', Hearings, Committee on Armed Services, US Senate, 101 Cong., 2nd sess., 11 September to 3 December 1990, 118.

35. Dilip Hiro, *Desert Shield to Desert Storm: The Second Gulf War* (London: HarperCollins, 1992), 426–33.

36. Fred Halliday, *Islam and the Myth of Confrontation: Religion and Politics in the Middle East* (London: I. B. Tauris, 1995), 97.

37. The Glaspie Transcript, 25 July 1990, in Sifry and Cerf, *Gulf War Reader*, 122–33; Halliday, *Islam*, 97; Hiro, *Desert Shield*, 428–31; Daniel Yergin, *The Prize: The Epic Quest for Oil, Money and Power* (London: Simon and Schuster, 1991), 772–4; Chomsky, *Deterring Democracy*, 196. See also: Yergin, *Prize*, 769–83.

38. National Security Directive 45, 20 August 1990.

39. Woodward, *Commanders*, 355; Schlesinger, Hearings, Committee on Armed Services, 118; Freedman and Karsh, *Gulf Conflict*, 431; Noam Chomsky, *World Orders: Old and New* (New York: Columbia University Press, 1994), 10.

40. Transcript of Perez de Cuéllar-Hussein meeting, 13 January 1991, as 'A Bitter cup of coffee in Baghdad', *Independent* (London), 14 February 1991. De Cuellar's office indicated that the release of the transcript was a breach of diplomatic protocol, and not the same as the version they had, though they did not have a problem with its substance. See also: Pierre Salinger with Eric Laurent, *Secret Dossier: The Hidden Agenda Behind the Gulf War* (London: Penguin, 1991), 212–21.

41. Glaspie Transcript, 25 July 1990, in Sifry and Cerf, *Gulf War Reader*, 122–33; Bush cited by Jonathan Mirsky, 'Reconsidering Vietnam', *The New York Review of Books* 28, no. 15 (10 October 1991), 44; NSD document cited by Maureen Dowd, *New York Times*, 23 February 1991; Robert W. Tucker and David C. Hendrickson, *The Imperial Temptation: The New World Order and America's Purpose* (New York: Council on Foreign Relations, 1992), 86–93, 152–9; David Ryan, 'Asserting US Power,' in Philip John Davies (ed.), *An American Quarter Century* (Manchester: Manchester University Press, 1995), 119.

42. George Bush, Responding to Iraqi Aggression in the Gulf, National Security Directive 54, the White House, 15 January 1991.

43. Richard Sobel, *The Impact of Public Opinion on U.S. Foreign Policy Since Vietnam* (New York: Oxford University Press, 2001), 152.

44. Philip M. Taylor, *War and the Media: Propaganda and Persuasion in the Gulf War* (Manchester: Manchester University Press, 1992); Douglas Kellner, *The Persian Gulf TV War*, (Boulder, CO: Westview Press, 1992); W. Lance Bennet and David L. Paletz (eds), *Taken by Storm: The Media, Public Opinion, and U.S. Foreign Policy in the Gulf* (Chicago, IL: University of Chicago Press, 1994).

45. Edward W. Said, *Culture and Imperialism*, (London: Chatto and Windus, 1993), 365; Paul Walker, 'The Myth of Surgical Bombing in the Gulf War', in Ramsey Clark, et. al., *War Crimes* (Washington, DC: Maisonneuve Press, 1992), 87; Victoria Brittain, *The Gulf Between Us: The Gulf War and Beyond* (London: Virago, 1991), ix; Rear Admiral Eugene J. Carroll and Gene R. La Rocque, 'Victory in the Desert: Superior Technology or Brute Force', in Brittain, *Gulf Between Us*, 53; Center for Defense Information, 'The U.S. as the World's Policeman? Ten Reasons to Find a Different Role', *The Defense Monitor* 20, no. 1 (1991); 'Arming Dictators', *The Defense Monitor* 21, no. 5 (1992); Middle East Watch, *Needless Deaths in the Gulf War: Civilian Casualties During the Air Campaign and Violations of the Laws of War* (New York: Human Rights Watch, 1991).

46. Thomas McCormick, *America's Half-Century: United States Foreign Policy in the Cold War* (Baltimore, MD: Johns Hopkins University Press, 1989), 1.

47. Ibid. (2nd edn), 246–52; Kennan cited in Noam Chomsky, *Deterring Democracy* (London: Verso, 1991), 53.

48. Gabriel Kolko, *Century of War: Politics, Conflict, and Society since 1914* (New York: The New Press, 1994), 450–1; Patrick E. Tyler, 'U.S. Strategy Plan Calls for Insuring No Rivals Develop', and excerpts from the plan, *New York Times*, 8 March 1992; Christopher Layne and Benjamin Schwarz, 'American Hegemony – Without an Enemy', *Foreign Policy*, no. 92 (Fall 1993), 9–10; Alexander L. George, 'Regional Conflicts in the Post-Cold War Era', in Geir Lundestad and Odd Arne Westad (eds), *Beyond the Cold War: New Dimensions in International Relations* (Oslo: Scandinavian University Press, 1993), 121–44; Ryan, 'Asserting US Power', 116–20.

49. George Bush, Review of National Defense Strategy, National Security Review 12, the White House, 3 March 1989.

CHAPTER 6   IRAQ AND VIETNAM:
THE UNBEARABLE WEIGHT OF DEFEAT

1. I would like to thank the British Academy who made it possible to research portions for this chapter. Another version of this can be found in John Dumbrell and David Ryan (eds), *Vietnam in Iraq: Tactics, Lessons, Legacies, Ghosts* (London: Routledge, 2007), 111–38.

2. Senator Robert Byrd cited by Norman Mailer, 'Only in America', *The New York Review of Books* 50, no. 5 (27 March 2003), 52.

3. Bob Herbert, 'The Agony of War', *New York Times*, 25 April 2005.

4. Jonathan Mirsky, 'Reconsidering Vietnam', *The New York Review of Books* 38, no. 15 (10 October 1991), 44.

5. Trevor B. McCrisken, *American Exceptionalism and the Legacy of Vietnam: US Foreign Policy since 1974*, (Basingstoke: Palgrave Macmillan, 2003).

6. Barry Rubin, 'The Real Roots of Arab Anti-Americanism', *Foreign Affairs* 81, no. 6 (November/December 2002), 84.

7. The Glaspie Transcript, 25 July 1990, in Micah L. Sifry and Christopher Cerf (eds), *The Gulf War Reader: History, Documents, Opinions*. New York: Random House, 1991, 125.

8. Ewen MacAskill, 'Blair gives strongest hint yet on taking war to Iraq', *Guardian* (London), 4 March 2002.

9. Brian Whitaker, 'Iraq plans urban warfare to thwart US', *Guardian* (London), 9 August 2002.

10. Thom Shanker, 'Regime Thought War Unlikely, Iraqis Tell US', *New York Times*, 12 February 2004.

11. See Arnold R. Isaacs, *Vietnam Shadows: The War, Its Ghosts, and Its Legacy* (Baltimore, MD: Johns Hopkins University Press, 1997), 76.

12. Andrew C. Emery, 'The Power of an Analogy: Vietnam, Operation Iraqi Freedom and the 2004 Presidential Election Campaign', unpublished thesis, University of Birmingham, October 2004.

13. Stephen Vlastos, 'America's "Enemy": The Absent Presence in Revisionist Vietnam War History', in John Carlos Rowe and Rick Berg (eds), *The Vietnam War and American Culture* (New York: Columbia University Press, 1991), 52–72.

14. W. R. Smyser memorandum to Secretary Kissinger, Lessons of Vietnam, 12 May 1975, NSA, Presidential Country Files for East Asia and the Pacific. Country File: Vietnam, Vietnam (23), Box 20, Gerald R. Ford Library.

15. Smyser memorandum to Kissinger.

16. Nomination of Robert M. Gates, US Congress. Senate, Select Committee on Intelligence, 99th Congress, 2nd session, 10 April 1986, 46–7.

17. Ibid.

18. Thom Shanker, 'Rumsfeld Favors Forceful Actions to Foil an Attack', *New York Times*, 14 October 2002; see also Donald H. Rumsfeld, 'Transforming the Military', *Foreign Affairs* 81, no. 3 (May/June 2002), 30–2.

19. See Chris Hedges, *War Is a Force That Gives Us Meaning* (New York: Anchor Books, 2003); David Campbell, *Writing Security: United States Foreign Policy and the Politics of Identity* (Minneapolis, MN: University of Minnesota Press, 1992).

20. Bob Woodward and Dan Balz, 'We Will Rally the World', *Washington Post*, <www.washingtonpost.com/wp-dyn/articles/A46879-2002Jan27.html>, 28 January 2002; Eric Schmitt and Thom Shanker, 'Administration Considers Broader, More Powerful Options for Potential Retaliation', *New York Times*, 13 September 2001.

21. Pew Global Attitudes Project, *Mistrust of America in Europe Even Higher, Muslim Anger Persists*, Pew Research Center for the People and the Press, 16 March 2004.

22. Maureen Dowd, 'I'm with Dick. Let's make War!', *New York Times*, 29 August 2002.

23. Michael Klare, 'United States: Energy and Strategy', *Le Monde Diplomatique* (Paris), November 2002.

24. Ed Vulliamy et al., 'Get Ready for War, Bush Tells America', *Observer* (London), 16 September 2001.
25. Toby Dodge, 'Iraqi army is tougher than US believes', *Guardian* (London), 16 November 2002; Barry R. Posen, 'Foreseeing a Bloody Siege in Baghdad', *New York Times*, 13 October 2002; Michael R. Gordon, 'Iraq Said to Plan Tangling the U.S. in Street Fighting', *New York Times*, 26 August 2002.
26. John F. Burns, 'Iraq Leader Exhorts His People to Draw Arms Against Invaders', *New York Times*, 20 March 2003; John F. Burns, 'As Allies Race North, Iraq Warns of Fierce Fight', *New York Times*, 24 March 2003; R.W. Apple, 'Bush Moves to Prepare Public for a Harder War', *New York Times*, 24 March 2003; Robert Pape, 'Wars Can't Be Won Only From Above', *New York Times*, 21 March 2003; Robert Fisk, '"America will have to fight street by street"', *The Independent on Sunday* (London), 9 March 2003.
27. Martin Woolacott, 'War is only feasible because Iraq isn't a threat to the US', *Guardian* (London), 20 September 2002.
28. See for instance the tracking of approval, Pew Research Center for the People and the Press, Presidential Approval, <http://pewresearch.org/datatrends/?NumberID=12>.
29. Julian Borger, 'Uprising in Iraq could derail Bush', *Guardian* (London), 7 April 2004.
30. Suzanne Goldenberg, '"Iraqification" key to return of US troops', *Guardian* (London), 8 November 2003.
31. Richard W. Stevenson, 'Public Doubt vs. Bush Vows', *New York Times*, 3 November 2003.
32. William Safire, 'Iraq War III', *New York Times*, 3 November 2003; Maureen Dowd, 'Death Be Not Loud', *New York Times*, 6 November 2003; Elisabeth Bumiller, 'Issue for Bush: How to Speak of Casualties?', *New York Times*, 5 November 2003; Giles Tremlett and Duncan Campbell, 'Body bag count puts strains on coalition', *Guardian* (London), 1 December 2003.
33. President George Bush, press conference, <www.whitehouse.gov/news/releases/2002/03/20020313-8.html> 13 March 2002; Don Oberdorfer, 'Tet: Who Won?', *Smithsonian Magazine* (November 2004).
34. President George W. Bush, Address to the nation, the White House, <www.whitehouse.gov/news/releases/2004/04>, 13 April 2004; Colonel Daniel Smith, 'The Psychology of War', *Foreign Policy in Focus* (7 April 2004); Representative Owens, House of Representatives, <http://thomas.loc.gov>, 21 April 2004.
35. Rory McCarthy, '22 killed as troops clash with Shias', *Guardian* (London), 5 April 2004; Rory McCarthy, 'Chaos killing and kidnap', *Guardian* (London), 9 April 2004; Jonathan Steele and Ewen MacAskill, 'Battles rage from north to south', *Guardian* (London), 8 April 2004; Rory McCarthy and Julian Borger, 'Death toll hits 600 in bloody siege of Falluja', *Guardian* (London), 12 April 2004.
36. Richard Norton-Taylor and Michael Howard, 'Peace in Iraq "will take at least five years to impose"', *Guardian* (London), 25 May 2005.
37. Richard Lock-Pullan, *US Intervention Policy and Army Innovation: From Vietnam to Iraq* (London: Routledge, 2006); Richard Lock-Pullan, 'Iraq and Vietnam: Military Lessons and Legacies', in Dumbrell and Ryan, *Vietnam in Iraq*.

38. George Bush and Brent Scowcroft, from *A World Transformed* (New York: Alfred A. Knopf, 1998), cited by Senator Levin, 'US Policy in Iraq', United States Senate, floor, 11 October 2004.

39. Peter W. Galbraith, 'How to Get Out of Iraq', *The New York Review of Books* 51, no. 8 (13 May 2004).

40. Jim McDermott, 'The Iraq War Just Keeps Getting Worse', House of Representatives, 4 May 2004; Lawrence J. Korb, '11-Step Program for Iraq Failure: The Bush Team is Repeating the Mistakes the US Made in Vietnam', Eye on Iraq, Center for Defense Information, 3 May 2004.

41. Galbraith, 'How to Get Out of Iraq'.

42. Edward W. Said, *Culture and Imperialism* (London: Catto and Windus, 1993), xii.

43. Powell cited in Lock-Pullan, *US Intervention Policy*, 139.

CHAPTER 7   THE TIPPING POINT:
BETWEEN BRING 'EM ON AND GOING SOUTH

1. Suzanne Goldenberg, 'We've Lost Battle for Baghdad, US Admits', *Guardian* (London), 20 October 2006; Simon Jenkins, 'America is Finally Waking Up to its Horrific Failure in Iraq', *Guardian* (London), 18 October 2006.

2. Jim Rutenberg and David S. Cloud, 'Bush, Facing Dissent on Iraq, Jettisons "Stay the Course"', *New York Times*, 24 October 2006; George Lakoff, 'Staying the Course Right Over a Cliff', *New York Times*, 27 October 2006.

3. Julian Borger, 'Rumsfeld Pays Price as US Sends Message to Bush', *Guardian* (London), 9 November 2006; Sheryl Gay Stolberg and Jim Rutenberg, 'Rumsfeld Resigns; Bush Vows to "Find Common Ground"', *New York Times*, 9 November 2006.

4. James A Baker and Lee H. Hamilton, co-Chairs, *The Iraq Study Group Report* (New York: Vintage Books, 2006), xiii–xvi, 32, 36.

5. Ibid., 11–12.

6. Maria Ryan, '"The need for judgement and prudence": Neoconservatives Confront the Limits of Regime Change, 1992–2006', conference paper, the British Association of American Studies, University of Leicester, 20 April 2007.

7. John Broder and Robin Toner, 'Report on Iraq Exposes a Divide Within the G.O.P.', *New York Times*, 10 December 2006.

8. John F. Burns, 'War Could Last Years, Commander Says', *New York Times*, 8 January 2007; Simon Tisdall, 'Once More Unto the Breach', *Guardian* (London), 11 January 2007.

9. Robert G. Kaiser, 'No More Illusions: Gone Forever Are the Barriers That Once Let Us Stand Apart', *Washington Post*, 16 September 2001.

10. Ibid.

11. Rajeev Bhargava, 'Ordinary Feelings, Extraordinary Events: Moral Complexity in 9/11', in Craig Calhoun, Paul Price and Ashley Timmer (eds), *Understanding September 11* (New York: The New Press, 2002), 321.

12. Susan Sontag, *Regarding the Pain of Others* (New York: Farrar, Straus and Giroux, 2003), 18.

13. Slavoj Žižek, *Welcome to the Desert of the Real: Five Essays on September 11 and Related Dates* (London: Verso, 2002), 13.

14. Tom Junod, 'The Falling Man', *Observer* (London), 7 September 2003.

15. Sontag, *Regarding*, 68.

16. Paul Bracken, 'Rethinking the Unthinkable: New Priorities for a New National Security', in Strobe Talbott and Nayan Chanda (eds), *The Age of Terror: America and the World after September 11* (New Haven: Perseus, 2001), 185.

17. George W. Bush, 'September 11 Remembered', the Pentagon, 11 September 2002.

18. Oliver Burkeman, 'Bush exploits suffering of 9/11, says Carter', *Guardian* (London), 25 October 2004.

19. Simon Schama, 'The Dead and the Guilty', *Guardian* (London), 11 September 2002.

20. Sontag, *Regarding*, 85–6.

21. National Security Council, National Strategy for Victory in Iraq, November 2005.

22. Sidney Blumenthal, 'Blinded by the light at the end of the tunnel', *Guardian* (London), 23 June 2005.

23. Simon Tisdall, 'No solution and no apology as president runs out of ideas', *Guardian* (London), 30 June 2005; Julian Borger and Richard Norton-Taylor, 'Bush's speech blurs fact with propaganda', *Guardian* (London), 30 June 2005; Douglas Jehl, 'Report Warned Bush Team About Intelligence Doubts', *Washington Post*, 6 November 2005.

24. Julian Borger and Richard Norton-Taylor, 'Bush exploited 9/11 in Iraq plea', *Guardian* (London), 30 June 2005; National Commission on Terrorist Attacks Upon the United States, *The 9/11 Commission Report* (New York: W. W. Norton, n.d.), 334.

25. Elliot Abrams, Richard Armitage, William Bennett, Jeffrey Bergner, John Bolton, Paula Bobriansky, Francis Fukuyama, Robert Kagan, Zalmay Khalilzad, William Kristol, Richard Perle, Peter Rodman, Donald Rumsfeld, William Schnider, Vin Weber, Paul Wolfowitz, James Woolsey and Robert Zoellick, Letter to President Clinton, <www.newamericancentury.org/iraqclintonletter.htm> 26 January 1998.

26. National Commission on Terrorist Attacks Upon the United States *9/11 Commission Report*, 334; Richard A. Clarke, *Against All Enemies: Inside America's War on Terror* (New York: The Free Press, 2004), 32.

27. Nicholas Lemann, 'How It Came to War', Letter from Washington, *The New Yorker*, 31 March 2003.

28. Brian Urquhart, 'World Order & Mr. Bush', *The New York Review of Books* 50, no. 15 (9 October 2003), 8–12.

29. Michael J. Glennon, 'How War Left the Law Behind', *New York Times*, 21 November 2002; Bruce Ackerman, 'The Legality of Using Force', *New York Times*, 21 September 2002; Ewen MacAskill et al., 'Doubts grow over legality of war', *Guardian* (London), 15 March 2003; Ewen MacAskill, 'Adviser quits Foreign Office over legality of war', *Guardian* (London), 22 March 2003.

30. George Bush, President Commemorates Veterans Day, Discusses War on Terror, the White House, <www.whitehouse.gov/news/releases/2005/11/print/20051111-1.html>, 11 November 2005.

31. Steven R. Weisman, 'Powell Calls His U.N. Speech a Lasting Blot on His Record', *New York Times*, 9 September 2005; Sidney Blumenthal, 'Bush's Other War', *Guardian* (London), 1 November 2003; Richard Norton-Taylor, '45 Minutes from a Major Scandal', *Guardian* (London), 18 February 2004; Julian Borger, '1,625 UN and US Inspectors spent more than two years searching hundreds of sites at a cost of over $1bn. Yesterday they delivered their verdict: There were no weapons of mass destruction in Iraq', *Guardian* (London), 7 October 2004; Julian Borger, 'Iraq WMD Report to Lay Blame on CIA', *Guardian* (London), 31 March 2005; Julian Borger, 'Interrogators "botched hunt for Iraq's WMD"', *Guardian* (London), 27 April 2005.

32. Julian Borger and Richard Norton-Taylor, 'US adviser warns of Armageddon', *Guardian* (London), 16 August 2002; and Julian Borger and Richard Norton-Taylor, 'Iraq attack plans alarm top military', *Guardian* (London), 30 July 2002; Ewen MacAskill, Duncan Campbell and Richard Norton-Taylor, 'Iraq Breeding Deadly World Jihadists, says CIA', *Guardian* (London), 23 June 2005.

33. Richard W. Stevenson, 'Acknowledging Difficulties, Insisting on a Fight to the Finish', *New York Times*, 29 June 2005.

34. Paul Krugman, 'The War President', *New York Times*, 24 June 2005; Memorandum to David Manning, 23 July 2002, reported in the *Sunday Times*, 1 May 2005, the Downing Street Memo, <www.downingstreet-memo.com/memos.html>.

35. Ted Honderich, *After the Terror* (Edinburgh: Edinburgh University Press, 2002), 125.

36. Ignacio Martín-Baró, 'Violence in Central America: A Social Psychological Perspective', in John Hassett and Hugh Lacey (eds), *Towards a Society that Serves its People: The Intellectual Contribution of El Salvador's Murdered Jesuits* (Washington, DC: Georgetown University Press, 1991), 333–46.

37. John F. Burns, 'First Case Against Hussein, Involving Killings in 1982, Is Sent to a Trial Court', *New York Times*, 18 July 2005; John F. Burns, 'First Court Case of Hussein Stems From Killings in Village in '82', *New York Times*, 6 June 1982; Robert Fisk, 'Saddam interrogation screened – in silence. The Question is: Why?', *Independent* (London), 14 June 2005.

38. Edward Wong, 'Iraq Asks Return of Some Officers of Hussein Army', *New York Times*, 3 November 2005.

39. Toby Dodge, *Iraq's Future: The Aftermath of Regime Change*, Adelphi Paper 372 (London: Routledge, 2005), 9–23.

40. Steven R. Weisman, *New York Times*, 9 September 2005.

41. Iraq Body Count, <www.iraqbodycount.net/>.

42. Susan Sachs, 'Arab Media Portray War as Killing Field', *New York Times*, 4 April 2003; Simon Jeffrey, 'Up to 7,000 Civilians Killed in War, Researchers Say', *Guardian* (London), 13 June 2003.

43. Rory McCarthy, 'US in Biggest Offensive Since Fall of Iraq', *Guardian* (London), 13 June 2003.

44. Peter Beaumont, 'Farah Tried to Plead with the US Troops but She was Killed Anyway', *Observer* (London), 7 September 2003; Bradley Graham, 'Enemy Body Counts Revived', *Washington Post*, 24 October 2005.

45. George W. Bush, Address to the nation, Fort Bragg, North Carolina, 28 June 2005, <www.whitehouse.gov/news/releases/2005/06/print/20050628-7.html>.

46. Bush, Address Fort Bragg, 28 June 2005.

47. David S. Cloud, 'Iraqi Rebels Refine Bomb Skills, Pushing Toll of G.I.'s Higher', *New York Times*, 22 June 2005; David S. Cloud, 'US General Sees No Ebb in Fight', *New York Times*, 24 June 2005; Rupert Cornwell, 'Beleaguered Bush Struggles to Reverse Tide of Pessimism Over Iraq', *Independent on Sunday* (London), 26 June 2005; David E. Sanger, 'Bush Declares Sacrifice in Iraq to Be "Worth It"', *New York Times*, 29 June 2005.

48. John F. Kerry, 'The Speech the President Should Give', *New York Times*, 28 June 2005.

49. Bob Herbert, 'Dangerous Incompetence', *The New York Times*, 30 June 2005; Editorial, *New York Times*, 29 June 2005.

50. Jason Burke, 'Al-Qaida is Now an Idea, Not an Organisation', *Guardian* (London), 5 August 2005; John Ward Anderson, 'October Toll Is 4th Highest for U.S. Troops in Iraq', *Washington* Post, 1 November 2005; Josh White, 'U.S. Military Death Toll in Iraq Hits 2000', *Washington Post*, 26 October 2005; Richard Morin, 'Bush's Popularity Reaches New Low', *Washington Post*, 4 November 2005.

51. Josh White, *Washington Post*, 26 October 2005.

52. Michael Ignatieff, *Virtual War: Kosovo and Beyond* (New York: Picador, 2000).

53. Michael R. Gordon, 'Dash to Baghdad Left Top U.S. Generals Divided', *New York Times*, 13 March 2006.

54. Robin Cook, 'Our Troops are Part of the Problem', *Guardian* (London), 15 July 2005.

55. Eric Schmitt, 'U.S. to Intensify Its Training in Iraq to Battle Insurgents', *The New York Times*, 2 November 2005.

56. Stanley Hoffman, 'Out of Iraq', *The New York Review of Books* 51, no. 16, 21 October 2004.

57. Condoleezza Rice, Iraq and US Policy, Senate Committee on Foreign Relations, 19 October 2005.

58. Toby Dodge, 'E is for Election. E is for Exit', *The Independent on Sunday* (London), 30 January 2005.

59. Ibid.; Cook, *Guardian*, 15 July 2005.

60. Hoffman, 'Out of Iraq'.

61. Peter Singer, *The President of Good and Evil: The Ethics of George W. Bush* (New York: Dutton, 2004), 174.

CHAPTER 8   IMPERIAL FRUSTRATIONS

1. Joseph A. Fry, 'Imperialism, American Style, 1890–1916', in Gordon Martel (ed.), *American Foreign Relations Reconsidered, 1890–1993* (London: Routledge, 1994), 67.

2. Michael Cox, 'Empire by Denial: The Strange Case of the United States', *International Affairs* 81, no. 1 (January 2005), 22–3.

3. See Samuel Flagg Bemis, *A Diplomatic History of the United States* (London: Jonathan Cape, 1937); Ernest R. May, *Imperial Democracy: The Emergence of America as a Great Power* (New York: Harper and Row, 1961); William Appleman Williams, *The Tragedy of American Diplomacy* (New York: Delta, 1959); Anders Stephanson, *Manifest Destiny: American Expansion and the Empire of Right* (New York: Hill and Wang, 1995).

4. See Andrew J. Bacevich, *American Empire: The Realities and Consequences of US Diplomacy* (Cambridge, MA: Harvard University Press, 2002); Robert W. Tucker and David C. Hendrickson, *The Imperial Temptation: The New World Order and America's Purpose* (New York: Council on Foreign Relations, 1992); Lloyd C. Gardner and Marilyn B. Young (eds), *The New American Empire* (New York: The New Press, 2005); Emmanuel Todd, *After the Empire: The Breakdown of the American Order* (London: Constable, 2003); Niall Ferguson, *Colossus: The Rise and Fall of the American Empire* (London: Allen Lane, 2004); Michael Mann, *Incoherent Empire* (London: Verso, 2003); Walden Bello, *Dilemmas of Domination: The Unmaking of the American Empire* (New York: Metropolitan Books, 2005).

5. Cox, 'Empire by Denial', 26; Mary Ann Heiss, 'The Evolution of the Imperial Idea and U.S. National Identity', *Diplomatic History* 26, no. 4 (Fall 2002), 511–40.

6. Richard K. Betts, 'The Political Support System for American Primacy', *International Affairs* 81, no. 1 (January 2005), 6.

7. President George Bush, Address to a Joint Session of Congress and the American People, the White House, <www.whitehouse.gov/news/releases/2001/09/20010920-8.html>, 20 September 2001.

8. Condeleezza Rice cited in Frances Fitzgerald, 'George Bush and the World', *The New York Review of Books* 49, no. 14 (26 September 2002), 80.

9. David Ryan, 'Mapping Containment: The Cultural Construction of the Cold War', in Douglas Field (ed.), *American Cold War Culture* (Edinburgh: Edinburgh University Press, 2005).

10. Norman Mailer, 'Only in America', *The New York Review of Books* 50, no. 5 (27 March 2003), 51.

11. President George W. Bush, Inaugural Address, the White House, <www.whitehouse.gov/press/inaugural-address.html>, 20 January 2001.

12. Anders Stephanson, 'A Most Interesting Empire', paper delivered to the symposium, 'Reviewing the Cold War: Interpretation, Approaches, Theory', Norwegian Nobel Institute, 1998; Anders Stephanson, 'A Most Interesting Empire', in Gardner and Young, *New American Empire*.

13. Serge Ricard, 'The Exceptionalist Syndrome in U.S. Continental and Overseas Expansionism', in David K. Adams and Cornelis A. van Minnen (eds), *Reflections on American Exceptionalism* (Keele: Keele University Press, 1994), 73.

14. David C. Hendrickson, 'The Course of Empire', *Harpers Magazine* 305, no. 1831 (December 2002), 16.

15. Timothy Garton Ash, 'The Peril of Too Much Power', *New York Times*, 9 April 2002.

16. Walter LaFeber, 'The Bush Doctrine', *Diplomatic History* 26, no. 4 (Fall 2002), 558.

17. Sources vary, but generally US defence budgets are larger than the next six to eight countries combined. William Wallace, 'Living with the Hegemon: European Dilemmas', in Eric Hershberg and Kevin W. Moore, *Critical Views of September 11: Analyses from Around the World* (New York: The New Press, 2002), 104.

18. Incidentally, it noted that the US will become 'increasingly vulnerable to hostile attack on the American homeland, and the US military superiority will not entirely protect us'.

19. Joseph S. Nye, *The Paradox of American Power: Why the World's Only Superpower Can't Go It Alone* (Oxford: Oxford University Press, 2002), 157–9.

20. Jessica T. Mathews, 'Estranged Partners', *Foreign Policy* (November/ December 2001), 48–9.

21. Nye, *Paradox*, 171; Mathews, 'Estranged Partners', 49–53; Michael Cox, 'American Power Before and After 11 September: Dizzy with Success?', *International Affairs* 78, no. 2 (2002), 264.

22. Eric Hobsbawm, 'America's imperial delusion', *Guardian* (London), 14 June 2003.

23. President George W. Bush, State of the Union Address, United States Capitol, Washington, DC, the White House, <www.whitehouse.gov/news/releases/2002/01/print/20020129-11.html>, 29 January 2002.

24. President George W. Bush, 'Graduation Speech at West Point,' the White House, <www.whitehouse.gov/news/releases/2002/06/print/20020601-3.html>, 1 June 2002.

25. Joseph Nye, 'The new Rome meets the new barbarians', *The Economist*, 23 March 2002.

26. Immanuel Wallerstein, 'The Eagle Has Crash Landed', *Foreign Policy* (July/ August 2002), 63.

27. Hendrickson, 'Course of Empire', 19.

28. G. John Ikenberry, 'America's Imperial Ambition', *Foreign Affairs* 81, no. 5 (September/October 2002), 58.

29. Chris Patten, 'Jaw-Jaw, not War-War', *Financial Times* (London), 14 February 2002.

30. Wallerstein, 'Eagle Has Crash Landed', 67.

31. Joan Didion, 'Fixed Opinions, or the Hinge of History', *The New York Review of Books* 50, no. 1 (16 January 2003), 58.

32. Ronald Steel, *Temptations of a Superpower* (Cambridge, MA: Harvard University Press, 1995), 49–50.

33. Ewen MacAskill, 'From Suez to the Pacific: US expands its presence across the globe', *Guardian* (London), 8 March 2002.

34. Ian Traynor, 'How American power girds the globe with a ring of steel', *Guardian* (London), 21 April 2003.

35. Gabriel Kolko, *Another Century of War?* (New York: The New Press, 2002), 60–1.

36. David Ryan, 'US Expansionism: From the Monroe Doctrine to the Open Door', in Philip John Davies (ed.), *Representing and Imagining America* (Keele: Keele University Press, 1996), 181; citing James Madison,

Federalist Paper No. 10, in the *Federalist Papers* 1788, ed. Isaac Kramnick (Harmondsworth: Penguin, 1987), 122–8; Martin Diamond, 'The Federalist', in Leo Strauss and Joseph Cropsey (eds), *History of Political Philosophy* (Chicago, IL: University of Chicago Press, 1981), 638; Isaac Kramnick, 'Editor's Introduction', *the Federalist Papers*, 41.

37. Richard Hofstadter, *The American Political Tradition: And the Men Who Made It* (New York: Vintage, [1948] 1989), 5.

38. See Isaiah Berlin, *Four Essays on Liberty* (Oxford: Oxford University Press, 1969); J. S. McClelland, *A History of Western Political Thought* (London: Routledge, 1996), 264–5.

39. James Rubin, 'The Historical Imperative', *Guardian* (London), 16 March 2002.

40. Melvyn P. Leffler, *A Preponderance of Power: National Security, the Truman Administration and the Cold War* (Stanford, CA: Stanford University Press, 1992).

41. Report by the Policy Planning Staff, PPS/23, Review of Current Trends in US Foreign Policy (24 February 1948), *Foreign Relations of the United States*, vol. 1, 1948.

42. Ibid., vol. 1, part 2, 526.

43. John Gray, *Al Qaeda and What it Means to be Modern* (London: Faber and Faber, 2003).

44. Wallerstein, 'Eagle Has Crash Landed', (2002), 60–8.

45. W. R. Smyser memorandum to Secretary Kissinger, Lessons of Vietnam, 12 May 1975, NSA, Presidential Country Files for East Asia and the Pacific. Country File: Vietnam, Vietnam (23), Box 20, Gerald R. Ford Library.

46. Cox, 'American Power', (2002), 275, note 48.

47. The White House, The National Security Strategy of the United States of America (NSS), 17 September 2002.

48. Defense Planning Guidance cited in Patrick Tyler, 'US Strategy Plan Calls for Insuring No Rivals Develop', *New York Times* 8 March 1992; Patrick E. Tyler, 'Goal of Blocking New Superpowers', *New York Times*, 24 May 1992.

49. US National Security Strategy, and accompanying papers, April 1982, document 8290283 (NSDD 32) System II, NSC Records, the Reagan Presidential Library.

50. Madeleine Bunting, 'Intolerant Liberalism', *Guardian* (London), 8 October 2001.

51. George Bush, Inauguration Speech, 20 January 2005, the White House, <www.whitehouse.gov/news/releases/2005/01/20050120-1.html>.

52. Eric Foner, *The Story of American Freedom* (New York: W. W. Norton, 1998), xv.

53. David Hackett Fischer, *Liberty and Freedom: A Visual History of America's Founding Ideas* (New York: Oxford University Press, 2005).

54. David Hackett Fischer, 'Freedom's Not Just Another Word', *New York Times*, 7 February 2005.

55. Fareed Zakaria, 'Writing Prose For A New Term', *Newsweek*, 15 November 2004.

56. Theodore Draper, 'Freedom and Its Discontents', *The New York Review of Books* 46, no. 14 (23 September 1999), 59.

57. Ngugi Wa Thiong'O, *Moving the Centre: The Struggle for Cultural Freedoms* (London: James Curry, 1993).
58. Carolyn Eisenberg, 'The New Cold War', *Diplomatic History* 29, no. 3 (June 2005), 424.
59. Joan Hoff, 'The American Century: From Sarajevo to Sarajevo', *Diplomatic History* 23, no. 2 (Spring 1999), 285–319; Melvyn P. Leffler, '9/11 and American Foreign Policy', *Diplomatic History* 29, no. 3 (June 2005), 397–400; John Lewis Gaddis, *Surprise, Security and the American Experience* (Cambridge, MA.: Harvard University Press, 2004); Lloyd C. Gardner, 'Angels in the Whirlwind', unpublished manuscript.
60. Offner characterises the Bush administration as rogue nation: it was not just about 9/11, but also about the ABM Treaty, the Kyoto Protocols, the International Criminal Court, the Comprehensive Test Ban Treaty, the disdain for the UN; 'I question both the means and the ends of the Bush administration. In my view, leaders who believe in democracy and freedom do not deceive, or lie to, their constituents so consistently, nor do they disdain Geneva Conventions and basic legal procedures. And government leaders who reject the long-established Westphalian doctrine of state sovereignty and non-interference in internal affairs, the UN Charter prohibition on use of force except in self-defense or by Security Council mandate, and the Nuremburg trials judgement that "preemptive" war is a crime, are practicing a revolutionary policy more suited to a "rogue" nation than a world leader.' Arnold A. Offner, 'Rogue President, Rogue Nation: Bush and U.S. National Security', *Diplomatic History* 29, no. 3 (June 2005), 435.
61. Kaizer Nyatsumba, 'America Must Understand Why the Third World still Distrusts its Power', *Independent* (London), 25 October 2001.
62. Ahdaf Soueif, 'Our Poor, Our Weak, Our Hungry', *Guardian* (London), 15 September 2001.
63. Khalil Shikaki, 'This is a War on Islam', *Guardian* (London), 11 September 2002; Susan Sachs, 'Intellectual Speaks of the Arab World's Despair', *New York Times*, 8 April 2003.
64. David Hirst, 'Out of the Crucible', *Guardian* (London), 11 June 2003.
65. Ibid.
66. Hani Shukrallah, 'We are All Iraqis Now', *Guardian* (London), 27 March 2003.
67. Patrick Cockburn, 'Invasion that's Become Bloody Anarchy', *Independent on Sunday* (London), 24 July 2005.

Bibliography

Achar, Gilbert. *The Clash of Barbarisms: Sept 11 and the Making of the New World Disorder.* New York: Monthly Review Press, 2002.

Adams, Nassau A. *Worlds Apart: The North-South Divide and the International System.* London: Zed Books, 1993.

Ali, Tariq. *The Clash of Fundamentalisms: Crusades, Jihads and Modernity.* London: Verso, 2002.

Anderson, Benedict. *Imagined Communities: Reflections on the Origin and Spread of Nationalism.* London: Verso, 2002.

Appleby, Joyce, Lynn Hunt and Margaret Jacob. *Telling the Truth about History.* New York: W. W. Norton, 1994.

Arnove, Anthony (ed.). *Iraq Under Siege: The Deadly Impact of Sanctions and War.* London: Pluto Press, 2000.

Arnove, Anthony. *Iraq: The Logic of Withdrawal.* New York: The New Press, 2006.

Ash, Timothy Garton. 'Anti-Europeanism in America', *The New York Review of Books* 50, no. 2 (13 February 2003).

Bacevich, Andrew J. *American Empire: The Realities and Consequences of US Diplomacy.* Cambridge, MA: Harvard University Press, 2002.

——. *The New American Militarism: How Americans are Seduced by War.* Oxford: Oxford University Press, 2005.

Bello, Walden. *Dilemmas of Domination: The Unmaking of the American Empire.* New York: Metropolitan Books, 2005.

Bennet, W. Lance and David L. Paletz. *Taken by Storm: The Media, Public Opinion, and U.S. Foreign Policy in the Gulf.* Chicago, IL: University of Chicago Press, 1994.

Bennis, Phyllis. *Before After: US Foreign Policy and the September 11th Crisis.* New York: Olive Branch Press, 2003.

Berger, John and Jean Mohr. *Another Way of Telling.* London: Writers and Readers Publishers Co-operative Society, 1982.

Berger, John. *About Looking.* New York: Vintage, 1991.

Berlin, Isaiah. *The Crooked Timber of Humanity: Chapters in the History of Ideas.* Henry Hardy (ed.). London: Fontana Press, 1990.

Betts, Richard K. 'The Political Support System for American Primacy', *International Affairs* 81, no. 1 (January 2005).

Bhargava, Rajeev. 'Ordinary Feelings, Extraordinary Events: Moral Complexity in 9/11', in Craig Calhoun, Paul Price and Ashley Timmer (eds), *Understanding September 11.* New York: The New Press, 2002.

Booth, Ken and Tim Dunne (eds). *Worlds in Collision: Terror and the Future of Global Order* London: Palgrave, 2002.

Bracken, Paul. 'Rethinking the Unthinkable: New Priorities for a New National Security', in Strobe Talbett and Nayan Chanda (eds), *The Age of Terror: America and the World after September 11.* New Haven: Perseus, 2001.

Brands, H. W. *Into the Labyrinth: The United States and the Middle East 1945–1993*. New York: McGraw-Hill, 1994.

Bresheeth, Haim and Nira Yuval-Davis (eds). *The Gulf War and the New World Order*. London: Zed Books, 1991.

Brigham, Robert K. *Is Iraq Another Vietnam?* New York: Public Affairs, 2006.

Brittain, Victoria. *The Gulf Between Us: The Gulf War and Beyond*. London: Virago Press, 1991.

Byrd, Robert C. *Losing America: Confronting a Reckless and Arrogant Presidency*. New York: W. W. Norton, 2004.

Buck-Morss, Susan. *Thinking Past Terror: Islamism and Critical Theory on the Left*. London: Verso, 2003.

Bulloch, John and Harvey Morris. *Saddam's War: The Origins of the Kuwait Conflict and the International Response*. London: Faber and Faber, 1991.

Burke, Jason. *Al-Qaeda: The True Story of Radical Islam*. London: Penguin, 2003.

Bush, George and Brent Scowcroft. *A World Transformed*. New York: Alfred A. Knopf, 1998.

Calhoun, Craig, Paul Price and Ashley Timmer (eds). *Understanding September 11*. New York: The New Press, 2002.

Callinicos, Alex. *Theories and Narratives: Reflections on the Philosophy of History*. Cambridge: Polity Press, 1995.

——. *The New Mandarins of American Power: The Bush Administration's Plans for the World*. Cambridge: Polity Press, 2003.

Campbell, David. *Writing Security: United States Foreign Policy and the Politics of Identity*. Minneapolis, MN: University of Minnesota Press, 1992.

Carroll, John. *Terror: A Meditation on the Meaning of September 11*. Melbourne: Scribe Publications, 2002.

Chomsky, Noam. *The Culture of Terrorism*. London: Pluto Press, 1988.

——. *Detering Democracy*. London: Verso, 1991.

——. *World Orders Old and New*. New York: Columbia University Press, 1994.

——. *9/11*. New York: Seven Stories Press, 2001.

Clark, Ramsey et al. *War Crimes*. Washington, DC: Maisonneuve Press, 1992.

Clarke, Richard A. *Against All Enemies: Inside America's War on Terror*. New York: The Free Press, 2004.

Coates, Ken (ed.). *Falluja: Shock and Awe*. Nottingham: Spokesman, 2004.

Cox, Michael. 'American Power Before and After 11 September: Dizzy with Success?' *International Affairs* 78, no. 2 (2002).

——. 'Empire by Denial: The Strange Case of the United States', *International Affairs* 81, no. 1 (2005).

Crockatt, Richard. *America Embattled: September 11, Anti-Americanism and the Global Order*. London: Routledge, 2003.

Cullather, Nick. 'Development? It's History', *Diplomatic History* 24, no. 4 (Fall 2000).

Didion, Joan. 'Fixed Opinions, or The Hinge of History', *The New York Review of Books* 50, no. 1 (16 January 2003).

Divine, Robert A. 'Historians and the Gulf War: A Critique,' *Diplomatic History* 19, no. 1, (Winter 1995).

Dodge, Toby. *Inventing Iraq: The Failure of Nation Building and a History Denied.* New York: Columbia University Press, 2003.

——. *Iraq's Future: The Aftermath of Regime Change.* London: Routledge, 2005.

Draper, Theodore. *A Present of Things Past.* New York: Hill and Wang, 1990.

Dumbrell, John and David Ryan (eds). *Vietnam in Iraq: Tactics, Lessons, Legacies and Ghosts.* London: Routledge, 2007.

Eisenberg, Carolyn. 'The New Cold War', *Diplomatic History* 29, no. 3 (June 2005).

Emery, Andrew C. 'The Power of an Analogy: Vietnam, Operation Iraqi Freedom and the 2004 Presidential Election Campaign', unpublished thesis, University of Birmingham, October 2004.

Engelhardt, Tom. *The End of Victory Culture: Cold War America and the Disillusioning of a Generation.* Amherst: University of Massachusetts Press, 1995.

Falk, Richard. *The Great Terror War.* Gloucestershire: Arris, 2003.

Farebrother, George and Nichiolas Kollerstrom (eds). *The Case against War: The Essential Legal Inquiries, Opinions and Judgements Concerning War in Iraq.* Nottingham: Spokesman, 2003.

Farouk-Sluglett, Marion and Peter Sluglett. *Iraq since 1958: From Revolution to Dictatorship.* London: I. B. Tauris, 1990.

Ferguson, Niall. *Colossus: The Price of America's Empire.* London: Allen Lane, 2004.

Fisk, Robert. *The Great War for Civilization: The Conquest of the Middle East.* London: Fourth Estate, 2005.

Fitzgerald, Frances. 'George Bush and the World', *The New York Review of Books* 49, no. 14 (26 September 2002).

Foley, Michael. *American Political Ideas: Traditions and Usages.* Manchester: Manchester University Press, 1991.

Foner, Eric. *The Story of American Freedom.* New York: W. W. Norton, 1998.

Foucault, Michel. *The Archaeology of Knowledge.* London: Routledge, 1991 [1969].

Fraser, Cary. 'Understanding American Policy towards the Decolonization of European Empires, 1945–64', *Diplomacy and Statecraft* 3, no. 1 (1992).

Freedman, Lawrence and Efraim Karsh. *The Gulf Conflict 1990–1991: Diplomacy and War in the New World Order.* London: Faber and Faber, 1993.

Fry, Joesph A. 'Imperialism, American Style, 1890–1916', in Gordon Martel (ed.), *American Foreign Relations Reconsidered, 1890–1993.* London: Routledge, 1994.

Fukuyama, Francis. *The End of History and the Last Man.* London: Penguin, 1992.

——. *After the Neocons: America at the Crossroads.* London: Profile, 2006.

Gaddis, John Lewis. 'A Grand Strategy of Transformation', *Foreign Policy* (November/December 2002).

——. *Surprise, Security and the American Experience.* Cambridge, MA: Harvard University Press, 2004.

Galbraith, Peter W. 'How to Get Out of Iraq', *The New York Review of Books* 51, no. 8 (13 May 2004).

——. *The End of Iraq: How American Incompetence Created a War Without End.* New York: Simon and Schuster, 2006.

Gardner, Lloyd C. *Economic Aspects of New Deal Diplomacy.* Madison, WI: University of Wisconsin Press, 1964.

Gardner, Lloyd C. and Marilyn B. Young (eds). *The New American Empire.* New York: The New Press, 2005.

George, Alexander L. 'Regional Conflicts in the Post-Cold War Era', in Geir Lundestad and Odd Arne Westad (eds), *Beyond the Cold War: New Dimensions in International Relations.* Oslo: Scandinavian University Press, 1993.

George, Alexander (ed.). *Western State Terrorism.* Cambridge: Polity Press, 1991.

George, Susan. *How the Other Half Dies.* London: Penguin, 1976.

Gills, Barry and Joel Rocamora. 'Low Intensity Democracy', *Third World Quarterly* 13, no. 3 (1992).

Gittins, John. *Beyond the Gulf War: The Middle East and the New World Order.* London: CIIR, 1991.

Gompert, David C. 'The EU on the World Stage', *Internationale Politik* (Transatlantic Edition) 3, no. 2 (Summer 2002).

Gordon, Joy. 'Cool War: Economic Sanctions as a Weapon of Mass Destruction', *Harper's Magazine* 305, no. 1830 (November 2002).

Graubard, Stephen R. *Mr. Bush's War: Adventures in the Politics of Illusion.* London: I. B. Tauris, 1992.

Gray, John. *Al Qaeda and What it Means to be Modern.* London: Faber and Faber, 2003.

——. *Heresies: Against Progress and Other Illusions.* London: Granta, 2004.

Gress, David. *From Plato to NATO: The Idea of the West and its Opponents.* New York: The Free Press, 1998.

Guyatt, Nicholas. *Another American Century? The United States and the World after 2000.* Sydney: Pluto Press, 2000.

Haass, Richard N. *The Opportunity: America's Moment to Alter History's Course.* New York: Public Affairs, 2005.

Hahn, Peter L. and Mary Ann Heiss (eds). *Empire and Revolution: The United States and the Third World since 1945.* Columbus: Ohio State University Press, 2001.

Halliday, Fred. *Cold War, Third World: An Essay on Soviet–American Relations.* London: Hutchinson Radius, 1989.

——. *Rethinking International Relations.* London: Macmillan, 1994.

——. *Islam and the Myth of Confrontation: Religion and Politics in the Middle East.* London: I. B. Tauris, 1995.

——. *Two Hours that Shook the World: September 11, 2001: Causes and Consequences.* London: Saqi Books, 2002.

Harrison, Paul. *Inside the Third World: The Anatomy of Poverty.* London: Penguin, 1979.

Hartz, Louis. *The Liberal Tradition in America.* New York: Harcourt, Brace, 1955.

Hauerwas, Stanley and Frank Lentricchia (eds). *Dissent from the Homeland: Essays after September 11.* Special edition of the *South Atlantic Quarterly.* Durham, NC: Duke University Press, 2002.

Hazen, Don et al. (eds). *After 9/11: Solutions for a Saner World.* San Francisco: AlterNet, 2001.

Hedges, Chris. *War Is a Force That Gives US Meaning*. New York: Anchor Books, 2003.

Heiss, Mary Ann. 'The Evolution of the Imperial Idea and U.S. National Identity', *Diplomatic History* 26, no. 4 (Fall 2002).

Held, David (ed.). *Prospects for Democracy: North, South, East, West*. Cambridge: Polity Press, 1993.

——. 'Violence, Law, and Justice in a Global Age', in Craig Calhoun, Paul Price and Ashley Timmer (eds), *Understanding September 11*. New York: The New Press, 2002.

Hendrickson, David C. 'The Course of Empire', *Harpers Magazine* 305, no. 1831 (December 2002).

Herman, Edward S. 'The Media's Role in U.S. Foreign Policy', *Journal of International Affairs* 47, no. 1 (Summer 1993).

Hershberg, Eric and Kevin W. Moore (eds). *Critical Views of September 11: Analysis from Around the World*. New York: The New Press, 2002.

Hertsgaard, Mark. *The Eagle's Shadow: Why America Fascinates and Infuriates the World*. London: Bloomsbury, 2002.

Hilsman, Roger. *George Bush vs. Saddam Hussein: Military Success! Political Failure?* Novato, CA: Lyford Books, 1992.

Hiro, Dilip. *Desert Shield to Desert Storm: The Second Gulf War*. London: HarperCollins, 1992.

——. *Iraq: A Report from the Inside*. London: Granta, 2002.

Hitchens, Christopher. *A Long Short War: The Postponed Liberation of Iraq*. New York: Penguin, 2003.

Hobsbawm, Eric. *Nations and Nationalism since 1780: Programme, Myth, Reality*. Cambridge: Canto, 1990.

——. *Age of Extremes: The Short Twentieth Century, 1914–1991*. London: Michael Joseph, 1994.

——. *The New Century*. London: Little Brown, 2000.

Hoff, Joan. 'The American Century: From Sarajevo to Sarajevo', *Diplomatic History* 23, no. 2 (Spring 1999).

Hoffman, Stanley. 'Out of Iraq', *The New York Review of Books* 51, no. 16 (21 October 2004).

Hofstadter, Richard. *The American Political Tradition: And the Men Who Made it*. New York: Vintage, [1948] 1989.

Hogan, Michael J. and Thomas G. Paterson (eds). *Explaining the History of American Foreign Relations*. Cambridge: Cambridge University Press, 1991.

Hoge, James F. and Gideon Rose (eds). *How Did This Happen? Terrorism and the New War*. Oxford: Public Affairs, 2001.

Hollander, Paul. *Anti-Americanism: Critiques at Home and Abroad, 1965–1990*. New York: Oxford University Press, 1992.

Honderich, Ted. *After the Terror*. Edinburgh: Edinburgh University Press, 2002.

Hunt, Michael H. *Ideology and US Foreign Policy*. New Haven: Yale University Press, 1987.

Huntington, Samuel P. 'Clash of Civilizations', *Foreign Affairs* 72, no. 3 (Summer 1993).

——. *The Clash of Civilizations and the Remaking of World Order.* New York: Simon and Schuster, 1996.

Hurrell, Andrew and Ngaire Woods (eds). *Inequality, Globalization, and World Politics.* Oxford: Oxford University Press, 1999.

Ignatieff, Michael. 'On Isaiah Berlin (1909-1997)', *The New York Review of Books* 44, no. 20 (18 December 1997).

——. 'Virtual War', *Prospect* (London) (April 2000).

——. *Virtual War: Kosovo and Beyond.* New York: Picador, 2000.

Ikenberry, G. John. 'America's Imperial Ambition', *Foreign Affairs* 81, no. 5 (September/October 2002).

Immerman, Richard H. 'Psychology', in Michael J. Hogan and Thomas G. Paterson (eds), *Explaining the History of American Foreign Relations.* Cambridge: Cambridge University Press, 1991.

Isaacs, Arnold R. *Vietnam Shadows: The War, Its Ghosts and Its Legacy.* Baltimore, MD: Johns Hopkins University Press, 1997.

Judt, Tony. 'Anti-Americans Abroad', *The New York Review of Books* 50, no. 24 (1 May 2003).

Karnow, Stanley. *Vietnam: A History.* Harmondsworth: Penguin, 1983.

Karsh, Efraim and Inari Rautsi. *Saddam Hussein: A Political Biography.* London: Brassey's, 1991.

Kellner, Douglas. *The Persian Gulf TV War.* Boulder, CO: Westview Press, 1992.

Kennan, George [X]. 'The Sources of Soviet Conduct', *Foreign Affairs* 25 (July 1947).

Kennedy, Liam. 'Remembering September 11: Photography as Cultural Diplomacy', *International Affairs* 79, no. 2 (March 2003).

Kennedy, Liam and Scott Lucas. 'Enduring Freedom: Public Diplomacy and U.S. Foreign Policy', *American Quarterly* 57, no. 2 (June 2005).

Kimball, Warren F. *The Juggler: Franklin Roosevelt as Wartime Statesman.* Princeton, NJ: Princeton University Press, 1991.

——. 'Foreword', in David Ryan and Victor Pungong (eds), *The United States and Decolonization: Power and Freedom.* London: Macmillan, 2000.

Kolko, Gabriel. *Century of War: Politics, Conflict, and Society since 1914.* New York: The New Press, 1994.

——. *Another Century of War?* New York: The New Press, 2002.

——. *The Age of War: The United States Confronts the World.* London: Lynne Reinner, 2006.

Kolko, Joyce and Gabriel. *The Limits of Power: The World and United States Foreign Policy, 1945–1954.* New York: Harper and Row, 1972.

Kuklick, Bruce. *Blind Oracles: Intellectual and War from Kennan to Kisinger.* Princeton, NJ: Princeton University Press, 2006.

Kuttab, Daoud. 'Why Anti-Americanism?' in Don Hazen et al. (eds), *After 9/11: Solutions for a Saner World.* San Francisco: AlterNet, 2001.

LaFeber, Walter. *America, Russia, and the Cold War* (7th edn). New York: McGraw-Hill, 1991.

——. 'The Bush Doctrine', *Diplomatic History* 26, no. 4 (Fall 2002).

Lake, Anthony. 'Confronting Backlash States', *Foreign Affairs* 73, no. 2 (March/April 1994).

Lapham, Lewis. *Theater of War.* New York: The New Press, 2002.

Lauterpacht, E. et al. (eds). *The Kuwait Crisis: Basic Documents*. Cambridge: Grotius, 1991.

Layne, Christopher and Benjamin Schwarz. 'American Hegemony – Without an Enemy', *Foreign Policy*, no. 92 (Fall 1993).

Layne, Christopher. 'America as European Hegemon', *The National Interest* 72 (Summer 2003).

Leffler, Melvyn P. *A Preponderance of Power: National Security, the Truman Administration, and the Cold War*. Stanford, CA: Stanford University Press, 1992.

——. '9/11 and American Foreign Policy', *Diplomatic History* 29, no. 3 (June 2005).

Lennon, Alexander T. J. (ed.). *What Does the World Want from America? International Perspectives on U.S. Foreign Policy*. Cambridge: MIT Press, 2002.

Lewis, Bernard. 'The Roots of Muslim Rage', *The Atlantic Online*, <www.theatlantic.com/issues/90sep/rage.htm>, September 1990.

Lieven, Anatol. *America Right or Wrong: An Anatomy of American Nationalism*. London: HarperCollins, 2004.

Lifton, Robert Jay. *Superpower Syndrome: America's Apocalyptic Confrontation with the World*. New York: Nation Books, 2003.

Lindley-French, Julian. 'Terms of Engagement: The Paradox of American Power and the Transatlantic Dilemma Post-11 September', Institute for Security Studies, European Union, *Chaillot Papers*, no. 52 (May 2002).

Liss, Sheldon B. *Radical Thought in Central America*. Boulder, CO: Westview Press, 1991.

Little, Douglas. *American Orientalism: The United States and the Middle East since 1945*. London: I. B. Tauris, 2003.

Lock-Pullan, Richard. *US Intervention Policy and Army Innovation: from Vietnam to Iraq*. London: Routledge, 2006.

——. 'Iraq and Vietnam: Military Lessons and Legacies', in John Dumbrell and David Ryan (eds), *Vietnam in Iraq: Tactics, Lessons, Legacies, Ghosts*. London: Routledge, 2007.

Lucas, Scott W. *The Betrayal of Dissent: Beyond Orwell, Hitchens and the New American Century*. London: Pluto Press, 2004.

Lundestad, Geir. *'Empire' By Integration: The United States and European Integration, 1945–1997*. Oxford: Oxford University Press, 1998.

MacArthur, Brian (ed.). *Despatches from the Gulf War*. London: Bloomsbury, 1991.

Mahajan, Rahul. *The New Crusade: America's War on Terrorism*. New York: Monthly Review Press, 2002.

Maharidge, Dale. *Homeland*. New York: Seven Stories Press, 2004.

Maier, Charles S. *Among Empires: American Ascendancy and its Predecessors*. London: Harvard University Press, 2006.

Mailer, Norman. 'Only in America', *The New York Review of Books* 50, no. 5 (27 March 2003).

——. *Why Are We At War?* New York: Random House, 2003.

Makdisi, Ussama. '"Anti-Americanism" in the Arab World: An Interpretation of a Brief History', in Joanne Meyerowitz (ed.), *History and September 11th*. Philadelphia: Temple University Press, 2003.

Mamdani, Mahmood. 'Good Muslim, Bad Muslim: A Political Perspective on Culture and Terrorism', in Eric Hershberg and Kevin W. Moore (eds), *Critical Views of September 11: Analyses from Around the World*. New York: The New Press, 2002.

Mann, Michael. *Incoherent Empire*. London: Verso, 2003.

Mathews, Jessica T. 'Estranged Partners', *Foreign Policy* (November/December 2001).

Matthews, Ken. *The Gulf Conflict and International Relations*. London: Routledge, 1993.

McAlister, Melani. *Epic Encounters: Culture, Media, and U.S. Interests in the Middle East, 1945–2000*. Berkeley, CA: University of California Press, 2001.

McCormick, Thomas. *America's Half-Century: United States Foreign Policy in the Cold War*. Baltimore, MD: Johns Hopkins University Press, 1989.

McCrisken, Trevor B. *American Exceptionalism and the Legacy of Vietnam: US Foreign Policy since 1974*. London: Palgrave Macmillan, 2003.

McMahon, Robert J. 'Toward a Post-colonial Order: Truman Administration Policies toward South and Southeast Asia', in Michael J. Lacey (ed.), *The Truman Presidency*. Cambridge: Cambridge University Press, 1989.

Melanson, Richard A. *American Foreign Policy since the Vietnam War: The Search for Consensus from Richard Nixon to George W. Bush*. 4th edn. Armonk: M. E. Sharpe, 2005.

Meyerowitz, Joanne (ed.). *History and September 11th*. Philadelphia: Temple University Press, 2003.

Middle East Watch. *Needless Deaths in the Gulf War: Civilian Casualties During the Air Campaign and Violations of the Laws of War*. New York: Human Rights Watch, 1991.

Miles, Hugh. *Al-Jazeera: How Arab TV News Challenged the World*. London: Abacus, 2005.

Mirsky, Johnathan. 'Reconsidering Vietnam', *The New York Review of Books* 38, no. 15 (10 October 1991).

Munslow, Alun. *Deconstructing History*. London: Routledge, 1997.

Naím, Moisés. 'The Perils of Lite Anti-Americanism', *Foreign Policy* (May/June 2003).

National Commission on Terrorist Attacks Upon the United States. *The 9/11 Commission Report*. New York: W. W. Norton, n.d.

Novik, Peter. *That Noble Dream: The Objectivity Question and the American Historical Profession*. Cambridge: Cambridge University Press, 1988.

Nye, Joseph S. *The Paradox of American Power: Why the World's Only Superpower Can't Go It Alone*. Oxford: Oxford University Press, 2002.

O'Brien, William V. 'Just-War Theory', in James P. Sterba (ed.), *The Ethics of War and Nuclear Deterrence*. Belmost, CA: Wadsworth, 1985.

Offner, Arnold A. 'Rogue President, Rogue Nation: Bush and U.S. National Security', *Diplomatic History* 29, no. 3 (June 2005).

Osterhammel, Jürgen. *Colonialism: A Theoretical Overview*. Princeton: Markus Wiener, 1997.

Packer, George. *The Assassins Gate: America in Iraq*. London: Faber, 2006.

Park, James William. *Latin American Underdevelopment: A History of Perspectives in the United States 1870–1965*. Baton Rouge: Louisiana State University, 1995.

Payne, Richard J. *The West European Allies, the Third World, and U.S. Foreign Policy: Post-Cold War Challenges*. New York: Praeger, 1991.

Pew Global Attitudes Project. *What the World Thinks in 2002*. Washington, DC: Pew Research Center for the People and the Press, 2002.

——. *Views of a Changing World*. Washington, DC: Pew Research Center for the People and the Press (June 2003).

——. *Mistrust of America in Europe Even Higher, Muslim Anger Persists*. Washington, DC: Pew Research Center for the People and the Press (March 2004).

Powell, Colin L. *A Soldier's Way*. London: Hutchinson, 1995.

Raban, Jonathan. *My Holy War: Dispatches from the Home Front*. New York: New York Review Books, 2006.

Record, Jeffrey. *Making War, Thinking History: Munich, Vietnam, and Presidential Uses of Force from Korea to Kosovo*. Annapolis: Naval Institute Press, 2002.

Ricks, Thomas E. *Fiasco: The American Military Adventure in Iraq*. London: Penguin, 2006.

Ridgeway, James (ed.). *The March to War*. New York: Four Walls Eight Windows, 1991.

Roberts, Adam. 'The Laws of War in the 1990–91 Gulf Conflict', *International Security* 18, no. 3 (Winter 1993/94).

Ross, Marc Howard. 'The Political Psychology of Competing Narratives: September 11 and Beyond,' in Craig Calhoun, Paul Price and Ashley Timmer (eds), *Understanding September 11*. New York: The New Press, 2002.

Rubin, Barry. 'The Real Roots of Arab Anti-Americanism', *Foreign Affairs* 81, no. 6 (November/December 2002).

Rumsfeld, Donald H. 'Transforming the Military', *Foreign Affairs* 81, no. 3 (May/June 2002).

Ryan, David. 'Asserting US Power', in Philip John Davies (ed.), *An American Quarter Century*. Manchester: Manchester University Press, 1995.

——. *US-Sandinista Diplomatic Relations: Voice of Intolerance*. London: Macmillan, 1995.

——. 'US Expansionism: From the Monroe Doctrine to the Open Door', in Philip John Davies (ed.), *Representing and Imagining America* (Keele: Keele University Press, 1996).

——. 'US "Colonialism" in Post-War Latin America', *The International History Review* 21, no. 2 (June 1999).

——. *US Foreign Policy in World History*. London: Routledge, 2000.

——. 'By Way of Introduction: The United States, Decolonization and the World System', in David Ryan and Victor Pungong (eds), *The United States and Decolonization: Power and Freedom*. London: Macmillan, 2000.

—— '"With One Hand Tied Behind Our Back": Collective Memory, the Media and US Intervention from the Gulf War to Afghanistan', in Bernhard May and Michaela Hönicke Moore (eds), *The Uncertain Superpower: Domestic Dimensions of U.S. Foreign Policy after the Cold War*. Opladen: Leske and Budrich, 2003.

——. 'Ten Days in September: The Creeping Irrelevance of Transatlantic Allies', *Journal of Transatlantic Studies* 1, special edition (Spring 2003).

——. 'Framing September 11: Rhetorical Device and Photographic Opinion', *European Journal of American Culture* 23, no. 1 (2004).

——. 'Mapping Containment: The Cultural Construction of the Cold War', in Douglas Field (ed.), *American Cold War Culture*. Edinburgh: Edinburgh University Press, 2005.

Ryan, David and Victor Pungong (eds). *United States and Decolonization*. London: Macmillan, 2000.

Ryan, Maria. 'Inventing the "Axis of Evil": The Myth and Reality of Intelligence and Policy Making after 9/11', *49th Parallel: An Interdisciplinary Journal of North American Studies*, no. 10 <http://artsweb.bham.ac.uk/49thparallel/currentissue/coll_mariaryan.htm>.

Said, Edward W. *Culture and Imperialism*. London: Chatto and Windus, 1993.

——. *The Politics of Dispossession: The Struggle for Palestinian self-Determination 1969–1994*. London: Chatto and Windus, 1994.

——. *Orientalism*. London: Penguin, 1995.

——. *Covering Islam: How the Media and the Experts Determine How We See the Rest of the World*. London: Vintage, 1997.

——. *Reflections on Exile and other Literary and Cultural Essays*. London: Granta, 2000.

——. 'The Clash of Ignorance', in Don Hazen et al. (eds). *After 9/11: Solutions for a Saner World*. San Francisco: AlterNet, 2001.

——. *From Oslo to Iraq and the Roadmap*. London: Bloomsbury, 2004.

Salinger, Pierre with Eric Laurent. *Secret Dossier: The Hidden Agenda Behind the Gulf War*. London: Penguin, 1991.

Sardar, Ziauddin and Merryl Wyn Davies. *Why Do People Hate America?* Cambridge: Icon Books, 2002.

Schivelbusch, Wolfgang. *The Culture of Defeat: On National Trauma, Mourning, and Recovery*. New York: Henry Holt, 2001.

Schwarz, Benjamin. 'Why America Thinks it has to Run the World', *The Atlantic Monthly* (June 1996).

Sciolino, Elaine. *The Outlaw State: Saddam Hussein's Quest for Power and the Gulf Crisis*. New York: Wiley, 1991.

Scraton, Phil (ed.). *Beyond September 11: An Anthology of Dissent*. London: Pluto Press, 2002.

Sen, Amartya. *Development as Freedom*. Oxford: Oxford University Press, 1999.

——. *Identity and Violence: The Illusion of Destiny*. New York: W. W. Norton, 2006.

Sherry, Michael S. *In the Shadow of War: The United States since the 1930s*. New Haven: Yale University Press, 1995.

Siekmeier, James F. *Aid, Nationalism and Inter-American relations – Guatemala, Bolivia, and the United States 1945–1961*. Lewiston, NY: Edwin Mellen Press, 1999.

Sifry, Micah L. and Christopher Cerf (eds). *The Gulf War Reader: History, Documents, Opinions*. New York: Random House, 1991.

Silberstein, Sandra. *War of Words: Language, Politics and 9/11*. London: Routledge, 2002.

Singer, Peter. *The President of Good and Evil: The Ethics of George W. Bush*. New York: Dutton, 2004.

Snyder, Jack. 'Imperial Temptations', and Stephen Peter Rosen, 'An Empire, If You Can Keep It', *The National Interest* 71 (Spring 2003).

Sobel, Richard. *The Impact of Public Opinion on U.S. Foreign Policy Since Vietnam.* New York: Oxford University Press.

Sontag, Susan. *Where the Stress Falls.* New York: Farrar, Strauss and Giroux, 2001.

——. 'Looking at War: Photography's View of Devastation and Death', *The New Yorker* (9 December 2002).

——. *Regarding the Pain of Others.* New York: Farrar, Straus and Giroux, 2003.

Soyinka, Wole. *Climate of Fear: The Reith Lectures 2004.* London: Profile Books, 2004.

Steel, Ronald. *Temptations of a Superpower.* Cambridge, MA: Harvard University Press, 1995.

Stephanson, Anders. *Manifest Destiny: American Expansion and the Empire of Right.* New York: Hill and Wang, 1995.

——. 'A Most Interesting Empire', paper delivered to the symposium, 'Reviewing the Cold War: Interpretation, Approaches, Theory', Norwegian Nobel Institute, 1998.

Sterba, James P. *The Ethics of War and Nuclear Deterrence.* Belmost, CA: Wadsworth, 1985.

Strauss, Leo and Joseph Cropsey (eds). *History of Political Philosophy.* Chicago, IL: University of Chicago Press, 1981.

Suskind, Ron. *The Price of Loyalty: George W. Bush, The White House, and the Education of Paul O'Neill.* New York: Simon and Schuster, 2004.

Talbott, Strobe and Nayan Chanda (eds). *The Age of Terror: America and the World after September 11.* New Haven: Perseus, 2001.

Taylor, Philip M. *War and the Media: Propaganda and Persuasion in the Gulf War.* Manchester: Manchester University Press, 1992.

Thiong'O, Ngugi Wa. *Moving the Centre: The Struggle for Cultural Freedoms.* London: James Curry, 1993.

Todd, Emmanuel. *After the Empire: The Breakdown of the American Order.* London: Constable, 2003.

Tucker, Robert W. and David C. Hendrickson. *The Imperial Temptation: The New World Order and America's Purpose.* New York: Council on Foreign Relations, 1992.

——. 'The Sources of American Legitimacy', *Foreign Affairs* (November/ December 2004).

United Nations Development Programme (UNDP). *Human Development Report 1992.* New York: Oxford University Press, 1992.

——. (UNDP). *Human Development Report 2000.* New York: Oxford University Press, 2000.

United States Senate. The Pike Report, reprinted as *CIA The Pike Report.* Nottingham: Spokesman Books, 1977.

Urquhart, Brian. 'World Order & Mr. Bush', *The New York Review of Books* 50, no. 15 (9 October 2003).

US News and World Report. *Triumph Without Victory: The Unreported History of the Persian Gulf War.* New York: Random House, 1992.

Vanaik, Achin. 'The Ethics and Efficacy of Political Terrorism', in Eric Hershberg and Kevin W. Moore (eds), *Critical Views of September 11: Analyses from Around the World*. New York: The New York Press, 2002.

Various. 'What we Think of America', *Granta* 77 (Spring 2002).

Vidal, Gore. *Perpetual War for Perpetual Peace: How We Got to be So Hated*. New York: Nation Books, 2002.

Vlastos, Stephen. 'America's "Enemy": The Absent Presence in Revisionist Vietnam War History', in John Carlos Rowe and Rick Berg (eds), *The Vietnam War and American Culture*. New York: Columbia University Press, 1991.

Wallace, William. 'Living with the Hegemon: European Dilemmas', in Eric Hershberg and Kevin W. Moore (eds), *Critical Views of September 11: Analyses from Around the World*. New York: The New Press, 2002.

Wallerstein, Immanuel. 'The Eagle Has Crash Landed', *Foreign Policy* (July/August 2002).

Walt, Stephen M. *Taming American Power: The Global Response to U.S. Primacy*. New York: W. W. Norton, 2005.

Walzer, Michael. *Just and Unjust Wars: A Moral Argument with Historical Illustrations*. New York: HarperCollins, 1992.

Waterbury, John. 'Hate Your Policies, Love Your Institutions', *Foreign Affairs* 82, no. 1 (January/February 2003).

Weinberger, Caspar W. *Fighting for Peace: Seven Critical Years in the Pentagon*. New York: Warner Books, 1990.

Westad, Odd Arne. *The Global Cold War: Third World Interventions and the Making of Our Times*. Cambridge: Cambridge University Press, 2005.

Wheeler, Nicholas J. 'Dying for "Enduring Freedom": Accepting Responsibility for Civilian Casualties in the War against Terrorism', *International Relations* 16, no. 2 (August 2002).

White House. *The National Security Strategy of the United States of America*. Washington, DC: The White House (September 2002).

Williams, Rowan. 'End of War', *The South Atlantic Quarterly* 101, no. 2 (Spring 2002).

——. *Writing in the Dust: Reflections on 11th September and its Aftermath*. London: Hodder and Stoughton, 2002.

Williams, William Appleman. *The Tragedy of American Diplomacy*. New York: Delta, 1961.

Williams, William Appleman et al. (eds). *America in Vietnam: A Documentary History*. New York: W. W. Norton, 1989.

Willis, Susan. 'Old Glory', *The South Atlantic Quarterly* 101, no. 2 (Spring 2002).

Wolf, Eric R. *Envisioning Power: Ideologies of Dominance and Crisis*. Berkeley, CA: University of California Press, 1999.

Woods, Ngaire. 'Order, Globalization, and Inequality in World Politics', in Andrew Hurrell and Ngaire Woods (eds), *Inequality, Globalization, and World Politics*. Oxford: Oxford University Press, 1999.

Wood, Robert E. 'From the Marshall Plan to the Third World', in Melvyn P. Leffler and David S. Painter (eds), *The Origins of the Cold War: An International History*. London: Routledge, 1994.

Woodward, Bob. *The Commanders*. New York: Simon and Schuster, 1991.

——. *Bush at War*. New York: Simon and Schuster, 2002.

——. *Plan of Attack*. New York: Simon and Schuster, 2004.

Zinn, Howard. *On War*. New York: Seven Stories Press, 2001.

Yergin, Daniel. *The Prize: The Epic Quest for Oil, Money and Power*. London: Simon and Schuster, 1991.

Žižek, Slavoj. *Welcome to the Desert of the Real: Five Essays on September 11 and Related Dates*. London: Verso, 2002.

Index